Groups in Social Work

GROUPS
IN SOCIAL WORK
APPLICATION OF SMALL GROUP THEORY AND RESEARCH TO SOCIAL WORK PRACTICE

Margaret E. Hartford

COLUMBIA UNIVERSITY PRESS
NEW YORK

Margaret E. Hartford holds the Ph. D. degree and is a professor of social work in the School of Applied Social Sciences at Case Western Reserve University, Cleveland, Ohio.

ISBN 0-231-03548-9 (cloth)
ISBN 0-231-08359-9 (paperback)
Copyright © 1971 Columbia University Press

Library of Congress Catalog Card Number: 71-181782
Printed in the United States of America
10

PREFACE

The idea of this book germinated in the years during which I had the opportunity to work with Dr. Grace Coyle on the development of a course on the theory of group behavior for social workers. As she stated, we have come to realize that small group theory can be separated from social group work practice theory and methods courses and taught as a unique body of content.[1] Dr. Coyle had developed the roots of such knowledge in her own research, which appeared in 1930 as *Social Process in Organized Groups*.[2] As we worked over this content with our colleagues Esther Test, Raymond Fisher, and Mary Louise Somers, a clearer formulation of group elements began to emerge. Dr. Somers'[3] analysis of "Four Small Group Theories" grew out of an effort to link some of the social science research findings on small groups to group work practice theory. My own study, "The Social Group Worker in the Pro-

[1] Grace L. Coyle, *Social Science in the Professional Education of Social Workers* (New York, Council on Social Work Education, 1958).

[2] Grace L. Coyle, *Social Process in Organized Groups* (New York, Richard R. Smith, Inc., 1930).

[3] Mary Louise Somers, "Four Small Group Theories: A Comparative Analysis and Evaluation of Selected Social Science Theory for Use as Teaching Content in Social Group Work" (unpublished Ph.D. dissertation, Western Reserve University, 1957).

cess of Group Formation,"[4] was another effort in this direction. In 1957, *Social Process in the Community and the Group*,[5] coauthored by Dr. Coyle and myself, gave a brief review of the course which we had been developing on a Russell Sage Grant.

At her death in 1962, Dr. Coyle was working on a new draft of her *Social Process in Organized Groups* to include some of the more recent research in the social sciences and in social group work practice. Although that work was never finished, this book is not an effort to complete it. I have moved to my own interpretations and arrangements of concepts. However, because of our twelve years of association, teaching and working, talking and thinking together, no doubt I have incorporated many of her ideas into my thinking. On the other hand, having worked over the material with several classes of students, and several institutes for social workers at both the masters and post-masters level for twenty-one years, I have made much of this material my own. During this time, knowledge about groups through research in the social sciences has burgeoned; i.e., sociology, psychology, anthropology, economics and political science, and the emergence of social psychology and its offspring, group dynamics. There have been also tremendous advances in social group work, group therapy, and group psychotherapy, and the uses of groups in business, industry, and armed forces, education, politics, and organized religion. The world is alive with group uses: group behavior, group theory, and group practice, some very appropriate, and some yet to prove their merits, some open to criticism as perhaps even harmful to the individual or to society.

This book is my effort to draw together small group theory, the findings of research, and experiences with groups which have proved useful in my teaching of group concepts, my consultation with group practitioners in social work, and in my own practice with groups. Through a review of the small group literature from theory and research, I have attempted to use those fragments of

[4] Margaret E. Hartford, "The Social Group Worker in the Process of Group Formation" (unpublished Ph.D. dissertation, University of Chicago, 1962).

[5] Grace L. Coyle, and Margaret E. Hartford, *Social Process in the Community and the Group* (New York, Council on Social Work Education, 1958).

knowledge which seemed applicable in forming a framework for understanding groups, which I hope may lead to some prescriptions for social work practice with people in groups.

The focus here is clearly on the uses of (1) groups in social work practice for the benefit of participants in personal enhancement, growth, support, rehabilitation, or change, where the individual participant is the target, and (2) groups for social change, action, amelioration of crises where the institution, community, or society is the target. Groups formed by agency or worker for individual and institutional or community change, as well as autonomous groups such as high school clubs, families, and gangs will be considered. No consideration is given to group supervision, institutional management, milieu direction, administration, or formal education, all of which exist in social work and employ the use of group knowledge, along with systems theory, organizational theory, and management theories. This is not to say that such facets of social work are not important, nor that group theory is not appropriate to them. It is merely to keep the focus here on groups as instruments of service in social work practice: casework, group work, community organization, multimethod practice, or social work generic practice, where such exists. My intent is to provide a basis for social workers to be more deliberate and purposeful in their decisions to use groups, in their efforts to create and form groups, and in their intervention and activity with groups, whether the aim is personal service to the participant or cooperative engagement of the members for some effect in the social situation or environment of the members.

I wish to acknowledge the special help and guidance which I have received in this production from many of my friends, colleagues, and students at Case Western Reserve University, by their questions, challenges, and suggestions. Also, I wish to acknowledge the special help of Helen Northen, Mary Louise Somers, and Mary Seguin. I should also like to acknowledge the help of my mother, who not only endowed me with some of the qualities that made this book possible but also provided me with the material comforts that enabled its production. Within the organization of Case Western Reserve University, Deans Herman D. Stein and John B.

Turner served facilitating roles by making time and support available, and Mrs. Marian Sidora provided technical assistance in the production of the manuscript.

Margaret E. Hartford

Cleveland, Ohio
May, 1971

CONTENTS

Groups in Social Work

GROUPS
IN SOCIAL WORK

Sources of Knowledge about Groups

With the increasing efforts to use groups as a major instrument for service in social work practice, and with a growing body of knowledge about the nature of group processes emerging in the social sciences, and to some degree within social work research, I will attempt in this book to link research and theory about groups with social work practice in groups.

The provision of social work and social welfare services through collectivities of two or more people with a worker has extended beyond the historic patterns of club and class work with children, youth, adults, and older adults in Y's, scouts, community centers, settlements, citizen-action programs, and adult education. Group services have also extended beyond therapeutic groups in clinics, hospitals, schools, and residential institutions. People are now being served in groups in almost every type of social welfare and social work service and for many kinds of personal, interpersonal, and social problems. The decade of the 1960's was the period of discovery and rediscovery of the small group in social work practice.

For social workers who have always used group work as their major means of service, the rediscovery has come with an improved understanding of groups through increased knowledge about group phenomena. The social sciences have produced more research and theory in aspects of small group behavior [1] than in any previous decade of their history. Behavioral scientists in sociology, social psychology, psychology, political science, and social anthropology have been formulating and testing hypotheses regarding the nature of group life and aspects of group phenomena. This theory provides the opportunity to improve the use of groups as a means of service in social work practice.[2] Since social work practitioners and theory builders have become acquainted with this research, they have extended their uses of groups. To a degree they have also produced research and developed theory on the nature of group phenomena.

More experienced social workers who have applied social science research findings to their own practice with groups have contributed to knowledge within social work, particularly in social group work and some aspects of casework and community organi-

[1] See particularly: A. Paul Hare, *Handbook of Small Group Research* (New York, The Free Press, 1962); Robert Golembiewski, *The Small Group* (Chicago, University of Chicago Press, 1962); Theodore Mills, *The Sociology of Small Groups* (Englewood Cliffs, N.J., Prentice-Hall, Inc., 1967); W. R. Bion, *Experiences in Groups* (New York, Basic Books, Inc., 1961); Dorwin Cartwright and Alvin Zander, *Group Dynamics* (3d ed., New York, Harper & Row, 1968); and, Helen E. Durkin, *The Group in Depth* (New York, International Universities Press, 1964).

[2] See particularly: Helen Northen, *Social Work with Groups* (New York, Columbia University Press, 1969); Robert D. Vinter, "Small Group Theory and Research: Implications for Group Work Practice Theory and Research," in Leonard Kogan, ed., *Social Science Theory and Social Work Research* (New York, National Association of Social Workers, 1960); William Schwartz, "Small Group Science in Group Work Practice," *Social Work,* VIII (October, 1963); and Saul Bernstein, ed., *Explorations in Group Work* (Boston, Boston University School of Social Work, 1965).

zation.[3] In community organization practice, groups have always been utilized for citizen action, neighborhood change, institutional change, conflict resolution, and the planning and coordination of community services. There is an increased employment of groups to engage people in action to bring about changes for themselves and others. The rediscovery of the small group in community organization has come particularly from developments in political science and organizational theory[4] in addition to social psychology and applied anthropology.

Social workers who have helped people as individuals to work on personal, interpersonal, and social problems primarily in a one-to-one interview method through social casework and counseling have discovered the group in two ways. First, they have moved in some instances toward reaching and treating whole families together or in subsections. They are discovering that there are not only group aspects to family life for which the small group theory

[3] For examples, see such articles as: Ralph Kolodny, "The Impact of Peer Group Activity on the Alienated Child," *Smith College Studies in Social Work*, XXXVII (February, 1967), 142–58; Margaret E. Hartford, ed., *Working Papers Toward a Frame of Reference for Social Group Work* (New York, National Association of Social Workers, 1962); Margaret E. Hartford, "The Preparation of Social Workers to Practice with People in Groups," *Journal of Education for Social Work*, III (Fall, 1967), 49–61; Elsa Leichter, "Interrelationship of Content and Process in Therapy Groups," *Social Casework*, XLVII (May, 1966), 302 ff; Rosemary Sarri and Maeda Galinsky, "A Conceptual Framework for Teaching Group Development in Social Group Work," in *Faculty Day Conference Proceedings, 1964* (New York, Council on Social Work Education, 1964); Louise Frey and Ralph Kolodny, "Illusions and Realities in Current Social Work with Groups," *Social Work*, IX (April, 1964); Barbara Bryant Solomon, "Social Group Work in the Adult Out-Patient Clinic," *Social Work*, XIII (October, 1968), 56 ff; and, Maxine Crow, "Preventive Intervention Through Parent Group Education," *Social Casework*, XLVIII (March, 1967), 161.

[4] See particularly: Ronald Lippitt, Jeanne Watson, and Bruce Westley, *The Dynamics of Planned Change* (New York, Harcourt Brace Jovanovich, Inc., 1958); Herbert Thelen, *Dynamics of Groups at Work* (Chicago, University of Chicago Press, Phoenix Books, 1954); John B. Turner, *Neighborhood Organization* (New York, National Association of Social Workers, 1968); James G. March, ed., *Handbook of Organizations* (Chicago, Rand McNally & Co., 1965); and, Hyman Weiner, "Social Change and Social Group Work Practice," *Social Work*, IX (July, 1964), 106–12.

gives understanding [5] but also they are recognizing that when they work with families they are intervening in small groups (no matter how disintegrated or dysfunctional). Social workers who have used the casework method primarily have also discovered that they may work with several clients together for some service functions including intake, orientation, diagnosis, and for treatment when clients have certain similarities of person or problem. They have discovered that if the aggregate of people can form into a group configuration, with the worker as an active participant taking a specified role, the group itself may provide a means and context for helping. The uses of groups by social caseworkers have been extended to many types of public and voluntary services and for a variety of ages and types of personal and social problems.[6]

[5] Frances Feldman, and Frances Scherz, *Family Social Welfare: Helping Troubled Families* (New York, Atherton Press, Inc., 1967); Virginia Satir, *Conjoint Family Therapy* (Palo Alto, Calif., Science and Behavior Books, 1964); Grace L. Coyle, "Concepts Relevant to Helping the Family as a Group," *Social Casework*, XLIII (1962); Gertrude Wilson and Gladys Ryland, "The Family as a Unit of Service," in *Social Work Practice, 1964* (New York, Columbia University Press, 1964); Alan Klein, "Exploring Family Group Counseling," *Social Work*, VIII (January, 1963), 23–29; Arthur Leader, "The Role of Intervention in Family Group Treatment," *Social Casework*, XLV (June, 1964), 327–32; and Albertina Mobley, "Group Application Interview in a Family Agency," *Social Casework*, XLVII (March, 1966).

[6] See as examples: Child Welfare League, *Group Methods and Services in Child Welfare* (New York, Child Welfare League of America, 1963); Norman Fenton and Kermit T. Wilse, eds., *Group Methods in the Public Welfare Program* (Palo Alto, Calif., Pacific Books, 1963); Family Service Association of America, *Group Treatment in Family Service Agencies* (New York, Family Service Association of America, 1964); Joyce Gale Klein, *Adult Education and Treatment Groups in Social Agencies* (doctoral dissertation, Washington, D.C., The Catholic University of America Press, 1960); Martin Strickler and Jean Allgeyer, "The Crisis Group: A New Application of Crisis Theory," *Social Work*, XII (July, 1967); United States Department of Health, Education, and Welfare, *Working with Groups* (Washington, D.C., U.S. Government Printing Office, 1963); Kermit Wilse and Justine Fixel, *Use of Groups in Public Welfare* (California State Department of Social Welfare, September, 1962); Ada Shaw Cyrus, "Group Treatment of 10 Disadvantaged Mothers," *Social Casework*, XLVIII (February, 1967), 80; Maxine Crow, "Preventive Intervention Through Parent Group Education," *Social Casework*, XLVIII (March, 1967), 161; and, Esther Appelberg, "The Cottage Meeting As A Therapeutic Tool," in Henry Maier, ed., *Group Work As Part of Residential Treatment* (New York, National Association of Social Workers, 1965), pp. 142–54.

When groups are used in social work practice, labels such as group treatment, group therapy, group work, social group work, community group work, group action, or group education are applied. The models of worker-to-member and member-to-member relationship in the context of the group may vary with auspice of service, purpose of service, capacity of participants, nature of defined problems, focus and stance of the worker, and phase and level of group development in time.[7] But regardless of label or model, when social work is practiced with people in groups, the elements of the configuration include a collection of individuals participating with each other and with a worker to accomplish some specific objective by being together. The social worker has a helping or facilitating role. Therefore, he needs to understand not only individual behavior but also the nature of group behavior so that he may maximize his own contribution in engaging the participants in their development of the group as an instrument for help, action, or change. Joyce Gale Klein,[8] a social worker, has stated "the change agent cannot successfully and consciously affect the focus of the group toward specific ends of education or treatment without some knowledge of and skill in [group process] elements." R. F. Bales,[9] a social scientist, has suggested that the therapist, educator, and club leader needs to know how to understand group processes enough to make effective interventions and take appropriate actions in groups.

[7] For discussion of comparison of models of social group work practice, see: Henry Maier, in *A Conceptual Framework for Teaching Group Work Method in the Classroom*, ed. by M. E. Hartford (New York, Council on Social Work Education, 1964); William Schwartz, in *Working Papers Toward a Frame of Reference for Social Group Work*, ed. by M. E. Hartford (New York, National Association of Social Workers, 1964); Catherine Papell and Beulah Rothman, "Social Group Work Models: Possession and Heritage," *Journal of Education for Social Work*, II (1966); and, Robert Vinter, "Social Group Work," in Harry L. Lurie, ed., *Encyclopedia of Social Work* (New York, National Association of Social Workers, 1965).

[8] Joyce Gale Klein, *Adult Education and Treatment Groups*, p. 118.

[9] Robert F. Bales, "Small Group Theory and Research," in R. K. Merton, Leonard Broom, and Leonard Cottrell, Jr., eds., *Sociology Today* (New York, Basic Books, Inc., 1959), p. 295.

The State of Knowledge
about Small Groups

As yet, there is no unified theory of small group processes either in social work practice or in the social sciences, although several people have attempted such formulation. Some early efforts were made in the 1920's and 1930's by social workers. Notable was the work of Grace L. Coyle, whose initial scheme was based upon her observations of actual groups within social welfare and the general society. Her work with women in industry through YWCA programs, with children's groups in settlement houses, and with discussion groups in the adult education movement led to her first effort to develop a formulation which appeared in *Social Process in Organized Groups*,[10] her doctoral dissertation, published in 1930. She drew upon the work of Simmel, Cooley, and MacIver, as well as some of her associates, Dewey, Sheffield, and Follett. Her formulation included the processes of group formation, membership selection, goal development, structural arrangement, leadership, creation of bond, group culture, group control, and collective thinking. Her application of these concepts to social work practice, as she employed them in her teaching, appeared in the book, *Group Work with American Youth*, in 1948.[11]

Coyle carried her work further through teaching group processes to social work students and by attempting to make bridges with the social science theory development and research in small groups in the 1950's. A preliminary statement of her last effort appeared in the pamphlet, *Social Processes in the Community and the Group*, 1958,[12] a syllabus for teaching small group theory to social work students.

W. I. Newstetter also pioneered in developing a scheme for un-

[10] Grace L. Coyle, *Social Process in Organized Groups* (New York, Richard R. Smith, 1930).

[11] Grace L. Coyle, *Group Work with American Youth* (New York, Harper & Row, 1948).

[12] Grace L. Coyle and Margaret E. Hartford, *Social Process in the Community and the Group* (New York, Council on Social Work Education, 1958).

derstanding and using group process by establishing exploratory and experimental research. Because of his concern about "the lack of generalized knowledge of the primary group" from which principles for practice with groups could be developed, he established a research project in 1926 in a children's camp, which continued for twelve years. The findings, published with research associates Marc Feldstein and Theodore Newcomb in 1938 as *Group Adjustment*,[13] dealt with the concepts of compresence, bond, interaction, and status, and showed that the needs of individuals could be fulfilled and people could grow individually through group associations. After some preliminary research, Newstetter set out to test, through a sociometric experiment in the living situation, Eubank's definition of a group. Eubank, in 1932, attempted to sum up definition of group that had appeared in sociological literature as follows: "[a group is] two or more individuals in a relationship of psychic interaction, whose relationship with one another may be abstracted and distinguished from their relationship with all others so that they may be thought of as an entity." [14] The major contribution of Newstetter's work was the demonstration that experimental research could be done in "natural" settings and that phenomena of groups could be studied and documented. Newstetter developed his work beyond the research in the children's camp and the extraction of records of groups in the settlement house made by his associates at the time, Clara Kaiser and Helen U. Phillips.[15] He redirected his thinking toward community organization and attempted to apply his formulation to what he called "the Social Inter-Group Work Process." [16]

[13] Wilbur I. Newstetter, Marc C. Feldstein, and Theodore Newcomb, *Group Adjustment* (Cleveland, Western Reserve University Press, 1938).

[14] E. E. Eubank, *Concepts of Sociology* (Boston, D. C. Heath & Co., 1932), p. 163.

[15] Clara Kaiser, ed., *The Group Records of Four Clubs at University Neighborhood Center* (Cleveland, School of Applied Social Sciences, Western Reserve University, 1930); and Helen U. Phillips, "Records Kept by Group Working Agencies: Their Form and Values" (unpublished Master's Thesis, Western Reserve University, 1927–28).

[16] Wilbur I. Newstetter, "The Social Inter-Group Work Process—How Does It Differ from the Social Group Work Process?" *Proceedings: National Conference of Social Work, 1947* (New York, Columbia University Press, 1948).

Most professional social workers who have specialized in the uses of groups in social work practice have learned some scheme of group processes that stems from a combination of these two sources, Newstetter and Coyle, with incorporation of some of the more recent social science research. The work of both Coyle and Newstetter suffered initially from the lack of research tools which are now available in the behavioral sciences, but their contributions have been used and modified by social workers in group practice, with fragmentary efforts at theory building.

While other group work authors, such as Gertrude Wilson, Clara Kaiser, and Gisela Konopka, acknowledged the need for a theory of group processes for group work practice, none of these people developed a total frame of reference on group processes or elements. Gertrude Wilson and Gladys Ryland,[17] for instance, in the text that was acknowledged as the basic reference for group work for many years, did not develop a comprehensive scheme of group behavior as such. They, too, used Eubank's definition of group and made a clear case for the need for knowledge about groups. However, while their one chapter on understanding the dynamics of group life refers to dimensions such as values and norms, interaction process, group acceptance and group structure, their discussion takes off from a focus on individual personality theory as people are related in the group.

Clara Kaiser, one of the leading teachers of social group work for many years, who also had been research director of Newstetter's research in University Settlement in the 1930's, wrote in 1959: "Since we have defined the social group work process as a purposive and disciplined way of affecting the group process, there must be some conceptual framework as to the nature and forms of group life to which this process is pertinent. . . . We can know much more about the sociological and psychological properties and behavior of groups than we could have a few years ago." [18] She goes on to suggest that some of the attributes of groups that have been

---

[17] Gertrude Wilson, and Gladys Ryland, *Social Group Work Practice* (Boston, Houghton Mifflin Co., 1948).

[18] Clara A. Kaiser, "The Social Group Work Process," in Marjorie Murphy, ed., *The Social Group Work Method in Social Work Education*, Vol. XI. A Project Report on Curriculum Study (New York, Council on Social Work Education, 1959).

incorporated into the group work practice knowledge include "how groups are formed, size of groups, degree of homogeneity with respect to age, sex, interests, cultural background, expressed or implicit purposes the group has for its members, nature of interests for group activity, group structure and controls, quality of interpersonal relations, *esprit de corps* or group feeling." She establishes the premise that there is a gap between the knowledge of the social scientists and group work practice and suggests that the gap could be bridged by closer and more effective collaboration between the social scientists and social group workers in not only increasing knowledge of group phenomena but also in improving methods for enriching and repairing individual and group life.

Gisela Konopka, whose books on group work have been widely used in teaching social work, acknowledges the necessity for theories of group process in one chapter of her book, *Social Group Work: A Helping Process*,[19] but deals only with subgroups, bond, formation, goal, and decision making. These she does not tie together in a clear framework of group processes.

The preoccupation of social workers using groups in the 1930's, 1940's, and into the 1950's was with the provision and extension of services, training of workers on practice methods, definition of role of the worker, but very little on analysis and definition of the internal processes in the groups. In the late 1950's and early 1960's, the Group Work Section and the Commission on Group Work of the National Association of Social Workers undertook efforts to build theory on use of groups. They attempted to develop a framework for understanding group processes and social worker interventions with groups, but their general conclusion was that theory development belonged in the hands of individuals and small groups of practitioners and educators, and could not be done by national associations or their committees.

The State of Social Science Theory

In the early emergence of the social sciences, little attention was paid to group processes as phenomena for theory or research.

---

[19] Gisela Konopka, *Social Group Work: A Helping Process* (Englewood Cliffs, N.J., Prentice-Hall, Inc., 1963), Chapter 4.

Among the few exceptions was LeBon, who described in *The Crowd* (1895), the phenomenon of interpersonal contagion readily applicable to small groups. He said, "Whoever be the individuals who compose the group, the fact that they have been transformed into a group puts them into a sort of collective mind which makes them feel, think, and act in a manner quite different from that in which each individual of them would feel, think or act in isolation." [20] In more recent years, Fritz Redl, among others, has picked up on the phenomenon of group contagion in his work with children in group treatment.[21]

McDougall also produced a similar theory in *The Group Mind* in 1920.[22] His theory endowed groups with certain cognitive aspects of the human mind, stating that groups function as a single human. While his formulation offered new insights into group behavior, we have since come to recognize that the individual personality and the small group are each described by a different order of social theory. McDougall's major contribution was the acknowledgment that a group as an entity could exist, that it had unique characteristics and qualities which could be studied and understood and that these qualities were different from the individual persons who composed the group and the society in which it existed.

Simmel developed theoretical formulations regarding group size including two- and three-person alliances,[23] also in the early 1920's. His conceptualization, including the nature of power alliances and the effects on interactions of various sizes of groups, particularly dyads and triads as they exist through time, increased knowledge of the nature of the interaction process within the small group and the different nature of interaction resulting from change

[20] Gustav LeBon, *The Crowd*, trans. by Fisher (London, A. Unwin, 1895).

[21] Fritz Redl, Norman Polansky, and Ronald Lippitt, "An Investigation of Behavioral Contagion in Groups," *Human Relations*, III (1950), 319–48; Fritz Redl, "Group Emotion and Leadership," *Psychiatry*, V (November, 1942), 573–96.

[22] William McDougall, *The Group Mind* (New York, G. P. Putnam's Sons, 1920).

[23] Georg Simmel, *The Sociology of Georg Simmel*, trans. and ed. by K. H. Wolff (New York, The Free Press, 1950).

in group size. Durkheim,[24] in his studies of suicide, emphasized the importance of the small group in supporting the individual within the wider society to give him some attachment, some sense of self-worth and belonging, and to provide for both personal and social control.

In one of his last works, *Group Psychology and the Analysis of the Ego*, Freud began a theoretical formulation of groups. In this volume published in 1922, he said, "Group Psychology is the oldest human psychology," [25] and then postulated that a group bond develops through the affectional ties of each member to a person in the role of leader and that this group bond leads to identification of members with each other, to group contagion and development of the capacity for empathy.

Perhaps the most significant contribution to the early developments of small group theory was the creation of the concept "primary group" by Charles Horton Cooley, the American sociologist who published his definition in 1909.[26] Cooley saw the small informal face-to-face groups, such as families, play groups, and friendship groups as primary in the sense that they were responsible for the initial development of values and standards of behavior. He said that primary groups provided for the members a sense of solidarity or mutual identification that resulted in the feeling of "we." About such groups he had two major hypotheses. First, socialization in childhood or the development of moral norms which continue into adulthood take place in primary group associations. Secondly, he suggested that small groups influence the behavior, reinforce and stabilize it in wider relationships in adulthood. Thus, he saw the study of primary groups as an important stream in American social theory. It has been suggested that his major ideas were apparently ignored for many years by sociologists, who were more concerned with developing research and theory about larger

[24] Emil Durkheim, *Suicide*, trans. by John A. Spaulding and George Simpson (New York, The Free Press, 1951).

[25] Sigmund Freud, *Group Psychology and the Analysis of the Ego*, auth. trans. by James Strachey (London, International Psychoanalytical Press, 1922).

[26] Charles H. Cooley, *Social Organization* (New York, Charles Scribner's Sons, 1909).

social phenomena. However, social workers made continuous use of his work.

These were, therefore, the major works in the 1920's used by the social workers who were beginning to question the nature of groups and to postulate theories about the groups that were being used at that time. Their practice in the social settlements was employing group methods for citizen education and action to improve working conditions in factories, to increase literacy, to effect Americanization and the transition from rural to urban life of both European immigrants and American migrants.[27] The leaders of youth movements who were developing programs in groups to affect moral standards and behavior of youth in the cities in the playground and recreation movement [28] were also attempting to make more explicit the uses of groups.

The early leaders of the adult education movement, Harrison Elliott, Alfred Sheffield, and Eduard Lindeman, set forth in the *Inquiry* [29] and in their individual writings their convictions that the functioning of a democratic government depended upon voluntary associations. Robert MacIver [30] and Mary Follett [31] also wrote on the merits of citizen participation in the operation of the democratic government. Grace Coyle's association with many of these people and their movements led her to interpret their ideas for social work theory. The YWCA work with industrial women workers

[27] Gaynell Hawkins, *Educational Experiments in Social Settlements*, American Association of Adult Education (New York, P. Grady Press, 1937); Loren M. Pacey, *Readings in the Development of Settlement Work* (New York, Association Press, 1950).

[28] Neva L. Boyd of Northwestern University developed some of the early theory regarding the use of various nonverbal media in recreation and informal education in groups.

[29] Harrison Elliott, Eduard Lindeman, and Alfred Sheffield worked together on a small paper called *The Inquiry*, which raised questions and offered opinions and ideas related to citizen involvement in social action and education. They each contributed significant independent publications in the area of the use of groups, such as Elliott's *Process of Group Thinking* (New York, Association Press, 1928); Sheffield's *Creative Discussion* (New York, The Inquiry, 1928); and, Lindeman's *Social Discovery* (New York, Public Press, 1924).

[30] Robert MacIver, *Community* (New York, The Macmillan Co., 1924).

[31] Mary Follett, *Creative Experience* (New York, Longmans Green, 1924), and *The New State* (New York, Longmans Green, 1918).

in education and action, the settlement groups for community action, the youth movements, and children's play and recreation groups all provided testing ground for postulates of the nature and significance of the small group. It became evident that hypotheses were needed which could be taught to workers so that their leadership of groups could be more effective and explicit. These were the forerunners of current social work theory on the use of groups which has come to be known as social group work practice.[32]

Through the years, as social work education moved from an apprenticeship type of training to a more theoretical and conceptual education, sequences of class and field practice were developed for social workers to learn to work with people in groups both in social group work and community organization practices. Maloney's [33] study shows that there was a continuous refinement of knowledge about group behavior within the schools of social work. Gradually it was recognized that small group theory as a part of individual and societal behavior theory was required knowledge for all social workers and not only the group specialists. As this content has been put into the curriculum of many schools of social work, better and clearer formulations of small group processes have evolved.[34]

Several strands of experimental work with people in groups developed in the 1930's. Ronald Lippitt, who was interested in youth work in the YMCA, undertook study with Kurt Lewin, a Gestalt psychologist, who had been much interested in the effect of social situations on behavior of individuals. They and others set up a classic series of experimental studies at the University of Iowa in which they considered the effects of certain types of leadership styles on the group structures which evolved and on members' be-

---

[32] Margaret E. Hartford, "Social Group Work 1930 to 1960: The Search for a Definition," in *Working Papers Toward a Frame of Reference for Social Group Work* (New York, National Association of Social Workers, 1964).

[33] Sara E. Maloney, "The Development of Group Work Education in Schools of Social Work in the U.S. 1919–1948," (unpublished D. S. W. dissertation, Cleveland, Western Reserve University, 1963).

[34] Grace L. Coyle, *Social Science in the Professional Education of Social Workers* (New York, Council on Social Work Education, 1958), pp. 30–36; Coyle and Hartford, *Social Process*, pp. 65–82.

havior.[35] While the results of their studies probably influenced the leadership styles and the group structures subsequently established in club leadership, particularly in American youth movements, criticism was expressed by many social work leaders that human emotions should not be the subjects of experimentation. The very valuable results of these and subsequent studies by these men had less effect on the use of groups in social work than they might, had there been more receptivity at the time to experimental methods of inquiry.

Dr. Lewin [36] and his associates went on to establish the Research Center for Group Dynamics at MIT and the National Training Laboratory at Bethel, Maine, where they continued to engage in many kinds of experiments in a variety of types of group phenomena. The Research Center moved from MIT to Michigan and the graduates of the program set up counterparts all about the country contracting for research in the armed forces, in business, in religious organizations, in education, and in some aspects of social work. Their contributions to the development of group theory have been tremendous from the research both in experimental groups and in real life groups pursuing long-term tasks. The influence of Lippitt and Lewin has been felt for propositions on the uses of group and many of the texts growing out of group dynamics experiments have been used in social work education. Nevertheless, a certain resistance to their contributions has continued. This resistance has been due in part to the Gestalt base of group dynamics, when social work was embracing a Freudian and ego psychological base. There has been objection also that findings from research on experimental groups or aggregates may not be applicable to treatment groups.[37] And some engaged in treatment felt one should

[35] Kurt Lewin, R. Lippitt, R. White, "Patterns of Aggressive Behavior in Experimentally Created 'Social Climates,'" in *Journal of Social Psychology*, X (1939), 271–99; or, R. Lippitt and R. White, "Leader Behavior and Members' Reactions in Three Social Climates," in Cartwright and Zander, *Group Dynamics* (1st ed., New York, Harper & Row, 1953), pp. 527–33.

[36] Kurt Lewin, *Field Theory in Social Science* (New York, Harper & Row, 1951).

[37] Grace L. Coyle, Memorandum on "The Bethel Laboratory for Group Development, 1948," to the Faculty of the School of Applied Social Sciences,

not experiment with the emotions and interpersonal responses of people. Fortunately, the attitude toward social research has changed. In recent years there has been a much greater acceptance throughout the whole social work profession of the group dynamics theory and research.[38] There also are recent social work developments, particularly in the area of behavior modification, socialization, and work almost exclusively on current social functioning of participants and clients, which has led some workers to look more closely at Gestalt psychology and the work of Lewin in field theory.

Another line of research was developed in the 1930's by Moreno and his associates, principally Helen Jennings.[39] Moreno, an Austrian psychiatrist, worked out an approach to the study of groups which he labeled "Sociometry," apparently from Freud's idea that the affectional bonds which attracted people to the group were the bases upon which the group formed. The interpersonal ties of members were examined and measured by the choices they registered of partners for work and play in particular types of activities. Jennings and Moreno together produced the "sociogram," a chart of interaction, choices, and responses. Perhaps because its psychological base was closer to social work, the approach developed by Moreno and Jennings has had greater acceptance. Many social workers have charted interaction patterns of group members from observations of participant interaction, and verbal and nonverbal responses. Thus, a modified sociometrics has entered social work practice as a means of taking quick readings and becoming more conscious of an interpersonal process that is going on within a group at a given time.

Western Reserve University (unpublished), and Robert Vinter, "Small Group Theory and Research Implications for Group Work Practice Theory and Research," in Kogan, ed., in *Social Science Theory and Social Work Research*, 1960, p. 125.

[38] Cartwright, and Zander, *Group Dynamics* (3d ed., 1968), Chapter I. Also, Northen, *Social Work with Groups*, p. 39.

[39] J. L. Moreno, *Who Shall Survive?* (Washington, D.C., Nervous and Mental Disease Publishing Co., 1934).

Helen Hall Jennings, *Leadership and Isolation* (2d ed., New York, Longmans Green, 1950).

The research of several other social scientists during the 1930's filtered through to some of the social work educators who were developing small group theory for the preparation of practitioners with groups. For instance, Clifford Shaw,[40] who wrote *The Jack Roller,* and F. Thrasher,[41] who wrote *The Gang,* worked in the University of Chicago and associated with the Institute of Juvenile Research to study the internal operations of autonomous street gangs. Their experiences in participating with delinquent youth in groups in the city and their documentation of activities led to modifications in work with autonomous groups, especially in settlements, community centers, and boys' clubs.

In 1937 another study appeared which had a profound effect on gang work—*Street Corner Society* by W. F. Whyte.[42] He examined the formal and informal social and political organization of the Italian community of Boston. As a participant-observer, he recorded in detail the inner workings of the street gang and the community club, whch revealed the effects of group life both on the individual participants and on the wider social and political structure of the community. Whyte observed the group concepts of interaction, structure, leadership, cohesion, and status. The works of Whyte, Thrasher, and Shaw gave some theoretical understanding for the street gang work that was revived in the 1950's and 1960's.

Theodore Newcomb,[43] who was associated with Newstetter, conducted a series of studies at Bennington College in Vermont on the effect of group associations on changes of attitudes of conservative students in the liberal college atmosphere. He found that as students became anchored in groups on the campus, their attitudes began to change consistently with the general social atmosphere of the surrounding college society. He concluded that the degree of

[40] Clifford Shaw, *The Jack Roller* (Chicago, University of Chicago Press, 1930).

[41] Frederic Thrasher, *The Gang* (Chicago, University of Chicago Press, 1927).

[42] William Foote Whyte, *Street Corner Society* (Chicago, University of Chicago Press, 1943).

[43] Theodore Newcomb, *Personality and Social Change* (New York, Dryden, 1943).

influence of the group on the individual depended to a large degree on the relationship of the individual to the group and that groups evaluate, rank, and reward members in part at least on their conformity to group norms. These studies not only provided a significant milestone on the possibility of research on "natural" groups but they also gave support to the potential effect of groups on their members, that is, provided new insights to the use of groups as means of changing attitudes of participants.

Muzafer Sherif,[44] a social psychologist, pioneered in research on the "autokinetic effect," the phenomenon of perceiving a still light to be moving if it is so dim in a dark room that the viewer has no reference points against which to measure its location. Although the light is stationary, individuals perceived the light to move back and forth varying distances. When estimates about the amount of movement were made in the presence of others, the judgments of observers were influenced by each other and converged toward a mean. When individuals were separated from the collectivities and asked to make judgments again, they maintained the judgment at which they had arrived with others rather than reverting to their previous independent judgment. Sherif's findings were reported on a discussion of social norms in 1936. His research is said to have had a profound effect on the development of experimental social psychology and small group research.[45] He also noted that the person who took the initiative generally was instrumental in establishing the group norms according to his judgment. However, after the group norm was established, if he changed his individual norm, he was no longer followed by the group. Sherif's further work on boys' gangs and the effects of "ego involvement" in which he showed the effect of group in maintaining norms alien to the surrounding society were frequently used by group work theorists.[46] Sherif's influence was seen in social work in the recognition that group influence may affect or change individual attitudes, and was

[44] Muzafer Sherif, *The Psychology of Social Norms* (New York, Harper & Row, 1936).

[45] Cartwright, and Zander, *Group Dynamics* (3d ed., 1968).

[46] Muzafer Sherif, and Hadley Cantril, *The Psychology of Ego Involvements* (New York, John Wiley & Sons, Inc., 1947).

put to work particularly in intercultural relations. Sherif's research on the self-selected groups of boys in camp produced some evidence of the value of voluntary group associations in building group morale and cohesion. He also showed that group cohesion could be increased by the presence of an external "enemy" by creating competing groups.

During the 1940's and 1950's, both sociologists and psychologists became more interested in the small group as a unit of study and for the extraction of concepts for theory building. It has been suggested that this was a period of rediscovery of the small group and that it resulted from serendipitous findings from other kinds of sociological study. Both Fred Strodtbeck [47] and Edward Shils [48] have drawn this conclusion. They cite, for example, the work of Lloyd Warner [49] and associates who discovered when they were studying the *Social Life of Modern Community* in the Yankee City series and later in community studies in the Midwest that the small group aspects of the family and the clique determined a person's values, class position, life style, and even facilitated his mobility. The findings from studies of social class led to hypotheses regarding factors in the small group which could be influential in connecting individuals with the wider society and social structure. A number of studies of small group organizations in the community followed.

In Samuel Stouffer's study of the effect of ideology and motivation on the combat record of the American soldier [50] in World War II, it was discovered that the small unit and group of friends provided greater incentive for survival and for improving combat functioning than did nationalistic and ideological incentives or the formal structure of the army. The degree of morale and unity

[47] Fred L. Strodtbeck, "The Case for the Study of Small Groups," *American Sociological Review*, XIX (December, 1954), 651–57.

[48] Edward Shils, "The Study of the Primary Group," in Daniel Lerner and H. D. Lasswell, eds., *The Policy Sciences* (Stanford, Calif., Stanford University Press, 1951), pp. 44–69.

[49] W. Lloyd Warner, Marchia Meeker, and Kenneth Eells, *Social Class in America* (Chicago, Social Science Research Associates, Inc., 1949).

[50] Samuel Stouffer et al., *The American Soldier, Combat and Its Aftermath* (Princeton, N.J., Princeton University Press, 1949).

within the combat teams exhibited a direct relationship to their combat record.

These studies, as well as the famous Roethlisberger [51] study of Western Electric, showed that the small work groups had more influence on production than company or corporate incentives. The Lazarsfeld [52] study of voting, *The People's Choice*, showed that people's voting was more influenced by their associates in clubs and by their families than by mass media and literature. These findings stimulated much interest in the study of group behavior as a means for social and attitudinal influence.

With all of these clues to the importance of groups in the functioning of society, some social scientists took a renewed interest in examining the inner processes of the small group. During the 1950's and 1960's there then emerged thousands of studies of various aspects of group life. Some of these were experimental, some were descriptive of phenomena in ongoing life groups. Many took one small aspect of a phenomenon to study. The field of social psychology seemed to come of age with a focus on interpersonal relations of man in society.[53] Applied anthropology also drew heavily upon small groups as instruments of social change. This recognition grew out of work in undeveloped countries and small group life in villages.

Golembiewski [54] refers to the growth of the study of small membership groups as "the most marked research trend in the post World War II social science revolution." He says that the "Johnny-come-lately boom in small group analysis is a composite of many elements" including the "usefulness of the small group concept for explaining behavior," which is incomprehensible by "individual psychology, or the influence of a macroscopic social unit."

[51] E. J. Roethlisberger, and W. J. Dickson, *Management and the Worker* (Cambridge, Mass., Harvard University Press., 1939).

[52] P. F. Lazarsfeld, B. Berelson, and Hazel Gaudet, *The People's Choice* (New York, Duel Sloan and Pearce, 1944).

[53] Gordon Allport, "The Historical Background of Modern Social Psychology," in Gardner Lindzey, ed., *The Handbook of Social Psychology* (Reading, Mass., Addison-Wesley Publishing Co., Inc., 1954), pp. 3–56.

[54] Robert Golembiewski, *The Small Group* (Chicago, University of Chicago Press, 1962), p. 17.

George C. Homans,[55] attempting to state a theory of groups based on an analysis of five types of small groups, produced *The Human Group,* which has been used by many social workers. His alignment of sentiments, activities, and interactions in a system of personal relations inside the group, and his positing an external system of the group in its social context, provides one framework for understanding and using groups.

The emergence of Group Dynamics from the Lewinian roots as mentioned earlier produced another framework for understanding group processes in the 1950's. While the major thrust of the published studies, writings, and theoretical propositions is said to be on research, the leadership of the group dynamics movement have also expended considerable energy on leadership training, on sensitizing participants to their own human interpersonal potentials, and, in fact, on some therapeutic endeavors. The concepts upon which they focus, as reflected in the most recent revision of the Cartwright and Zander publication of *Group Dynamics,*[56] include composition of membership, cohesion, pressures to uniformity, power and influence, leadership, motivation, and structure.

Significant in the development of theory about small groups was the extensive research on the interaction process in groups by Robert F. Bales,[57] begun in the 1940's. Bales noted the quantity and quality and type of actions taken by participants in problem-solving groups, and he developed a scheme for classifying the types of contributions made by participants. One of the valuable outcomes of Bales's research was the finding that in any group engaged in problem solving, work on the task and work to maintain the group functioning were produced simultaneously. He found there were *instrumental* or task activities and *social-emotional* or affective responses, and that these kinds of responses and actions by members needed to be taken into account in examining the process of the group. His work also gave a preliminary impetus to the study of

[55] George C. Homans, *The Human Group* (New York, Harcourt Brace Jovanovich, Inc., 1950).

[56] Cartwright, and Zander, *Group Dynamics* (3d ed., 1968).

[57] Robert F. Bales, *Interaction Process Analysis* (Reading, Mass., Addison-Wesley Publishing Co., Inc., 1950).

phasing as his research produced evidence that groups pass through a process of phases in their organization and problem-solving process. Although Bales initially studied experimental groups, his work has been carried on continuously in real life groups with specific tasks, such as labor negotitations, community organization committees, therapy groups, jury deliberations, and classroom activities. Social workers have found his scale quite helpful in analyzing the group interactions, and phase development in both person-focused groups and task-focused groups, and also for understanding the importance of the orientation period while a group settles down to do its work.

Hare, Borgatta, and Bales [58] have evolved another conceptual framework of the group as a system of social interaction. In their volume, *Small Groups: Studies in Social Interaction,* published in 1955 and revised in 1966, they look at the phenomena of communication networks, interaction and equilibrium, group size, composition and subgroups, role differentiation and leadership. Hare himself developed a more detailed formulation in the studies he chose to include in his *Handbook of Small Group Research,*[59] published in 1962. This framework consisted of group process and structure, including norms and control, the decision process, roles, and interpersonal choice; interaction variables of personality, social characteristics of members, group size, tasks, communication networks, and leadership and group productivity.

Theodore Mills, viewing the group from a sociological perspective, has attempted to develop a scheme for understanding the small group as a social system. While he examines a variety of models of groups, he actually discusses the group elements of behavior and group emotion, norms and normative control, group goals, group management and authority, and group growth. His formulation appears primarily in his *The Sociology of Small Groups.*[60]

There is also a framework suggested by Robert Golembiewski in

[58] A. Paul Hare, E. F. Borgatta, and R. F. Bales, *Small Groups: Studies in Social Interaction* (rev. ed., New York: Alfred A. Knopf, Inc., 1965).

[59] Hare, *Handbook.*

[60] Mills, *Sociology of Small Groups.*

The Small Group.[61] He says, "Researchers have developed a wide range of variables describing small group properties and processes. It would be presumptuous to pick one set of concepts adequate for group descriptions at this time. One need not be incautious to begin the task of specifying a set of useful group properties." [62] Golembiewski then states his scheme for understanding groups, including leadership, roles, styles, atmosphere, personality, cohesion, and norms.

No discussion of the evolution of theory of small groups useful to social workers would be complete without inclusion of what has been called group therapy or group psychotherapy. It grew from some of the same roots as social work. Slavson,[63] for instance, was one of the pioneers in the group work aspect of social work and in the 1930's split off to develop his group therapy approach. Today group uses for therapeutic purposes have been expanded by a large number of professionals, referred to as group therapists or group psychotherapists. Their professional base may be social work, psychology, or psychiatry. Some research and much writing is produced by these people.

Recent writers who have attempted to examine the theoretical aspects of groups for use in therapeutic situations are several. Notable is the work of Helen Durkin, whose study, *The Group in Depth,*[64] reviews and assesses various schools of thought, theories, and approaches to understanding group processes. Max Rosenbaum and Milton Berger,[65] in their book, *Group Psychotherapy and Group Function,* also have put together articles dealing with some of the group processes. In a paper called "Memorandum on Group Theory," David Rapaport [66] attempted to list group ele-

[61] Golembiewski, *The Small Group.*

[62] Robert Golembiewski, "Small Groups and Large Organizations," in James G. March, ed., *Handbook of Organizations,* Chicago, Rand McNally & Co., 1965.

[63] S. R. Slavson, *The Practice of Group Therapy* (New York, International Universities Press, 1947).

[64] Durkin, *The Group in Depth.*

[65] Max Rosenbaum, and Milton Berger, *Group Psychotherapy and Group Function* (New York, Basic Books, Inc., 1963).

[66] David Rapaport, *The Collected Papers of David Rapaport,* ed. by Merton M. Gill (New York, Basic Books, Inc., 1967).

ments that he had observed, including cohesion, group code, leadership, structure and subdivision, group goals, interaction, morale, activity, and decisions. His major approach was to examine how groups change in these processes and how changes can be induced. These are only a few of the psychotherapists who have endeavored to write about groups.

Perhaps one of the most prolific in writing about group theory as applied to therapy is Eric Berne,[67] whose several books about group theory have had wide circulation, including *The Structure and Dynamics of Organizations and Groups.*

Thus, it is possible to see that as social workers began their exploration of group theory, few resources were available in social work or in the social sciences. As they moved ahead on their own, social workers' concern was more with service to people in and through groups than it was in theory development *per se.* As social science theory appeared, it was seized upon and incorporated within the teaching and the theory for practice of social group workers. As yet, however, few group workers have formulated questions for social science research, although a few have formulated questions for their own research, largely for doctoral dissertations or in other aspects of the academic setting. Group work practitioners have produced very little research or theory development from their own practice with groups. The borrowing to date seems to go principally in one direction—from social science to social work.

Notable among the recent writers in social work who have attempted to reformulate social science concepts of the group for social work use are Robert Vinter and his colleagues at the University of Michigan.[68] Vinter recommended that more research be undertaken and encouraged his colleagues to develop questions for further study.[69] Similar is the work of Saul Bernstein and his colleagues at Boston University.[70] Their close association with Robert

[67] Eric Berne, *The Structure and Dynamics of Organizations and Groups* (Philadelphia, J. G. Lippincott Co., 1963).

[68] Robert Vinter, ed., *Readings in Group Work Practice* (Ann Arbor, Campus Publishers, 1967).

[69] Vinter, "Small Group Theory and Research," in Kogan, ed., *Social Science Theory and Social Work Research.*

[70] Bernstein, *Explorations in Group Work.*

Chin and Kenneth Benne, who are leaders in the National Training Laboratory for Group Dynamics, has brought some merger of
research and group practice. Two authors who have been concerned with practice application and theory development *per se*
are Helen Northen and William Schwartz. Dr. Northen's major
work, *Social Work in Groups*,[71] touches upon and uses small group
theory in her chapters on the social work practice related to phases
of groups. She presents concepts tested in research carried on by
doctoral students under her tutelage. William Schwartz has engaged to a large extent in developing theory about the functions of
the social worker in the group, but he also implies the use of small
group theory.[72] He has drawn heavily upon systems theory. While
none of the above writers has produced what Robert Merton calls
a "middle range" theory of small groups, they have begun to set
down descriptive and analytical hypotheses which may be tested,
and have made more explicit knowledge available for understanding and working with people in groups. Some recent doctoral dissertations in schools of social work also attempt theory building.[73]

Mention should be made here of the emergent theory regarding
the small group aspects of family life, contrary to the view of the
family as a social institution. The interactional theory, drawing on
Cooley's view of the small primary group as a socializing process,
of which the family is one, and Burgess' view of the family as a
unit of interacting personalities, postulates that the family is a

[71] Northen, *Social Work with Groups.*

[72] Schwartz, "Small Group Science and Group Work Practice," *Social Work,*
VIII (October, 1963).

[73] For instance, see: Florence Cleminger, "Congruence Between Members
and Workers on Selected Behaviors of the Role of the Social Group Worker"
(unpublished D.S.W. dissertation, University of Southern California, 1965);
Francis J. Pierce, "A Study of the Methodological Components of Social Work
with Groups" (unpublished D.S.W. dissertation, University of Southern California, 1966); Marjorie W. Main, "An Examination of Selected Aspects of the
Beginning Phase in Social Work with Groups" (unpublished Ph.D. dissertation, University of Chicago, 1965); Henrietta Saloshin, "Development of an
Instrument for the Analysis of Social Group Work Method in Therapeutic Set-
tings" (unpublished D.S.W. dissertation, University of Minnesota, 1954); and,
William I. Shalinsky, "The Effect of Group Composition on Aspects of Group
Functioning" (unpublished D.S.W. dissertation, Cleveland, Western Reserve
University, 1967).

small group. The family can be studied, understood, and treated as a self-contained small group according to this position. Jay D. Schvanveldt [74] maintains that the "unique, differentiating characteristic of the interactional approach is that it is based on the action of the family resulting from the communication process. It views family behavior as an adjustive process where cues are given and individual members respond to these stimuli." The small group framework has been particularly useful in the preparation of case histories, gathering data about families in crisis, and intervening in the processes of the interpersonal relationships among family members. Christensen [75] has noted that the approach to the family as a small group has permitted those who work with families to view each individual member within the changing group and also provide for isolation and specification of potential sources of difficulty as family members interact with each other and the wider society. Coyle and Somers both refer to the group processes which apply to families. Coyle [76] makes direct application of the processes of group formation and composition, development of structure, interpersonal relationships, control and authority associated with roles, communication systems and the decision-making process, the emergence of values, norms and cohesion. Somers [77] also considers the group dimensions of family group formation, family group problem solving, and the development of family group cohesion. Somers says, "The nuclear family in our culture can be thought of as a small group and is generally recognized as one of the most crucial in maintaining the integrity of the individual and of society." Therefore, in our analysis of small group process, we will periodically refer to the application of particular group dimensions to the

[74] Jay D. Schvanveldt, "The Interactional Framework in the Study of the Family," in F. Ivan Nye and Felix M. Berardo, eds., *Emerging Conceptual Frameworks in Family Analysis* (New York, The Macmillan Co., 1966), pp. 97–99.

[75] H. T. Christensen, *Handbook on Marriage and the Family* (Chicago, Rand McNally & Co., 1964), Chapter I.

[76] Grace L. Coyle, "Concepts Relevant to Helping the Family As A Group," *Social Casework*, XLIII (July, 1962), 347–54.

[77] Mary Louise Somers, "Group Process Within the Family Unit," in *The Family As Client*. National Association of Social Workers, Pacific Northwest Regional Institute, 1968.

family as one example of a continuous autonomous group, utilized and served in social work practice.

Definition of Group

We have considered the early and more recent efforts at conceptualization of small group processes within social work, some of the sources of knowledge about groups in the social sciences which we will draw upon, and some of the parallel developments in conceptualization in group therapy, but we have not yet defined "group." The definition of "group" is crucial to type of theory and research which is useful in building a scheme for understanding group behavior.

For purposes of this book, a small group is defined as at least two people—but usually more, gathered with common purposes or like interests in a cognitive, affective, and social interchange in single or repeated encounters sufficient for the participants to form impressions of one another, creating a set of norms for their functioning together, developing goals for their collective activity, evolving a sense of cohesion so that they think of themselves and are thought of by others as an entity distinct from all other collectivities.

This definition takes account of size, location, frequency of meeting, purpose for convening, and goals for group activity which emerge out of the interaction. It also contains the notion of mutual influence, the adoption of group norms, and the establishment of a sense of bond in the group cohesiveness that grows out of the members' attachment to one another and to the group-as-a-whole.

The small group as instrument for providing service or help within the social work context includes the social worker as a group member with a defined professional function and role. Usually, the social work group is formed within or brought into the social welfare setting (an agency or a program).

A simple collection of people is sometimes erroneously referred to as a group. People in a waiting room, at a reception, or traveling on a bus are sometimes called a group. Such a gathering, however, is an aggregate—people bounded by location and usually experiencing common influences. The first convening of any collection of people is an aggregate until they interact and begin to take on meaningful relationships and establish some form. Parsons [78] distinguishes a group having organization from an aggregate or a category of people. He says an aggregate is a gathering of people without a common bond or significant interaction. Examples would be the unorganized residents of a neighborhood, people waiting in a clinic, the audience of a play. A category or class of people are those who share some characteristic, and are therefore thought of together or as similar, but who are not organized. For instance, all students, all delinquents, all older adults, all Italians, all social workers may be thought of together, and sometimes referred to as a group. Sometimes they are erroneously asked to be represented as if they were organized and had a single point of view. Since social work services may be organized fallaciously when it is assumed that either an aggregate or a category is a group, it is crucial to make clear this difference.

In social work settings, people with similar problems are brought together with a worker who serves as therapist and talks with or counsels individual members while others observe. All who are present may benefit from what they observe and hear, regardless of whether or not the conversation focuses on their problems, concerns, or interests. Interpersonal interaction is, however, at a minimum and generally all persons present are not engaged in working together or sharing their thoughts and feelings about the problems. Such treatment situations may be more aggregational than group and in them the potential for group help or group work is not maximized. Similarly, in some activity or interest groups where the members are engaged in parallel work, such as painting, crafts, or individualized sports, no group actually exists unless some interaction and corporate activity is undertaken. A collection of representatives of groups or organizations, such as a citizen-action council, is not a group until the members begin to interact together in the new organization. Such a collection is sometimes

[78] Talcott Parsons, and Edward Shils, *Toward A General Theory of Action* (Cambridge, Mass., Harvard University Press, 1951).

thought of or referred to as a group when in fact it is an aggregation of individuals engaged in activity at the same time and place with interaction and emotional responses at a minimum.

A group creates its own style or culture which characterizes the particular collection of persons as separate from their outside setting, or what Homans refers to as external system.[79] Such culture, once established, also influences the behavior, customs, and styles of interaction of the members, or what Homans refers to as the internal structure.

The difference between aggregates and groups may render some research findings more or less useful in building knowledge about groups, at least about groups with continuity, purpose, and focus. Many studies, particularly experimental ones, are based on the responses of hired subjects who have been brought together briefly with no interpersonal attachment and no motivation to remain together nor to work on any matter of vital concern and who therefore do not have the same qualities as ongoing natural groups. The social scientists engaged in this type of research, however, have made some valuable contributions regarding certain types of task-oriented problem-solving processes, as may become apparent when research is reviewed later in this text.

In the next chapter we will examine some research on the human uses to which groups may be put. Findings from social research will equip us to establish a set of categories for group uses.

[79] Homans, *The Human Group.*

SOCIAL SCIENCE FINDINGS
ON THE USES OF GROUPS

Within social work practice, the increasing interest in groups introduces a new imperative to understand the possibilities of group
methods. Groups are effectively used to support individuals in
growth, rehabilitation and change, and for prevention of social and
personal breakdown. A group can also be used for the development and change of the group's own environment, for modifying
systems, and for changing some of the institutions of society. A
more definitive understanding, however, still is needed of those situations and circumstances for which a group may be the most appropriate means of social work service delivery.

Questions remain unanswered as to the nature of people and
problems for which groups are the most effective means of service,
and those for which they are not indicated, as to the purposes and
goals most readily achievable in groups, and purposes and goals
which are more readily achieved by individuals working alone.
These kinds of questions frequently emerge when consideration is

being given to use of group methods, especially for the first time. In this chapter we will examine some of the social science theory and research on effectiveness of group experience and the purposes for which groups have proved useful.

While experience in social work practice has produced evidence for the position that certain ends can be achieved through practice with people in groups, there has been relatively little rigorous research to establish empirically that group methods produce expected results. One sees in social work writings, especially in descriptions of practice, conclusions that certain types of problems are amenable to treatment or action for change through group activity. Groups have been used when they somehow seemed to be the appropriate means of service for social development, preparation for new experiences, teaching or changing values, modification of life style, problem solving, community and social planning, and many other purposes. We nevertheless have no clear prescriptions for group use, nor any classification within social work practice of problems which may be better served through group than by individual methods. Therefore, it seems high time to attempt a fairly primitive and commonsense classification, based on the uses of groups to achieve particular objectives with given targets. These targets are: (1) the individual member; (2) problems in interpersonal relationships; (3) small systems in neighborhood, community, or institution; and (4) large systems of institutions, regions, states, or nations.

Social science research on groups has produced theory and evidence on the effects of groups in achieving certain results with individuals, with problem solving, and with influencing or changing the system or societal situation outside of the group. Our classification of this research serves merely to group studies, and to permit conclusions about present or potential group use in practice. While for any member a group may have a primary purpose or use, the group can usually be said to have secondary purposes as a whole, and differential effects for individual members. Also, groups may have different meanings through time; the purposes of some change and their usefulness increases or decreases.

Social science theoretical formulations and studies permit us to propose the following categories of group use:

1. *For effect on participants:* socialization-resocialization, acquiring or changing concept of self, identity, motivation; attitude formation and change, formation and modification of values and beliefs; behavioral change; achieving a sense of belonging and support; education.

2. *For collective problem solving:* work on common or joint tasks, particularly in the area of ideas, group thinking, cognitive, emotional, or social, or individual, group or social situation.

3. *For change in social situation or conditions outside the group:* (a) modification of the institution or social system within which the group exists, or (b) of the social situation—including the community or society—through pressure, dissemination of information, or organization; modification of attitudes of outsiders.

Group Effect on the Participants

Socialization—Role Induction

Cooley,[1] one of the earliest group theorists, postulated that it was by group experience that the individual becomes socialized. Socialization is "the sequence of social learning experiences that result in the integration of the individual into a society." [2] Social learning implies that the individual takes on values, norms, acceptable behavior, and life style through interaction with others. The socialization of the individual proceeds throughout his life [3] through contacts with other people and through the institutions of society. This adaptation process seems to be most influenced by

[1] Charles H. Cooley, *Social Organization* (New York, Charles Scribner's Sons, 1909).

[2] John W. McDavid, and Herbert Harrari, *Social Psychology* (New York, Harper & Row, 1968), p. 39.

[3] Orville Brim, and Stanton Wheeler, *Socialization after Childhood* (New York, John Wiley & Sons, Inc., 1966).

small groups: family, friendships, and peers, school groups, play groups, occupational and associational groups. Cooley [4] said that the group is the medium and the context for producing changes in members that endure beyond the existence of the group. These changes, he said, appear in attitudes, personality traits, interests, or skills, and occur during and after interaction among members of a group.

Cartwright [5] also observed that the "behavior, attitudes, beliefs and values of the individual are all firmly grounded in groups to which he belongs." "What he believes to be true and good, whom he loves and hates, what beliefs and prejudices he holds, are highly influenced by his group membership." Cartwright concludes that "whether [people] change or resist change will be influenced by their groups."

The socialization process is sometimes referred to as "learning the rules of the game," that is, becoming acculturated to social expectations of the cooperative game of living in society. Helanko [6] took the phrase literally in setting up a research to determine when and how people from infancy through young adulthood learned to comprehend the rules of games, played spontaneously. He made extensive observations in a longitudinal study of children's play and game activities after the style of Piaget. He concluded that during their socialization, people learn to behave in a system of pairs and gradually extend themselves to increasingly larger groups. He noted that children ages one to three were preoccupied with motor development or mastery of physical skills. They had no comprehension of rules. They played in aggregations, with mostly egocentric behavior. He observed some primitive pairs

[4] C. H. Cooley quoted in Henry Riecken and George Homans, "Psychological Aspects of Social Structure," in Gardner Lindzey, ed., *Handbook of Social Psychology* (Reading, Addison-Wesley Publishing Co., Inc., 1953).

[5] Dorwin Cartwright, "Achieving Change in People," in Warren G. Bennis, Kenneth Benne, and Robert Chin, eds., *The Planning of Change* (New York, Holt, Rinehart & Winston, Inc., 1961), p. 698.

[6] R. Helanko, "Sports and Socialization," in Neil J. Smelser and William T. Smelser, *Personality and Social Systems* (New York, John Wiley & Sons, Inc., 1963).

but no actual group attachments, and no sports activities. At age five, children were still mostly egocentric but beginning to move out to others. Some competition began to enter children's games at ages of six or seven when cooperation was beginning to emerge, though children tended still to be egocentric. Some worked in pairs in their free play. Some rules began to be important and by ages seven to nine, rules were sacred and absolute. The play-gang stage was emerging, primitive groups with which solidarity and fluid organization and primitive sports were played.

Age nine seemed to be a turning point in the emergence of groups and Helanko classified the gang age as nine to sixteen, though he divided it into two subperiods—nine to twelve and twelve to sixteen. In this period he noted, children learn to behave in primary groups in the company of their equals, such as neighborhood boys, or school yard groups, with strong solid in-group feeling with strong internal pull for the members. There was highly organized activity in sports and games. The nine to twelve period he characterized with intensive interaction, a closed circle, and firm organization repellent to others in groups numbering six or seven.

In the gang-age period of twelve to sixteen, he observed a tendency to codify rules which were regarded as related to the game. Gangs frequently reformed or widened to include a new configuration of people or a second gang. As they neared age sixteen, the older members withdrew. In some cases the upper age groups included girls, and there was some pairing off and leaving the group. Sports in this age level were highly structured, demanding a high level of cooperation.

By age sixteen boys seemed to lose interest in games, and where all members were about the same age, groups terminated at age seventeen. By eighteen, former members had paired off with either best friends of the same sex or girl friends, or both, but relationships tended to be individualistic. Activities were dancing or pair sports. From sixteen to twenty-four there was a preoccupation with finding a partner and social position in the wider society, and the formation or joining of social clubs and associations which tend toward secondary groups around beliefs or movements, but with less investment of self.

This rather extensive longitudinal study supports some common-sense beliefs about grouping based on observation of children that have been considered relevant to group practice for some time. It has implications for group uses toward the specific ends of socialization and teaching of values and norms at specific ages. For instance, an effort to organize groups of nursery-age children may be futile, while small groups of children from ages seven on may be useful if the purpose of the group is socialization and the development of self-control and self-managed groups. It also suggests guides for working with people who have suffered social deprivations or interruptions of normal social development due to physical or emotional handicaps or illnesses. There may also be implications for resocialization or modification of internalized roles from a subsystem of society, such as use of groups for the modification of racist attitudes, delinquent behavior, or other antisocial life styles detrimental to physical or social well-being.

Identity and Self-Concept

Not only do one's values, beliefs, and behaviors seem to stem from his interaction with others, but one's very impression of himself or herself—one's identity, one's assessment of his own worth, also develop from associations with others.

Mead [7] theorized that a person's perception of himself came almost totally from the image he had perceived in the responses of others to him. He wrote of the "looking-glass self"—the self one sees reflected in the way others respond to him. He also wrote of the "significant others" in one's life—those people who take on meaning for one and influence one's impression of self. Thus a person may be socialized to certain expectations of himself in light of what his associates teach him to expect, and how he considers that he measures up to or deviates from the expectation of those about him. Although his sense of adequacy may come from his actual successes and failures in achievement, his standards of expectation

[7] G. H. Mead, *Mind, Self, and Society* (Chicago, University of Chicago Press, 1934).

for himself are culturally derived from the expectation of those significant others in his life. The responses that he receives from those about him give him some measure of himself. A person is apt to approve those factors in himself that others approve, and disapprove of those features which he feels are criticized.

In an effort to test Mead's theory, Manis [8] studied men in small living groups in residences and discovered that over time a person's conception of himself tended to change in the direction of others' expectations of him. Where the group's conception of the person differed from the person's conception of self, over time, the person changed toward group expectations of him; the group did not modify its expectations of the man. Revisions in the person's sense of himself tended to be in an improvement in evaluation of self, and his change was more greatly influenced by opinions of friends or people who had significant meaning to him, than by people who knew him but were not close personal friends.

Sears and Sherman [9] also conducted studies on the origins of self-approval and found evidence that self-evaluation stemmed from responses of others and standards set by significant others. They found that over a period of time "changes in children's physical development, scholastic achievement and socially desirable behavior were closely related to differential treatment by teachers, peers, and families, and this in turn resulted in considerable change in self-esteem." McDavid and Harrari [10] conclude that "being liked and approved by others provides one important basis for liking and approving oneself."

Golembiewski [11] theorized similarly that "friendships and affections are available often only in group interaction. A person's conception of self and the preservation of that self-conception are very often group products. These gratifications attract people to

[8] Melvin Manis, "Social Interaction and the Self Concept," *Journal of Abnormal and Social Psychology*, LI (1955), 362–70.

[9] Pauline S. Sears, and V. S. Sherman, *In Pursuit of Self-Esteem* (Belmont, Calif., Wadsworth Publishing Co. Inc., 1964).

[10] McDavid and Harrari, *Social Psychology*, p. 229.

[11] Robert Golembiewski, *The Small Group* (Chicago, University of Chicago Press, 1962), p. 23.

groups." He suggested further that groups provide a frame of reference or an anchor for the individual and his behavior.

If one's sense of self, then, derives from one's contacts in various associations and groups, it would follow that movement into and among various social groups in which there are *different* expectations of a person might result in role conflicts and confusions. McDavid and Harrari [12] suggest that "to the extent that participation in groups introduces varied new elements into the self-concept, internal conflicts within . . . the self-concept are likely to increase as the number of group identifications in which the person engages increase." On the other hand, if a person with many associations synthesizes the many expectations of himself in his various associations, he broadens and strengthens his self-image.

These postulates suggest that although one may have a particular image of self, this assessment of himself could be changed through group experience and that if one wished to induce such changes in a person, particularly to improve his sense of self—and to modify his socialization process—this might be arranged through group assignment or planned group experiences. A carefully designed group could offer a corrective self-assessment. Groups, in which most members feel themselves to be failures as people and in particular roles, may provide experiences where members succeed and achieve a measure of satisfaction. This experience may then improve their capacity to function in other areas of their lives. Observations of children who were poor achievers in school showed their performance improved after having a group experience wherein their personal esteem was improved. Some groups of young mothers who were welfare recipients showed considerable improvement in their parenting roles and in their sense of self when they participated in activities that were successful and made them feel more adequate and important.

Some of the research and training done under the auspices of National Training Laboratories for Group Dynamics has been concerned with this phenomenon of modifying a person's self-concep-

---

[12] McDavid and Harrari, *Social Psychology*, p. 231.

tion and individual behavior. Bradford, Gibb, and Benne [13] say that in the *T* Group, members "must establish a process of inquiry in which data about their own behavior are collected and analyzed with the [group] experience that generates the behavior." Through group discussion the participant sees himself in interactions with others and while looking at and helping others, he becomes more sensitive to his own "motives, feelings and strategies in dealing with other persons." He also discovers the reactions he produces in others as he interacts with them.

Within constructed groups, it has been found that people can be deliberately helped to reflect themselves, and also modify their behaviors and styles in such a way that they may be more effective in all social and interpersonal relations. While some of the effects in this process are similar to group psychotherapy and other therapies, sensitivity training makes use of a focus on the present reality and current functioning of the well part of people, rather than the unconscious behavior or pathological aspects frequently involved in therapy. This method utilizes learning theory techniques of reinforcement, feedback, and conditioned response rather than dynamic, developmental, psychoanalytic theory. Over time, the experiences of the groups created under the various branches of *T* groups or sensitivity training would tend to demonstrate that the formation of self-image and social behavior not only derives from group experiences throughout life but also can be modified and made more socially effective through guided group experience.[14] The changes in the person from this experience are thought to be cognitive and to include increased self-awareness, emotionally changed attitudes, and behaviorally changed interpersonal competence, according to Schein and Bennis.

Education and Learning

Education is an individual phenomenon, that is, a person must be responsible for his own learning, for taking on his own knowl-

[13] Leland Bradford, Jack R. Gibb, and Kenneth Benne, *T-Group Theory and Laboratory Method* (New York, John Wiley & Sons, Inc., 1964), pp. 1–3.

[14] Edgar Schein, and Warren Bennis, *Personal and Organizational Change through Group Method* (New York, John Wiley & Sons, Inc., 1965).

edge, but a great deal of learning goes on in groups. Research has been done on the effects of various group experiences on learning. In one experiment,[15] methods of teaching employing the lecture-demonstration with teacher-directed discussion were compared with a group approach where students had free choice of topics, direction of discussion, and expression of opinion within the framework of the focus of the course. The teacher-directed group made higher grades on the final exam than did the group-focused group, but the students in the experimental group were more satisfied with the course. It was obvious that the effectiveness of the learning experience and satisfaction of the learner are not equivalent.

Gardner Murphy [16] in studying the use of the group in education found that "where there was a chance for more classroom discussion among students there was a group morale that resulted in a collective learning process." He notes the importance of empathy, sympathy, and support of individual problem-solving approaches that occur in the group. Murphy suggests further that "in educational group experiences there is a realignment and reorganization of the affective ties of each person with his fellow, so that as the subject matter becomes meaningful to him, his social relationships with those who are coping with the same subject matter, become more precious to him, and he as a learner identifies with others who are learning at the same time."

Roseborough [17] found that students participate more in permissive class sessions than in structured discussions and find them more interesting, but felt more adequately prepared from the teacher-directed sessions. However, this study revealed no difference in the grades of students in either style. He concluded that the students' own purposes and values govern their reactions to more or less constricted participation, and that some will learn better under one method and some under the other. This may also depend on their personalities and previous socialization processes.

[15] Mary E. Roseborough, "Experimental Studies of Small Groups," *Psychological Bulletin*, L (1953), 275–303.

[16] Gardner Murphy, "Group Psychotherapy in Our Society," in Max Rosenbaum and Milton Berger, *Group Psychotherapy and Group Function* (New York, Basic Books, Inc., 1963), pp. 33–41.

[17] Roseborough, "Experimental Studies," *Psychological Bulletin*, L (1953).

In another study, students [18] were asked to prepare for an examination independently. After they had completed the exam, all were given an opportunity to restudy in light of their results; members of one group, however, were asked to study alone, while members of another group had the opportunity to discuss the questions and the material with each other. On the whole, the students who discussed the results did better on the retest, suggesting that the opportunity to talk together gave some new insights and understanding to individuals that they had not achieved alone. This modification in their views, then, was evident in the retest.

In an experiment [19] of a class developed by this writer, after several class sessions employing the lecture-discussion method structured by the instructor, students were asked to work in self-selected small task groups around topics which they also chose from an outline prepared by the instructor, and to prepare class presentations for their classmates. In evaluating the experience, students agreed that they had had an opportunity to learn more about group behavior through experiencing it and analyzing the process together with their classmates, but they felt that they suffered a loss in cognitive content or the development of theory about small groups in the presentations of their classmates. They felt their classmates could not master, organize, and present the theory for learning purposes to each other as well as the instructor. The emotional and experiential aspects of student-conducted study were rated high, while the mastery of content was rated as low.

Similarly, Faw [20] found in a classroom experiment that students doubted the intellectual adequacy of the experimental group and also felt that they had not received as much information and knowledge as in the instructor-centered group, but they felt they experienced emotional and social value from the group-centered learning.

[18] J. Levine, and J. Butler, "Lecture vs. Discussion in Changing Behavior," *Journal of Applied Psychology,* XXXVI (1952), 29–33.

[19] Classroom experiment in Group Behavior Course at Case Western Reserve University, Fall, 1969.

[20] V. A. Faw, "A Psychotherapeutic Method of Teaching Psychology," *American Psychologist,* IV (1949), 104–109.

Formation or Modification of Values,
Beliefs, Attitudes, and Attitude Change

As suggested in the socializing process, a person seems to take on his beliefs of right and wrong, good and bad, true and false, beautiful and ugly, from those about him. Initially these cultural attributes come from his family contacts but very quickly come from the "street," that is, play groups, peer groups, and throughout life from significant others in his reference groups. The Asch [21] experiments show the effect of group pressure in changing one's expressed opinion, although whether they show actual changes in opinions or merely in public expression of opinions is difficult to say. People do yield in their opinions to pressures of the opinions of those about them.

In the experiments conducted by Asch, members were asked to express their opinions about their observations. In each small group, only one person was the subject of the experiment, the others were allies of the tester. The allies all reported that their judgments on an observation were consistent with each other but in disagreement with the subject. In 36.8% of the tests, the subject changed his mind about his answer in conformity with the group pressure. The conclusion may be drawn that people tend to respond in order to be consistent with those about them. At least on matters in which they do not have a high investment, they are willing to go along with the group in their public expressions of opinion. In replications of these tests where the group members knew each other and had meaning for each other, conformity was even higher.[22]

"When an individual is in a social situation he tends to react toward himself in the same way that he thinks others would react to him," according to Mead.[23] This behavioral effect of the social situ-

[21] Solomon Asch, "Opinions and Social Pressure," *Scientific American*, CXCIII (1955), 31–35.
[22] B. Musner, "Studies in Social Interaction," *Journal of Social Psychology*, XLI (1955), 259–70.
[23] Mead, *Mind, Self, and Society*.

ation gives indication of considerable group influence on an individual's functioning. One may observe in family discussions, committee deliberation, and conversations among friends, where people are merely expressing themselves, and where no one has the delegation to assume a particular position or to advocate a point of view, that people tend to move toward the collective group opinion.

Thus, most people seem to yield to the pressures of those about them to act or react in what they consider to be socially acceptable ways. The group may have very strong influences on thought, belief, and behavior. Hare [24] says that the "basic tendencies of the individual are never seen in their raw form. All intended behavior is modified to some extent before it becomes overt. . . . Some individuals . . . are relatively insensitive to pressures but a person cannot remain a social being, a person, and stand wholly apart from social pressure." If this is true, then group experience would exert a fairly strong control over overt expressions of feelings, beliefs, and opinions, at least within the group, and might also carry over outside of the group, if the group has significant meaning to the person.

In another citation, Hare says "when an individual's norms and goals are in accord with those of the group, his behavior will meet with approval. . . . If the individual finds that his behavior deviates from group norms he has four choices: to conform, to change the norm, to remain a deviant, and to leave the group." Of course, he may also be removed from the group without his consent.[25] Strong, then are the social pressures to believe and behave in accordance with the group. The individual, by the process of group pressure, is molded into shape, either by changing himself, his attitudes, beliefs, style of behaving, or values in accordance with his group, or he leaves the group.

It should be remembered, of course, that while the individual is taking on the color of the group, he, too, is part of the group and may be helping the group culture to change. He is not solely a

[24] A. Paul Hare, *Handbook of Small Group Research* (New York, The Free Press, 1962), p. 169.
[25] *Ibid.*, p. 24.

captive. It should also be remembered that 36.8% of the subjects in the Asch experiments changed, and 24% never did. Many variables may intervene to condition how much influence a particular group experience will have on a member.

Some of the factors that will affect group influence upon the member and vice versa are: the significance of a particular group in relation to other groups of which the individual is a member; the amount of attachment a person has to other people in the group; the type of group culture, that is, group values and norms; the status of the person in the particular group; the rewards for conformity or the sanctions for nonconformity in the particular group.

Kelley and Thibaut [26] state that the individual acquires his thought and judgment habits largely through interaction with other people. This observation was made similarly by Piaget in his extensive studies of children's behavior. He noted that the child formed his values and judgments in his associations with others in his world.

The individual not only acquires his values and beliefs in his associations, but Cartwright and Lippitt [27] found that "the individual needs social support for his values and social beliefs." They say "he needs to be accepted as a valid person, as a member of the group he values. Failure to maintain such a group membership produces anxiety and personal disorganization. On the other hand, group membership and participation cost the person his individuality—if he is going to receive support he must give support and hold some common values and beliefs."

Lewin [28] makes a similar observation when he says "when an individual tries to diverge too much from group standards he will be ridiculed, treated severely, and finally ousted from the group."

[26] Harold Kelley, and John W. Thibaut, "Experimental Studies of Group Problem Solving and Process," in Gardner Lindzey, ed., *Handbook*, pp. 735–85.

[27] Dorwin Cartwright, and Ronald Lippitt, "Group Dynamics and the Individual," in Bennis, Benne, and Chin, eds., *The Planning of Change*, (New York, Holt, Rinehart & Winston, Inc., 1961), p. 264 ff.

[28] Kurt Lewin, *Field Theory in Social Science* (New York, Harper & Row, 1951).

Behavioral Change

Many experiments have been undertaken to test the effectiveness of the group in changing attitudes and behaviors. These experiments and experiences have included such areas as changing food customs and the use of less familiar food products, child-rearing habits, racial attitudes, control of obesity, control of drug use, alcoholism, and smoking.

Some of the research now regarded as classic was done by Lewin during World War II on modification of use of foods due to shortages. Lewin found that use of a lecture giving accurate and adequate information had little effect in changing practice. When the lecture was followed by group discussion and public commitment to group members to try to change habits, and when the members knew that they were to report back on their experiences, there was a higher ratio of actual change in practice. The group attachments had more meaning for the individuals than the cognitive information and intellectual awareness.

Similarly, the experiences of Alcoholics Anonymous, Synanon, Weight Watchers, and Take Off Pounds Sensibly (TOPS), and the various organizations to stop smoking have produced results in the way of control exercised by group support, group sanctions, or group criticism and ridicule, where the other members take on meaning and influence, and thereby cause a person to modify behaviors. Pledges to change one's behavior, given to meaningful others in one's group, apparently have influence, stemming from the socialization process and the definition of self-image that are socially imposed and internalized to an individual's basic character and behaviors. Some of the work in behavioral modification therapy follows these precepts.[29] The influence over an individual's behavior comes not only from his desire to be accepted and his fear of negative sanctions from other group members if he deviates but also from his sense of responsibility for the group, in not letting down group expectations and standards. As the group becomes more modified and important to the member, it will have more influence over his overt behavior and expressed views.

[29] William Glasser, *Reality Therapy* (New York, Harper & Row, 1965).

Presence of others creates new motivational implications for each group member according to Collins and Guetzkow.[30] They say, "many of the goals and rewards which an individual values are available only in the presence of others. High productivity is rewarded by others and therefore productivity increases." Some of the studies of motivation also show the effectiveness of group experience in encouraging individuals to change. It has been suggested that in their quest for approval and recognition by the group, individuals may express their dependence on the help of others to achieve their individual goals. They may use the group as a teacher, or source of information, or for a means of testing out ideas. They may also use the group to relieve fears or anxieties. Grinker and Spiegel [31] in their study of air force pilots showed that the men were considerably less anxious and more reassured in the company of their crew whom they knew well and depended upon. They showed the value to the person of praise, verbal approval, social acceptance and rewards from his group and also the personal effects of criticism, disapproval, social rejection and punishment to keep the person in line with group expectations.

Some of Allport's [32] studies showed that people working in the presence of others, doing the same things but not necessarily together or collectively, resulted in more vigorous performance on the part of individuals, than in people working alone. In other words, they were stimulated by each other's activity. The improvement in their work was in thought and motor activity though the quality of their work was not improved. For although people solved more problems and worked faster when stimulated by the presence of others, they also made more errors. He found that there was a tendency for these same people to work more slowly in isolation. Dashiell [33] in similar studies found that competition

[30] Barry Collins, and Harold Guetzkow, *A Social Psychology of Group Processes for Decision Making* (New York, John Wiley & Sons, Inc., 1964).

[31] R. R. Grinker, and J. P. Spiegel, *Men Under Stress* (New York, McGraw-Hill Book Company, 1945).

[32] Floyd Allport, "The Influence of the Group upon Association and Thought," *Journal of Experimental Psychology*, III (1920).

[33] J. F. Dashiell, "Experimental Studies of the Influence of Social Situations on the Behavior of Individual Human Adults," in C. Murcheson, ed., *Handbook of Social Psychology* (Worcester, Mass., Clark University Press, 1935).

among members, working in each other's presence, provided the basis for the observed increase in production, but decrease in the quality of the product. It could be concluded that the group or collective effect could prove a stimulus for individual achievement and production even though this may not be interaction or collective problem solving. In summary, then, people working in the presence of others on independent work, such as reading, writing, or problem solving, turned out a physically greater quantity of work. Their motivation was increased, but there was lesser quantity or quality in intellectual processes or concentration. Also, the presence of periodic distractions increased the tensions and caused some variations in outputs.

Hare [34] shows evidence to support the finding that if an individual working in the presence of others has to give some attention to social-emotional tasks, that is, must lend support and approval to others, he may be diverted somewhat from his task and therefore the quantity and quality of his activity on the intellectual task may be lessened. Another influence on achievement is level of performance of the others, in whose presence a person is working. If all are doing well, then they may motivate each other to higher achievement, but if many are not doing well, they may tend to lower each other's goals.

If social scientists have discovered that groups have significant influence in the formation of attitudes and values and in establishing expected behaviors and, further, that it is from group experience that an individual may change his beliefs, his values, his way of thinking, and some of his behavior, then it seems reasonable to propose that groups could be established and utilized within social work practice to achieve these specific ends. As a matter of fact, the early youth services, the Y's, scouts, and other youth groups were established initially for the purpose of influencing values, standards, and behavior of their members. In the early years of their experience they were called "character building," clearly designating their value development, value change motives. Various adult social movements within social work have also had the goal of attitude change of members.

[34] Hare, *Handbook*.

In more recent years, groups have been employed within social work to influence values of delinquents, to modify the life style of dependent, low-income, and culturally deprived people, to modify both white racist and black racist attitudes, to enhance self-image through the provision of opportunities to become adequate and powerful in the group and for ego supportive therapeutic experiences.

The research and theory on group uses in development and change of the person encourage predictions that the establishment of groups or intervention in already existent autonomous ones for the purpose of developing or changing the individual members are indicated. It should be noted that the research suggests that mere presence in an aggregate may have some influence on the individual, as per the findings of Sherif and Asch already noted, but that the real thrust of individual growth and change involves engagement with others, development of attachments that assume significance to members, interaction with others, and commitment to group goals and objectives.

The implications are that the convening of people may influence their functioning at least while they are together, but for lasting effect, for significant changes in attitude, or behavior, the group must acquire continuing significance in the life of the member. The aggregate would, therefore, need to be developed into a well-formed group over time with significant interpersonal attachments and the individual to be significantly influenced would need to endow the group with importance for himself. Furthermore, the conclusion may be drawn that if the service goal is change in the individual, groups may well have more effect in reinforcement and support than when an individual gains understanding of the problem and motivation to change by himself or with an individual counselor. The phenomenon of commitment in the collective presence lends support to one's decisions, beliefs, and actions.

Changes in Groups

We have thus far focused on the influence of group experience upon members and the possibility of groups created for purposes of development and change of the person. What are the possibilities in intervening in groups that already exist? Lewin [35] considered the effects of attempting change in autonomous groups, or groups already existing within society. Gang groups, friendship groups, or autonomous cliques in subgroups within hospitals, institutions, schools, or other wider associations often appear. When the members have formed the group autonomously, what are some of the factors implicit for a social worker who would intervene to bring about some changes in the individuals?

Lewin suggests that inasmuch as attempts to change an individual outside of his group may make him a deviant, the problem is to change the group level of values, behaviors, or beliefs. This process must take place through discussion and decision making in the group, to weaken the forces that oppose desirable changes and then to develop through further discussion some clear idea of a new kind of behavior or activity. According to Lewin, once this process has been engaged in, the group decision "freezes" the activity level at a new point and the individual is brought along by the very forces that caused him to resist change in the first place. That is, if a person's standards and beliefs are reinforced by a strong peer group clique, friendship group, family, or other reference group, he will not wish to differ from them in modifying his values or his activities. These group influences are a great deal stronger than any rational or logical suggestions of change. The group as a whole, therefore, must change, and in that process the individual members will not only change, but reinforce each other in the change.

Lewin postulates that where there is an enduring group with relatively high interaction, the individual would have higher commitment to the group than to others outside; therefore, it would be easier to change the behavior of the individuals as a group than to change them one by one. He suggests further that when it seems impossible to change the standards of an entire group, a small segment may be formed or worked with, especially people with problems like delinquents or chronic alcoholics. Lewin found it was necessary to insulate them from the larger group, the neighborhood

[35] Kurt Lewin, "Forces Behind Food Habits and Methods of Change," *National Research Council Bulletin,* CVIII (1943).

of delinquents or the social circles of alcoholics in order to reduce the forces that supported the individual's behavior at the old level.

The concept of "cultural island" emerged from this research. Specifically, some of the people were removed from their surroundings to a camp, workshop, or other group where their changes were reinforced over a period of time in the new group setting in a special therapeutic or change-related subculture so that the modified standards or behaviors could be reinforced long enough to become incorporated in the habits of the individual member. The pressure of some of his other reference group members helped a subgroup to build in supports for the individual's return to the original, now alien, culture. This process has been attempted for professionals, such as teachers, social workers, and police, in an effort to modify racial attitudes. It has also been used with youth leaders from churches, schools, and isolated segregated communities to give an experience in intercultural and international living and modify biases and prejudices. This phenomenon has also been the theoretical basis for the structure of some of the marathon *T* groups and sensitivity training groups.

Some of the work in treating families as whole units makes use of this theory. If individual members need to change, and if the behaviors and values emerge within the family, then it would follow that change can take place by affecting the entire family. Lippitt [36] added to Lewin's theory of group training and retraining the suggestion that when two or more people are retrained together they constitute a subgroup in which the newly learned attitudes and activities constitute a group standard and they reinforce each other in retaining the change. The Asch [37] experiments show that an individual is more likely to hold to his beliefs if he has the encouragement of even one other person in the face of social pressure to modify. A small group is, therefore, an even greater reinforcer.

Following this idea, some of the training projects to eliminate poverty in the Office of Economic Opportunity to develop individuals and leadership have had groups of parents from a neighbor-

[36] Ronald Lippitt, Jeanne Watson, and Bruce Westley, *The Dynamics of Planned Change* (New York, Harcourt Brace Jovanovich, Inc., 1958).

[37] Asch, "Opinions and Social Pressure," *Scientific American*, CXCIII (1955).

hood associated with groups of children in Head Start programs. In these groups the idea was not only that parents would support each other, and children support each other, but also that parents would reinforce the children's growth and change or resocialization. In some youth counseling services, groups of parents for interpretive and supportive purposes have been associated with therapeutically oriented adolescent groups. Relatives of patients have been worked with along with patient groups in alcoholism, emotional disorders, mental and physical handicaps, and certain physical disease entities, such as cancer and T. B.

Lazarsfeld [38] found in a study of political habits that people followed patterns of voting both for candidates and issues that reflected their friends, family, or occupational colleagues. In general, a person made his voting decision, not upon knowing the candidate, nor on the propaganda or promotional campaigns, but on what the people in his various reference groups thought. Therefore, in convincing individuals how to vote, the most effective means to influence individuals was to work through organized groups, and group deliberations. Voting is, of course, a private and individual activity, however, the individual decision reflected group discussion and decision.

In examining social class and status, W. Lloyd Warner [39] found that an individual's status in society was determined first by his family of origin, parents, and siblings, and secondly by his social associations and cliques. With increased income, amount of education, change in occupation, and area of residence, he could change his social position in adulthood if he could gain entry into the small group associations that designated status. Obviously to gain entry into certain clique groups or social associations means acceptance of values, norms, and standards of behavior, and behaving in specified ways acceptable to such groups. Such performance may be equally true for one who wishes to be socially upward mobile, as for one who wishes to be professionally relevant to people in lower-class or poverty subcultures. It would hold for crossing ra-

[38] P. F. Lazarsfeld, B. Berelson, and Hazel Gaudet, *The People's Choice* (New York, Duel Sloan and Pearce, 1944).
[39] W. Lloyd Warner, and Paul Lunt, *Social Life of a Modern Community* (New Haven, Yale University Press, 1941).

cial, ethnic, or any subcultural lines either personally or professionally and have relevance for subgroup functioning. Status and performance, as well as access, would be closely related in the modification of an individual's behavior and values.

Berelson and Steiner [40] also support the idea of group change through an interaction process as opposed to individual change. They say that active discussion by a small group to determine goals, to choose methods of work, to reshape operations, or to solve problems is more effective in changing group practice than separate instruction of individual members. Group activity, they think, brings about better motivation and support for change and better implementation and productivity of new practice.

Coch and French [41] found in their research in industry that where workers were encouraged to participate in group deliberation and decision making around change in procedures that there was less expression of aggression to supervisors, less drop in production, and quicker recovery from any production drop, less quitting, and a higher final rate of production. When orders were handed down from above with no group participation, no suggestions or feedback, there was considerable grumbling, some work stoppages, absenteeism, and slowdown in production. Bavelas [42] similarly found that while encouragement and incentives from management did not improve individual piecework production rate, a group decision by workers after discussion did result in improvement. Such findings offer strong support for engaging people in group deliberation and for the effect of group contagion on individual and group performances.

Task Groups for Problem Solving

The use of groups for problem solving is another area in which there has been theoretical formulation and research. The question

[40] Bernard Berelson, and Gary A. Steiner, *Human Behavior* (New York, Harcourt Brace Jovanovich, Inc., 1964).

[41] L. Coch, and J. R. P. French, Jr., "Overcoming Resistance to Change," *Human Relations,* I (1948), 512–32.

[42] A. Bavelas, "Morale and the Training of Leaders," in G. Watson, ed., *Civilian Morale* (New York, Reynal & Hitchcock, 1942).

frequently arises as to whether individuals working alone or in groups are more effective in finding solutions to problems. G. Murphy [43] says, "It is a waste of time to ask if [people in] groups think more efficiently than the individuals that compose them. In some situations one individual has the necessary information or skill or both and can do better than any arrangement of individuals in group. In other situations there are scattered bits of information and potential insights which can become integrated in the group setting so that the group thinks a good deal more efficiently than the individual members. Sometimes the benefit is not in creative contributions, but rather the enhancement of a critical capacity to see blind alleys or false assumptions."

Group problem solving is a process whereby people work together to contribute individually and collectively to a common solution for some problem. Some differences are apparent between the types of problems which lend themselves to group solutions and those which do not. For instance, Hare [44] concluded in a survey of considerable research on problem solving, that "the superiority of the group over the individual with respect to productivity is usually greater on manual problems than on intellectual tasks." He found that the group lost its superiority in accuracy and efficiency if no division of labor was required, if the group had to spend too much time and energy on its own development and control, or if the group level of productivity was lower than that of the separate individuals. Furthermore, group problem solving generally took more time for the same amount of return as individual activity. Groups tended to be more accurate because of the greater number of checks and balances. After group deliberation over a problem, the individual member tended to be more accurate in his own judgment. Recall is greater for groups than individuals, because there seem to be more resources for memory in the group.

Kelley and Thibaut [45] warn against personalizing the group in

[43] Gardner Murphy, "Group Psychotherapy," in Rosenbaum and Berger, *Group Psychotherapy and Group Function.*

[44] Hare, *Handbook,* p. 363.

[45] Harold Kelley, and John W. Thibaut, "Experimental Studies of Group Problem Solving and Process," in Lindzey, ed., *Handbook,* pp. 735–85.

the problem solving process. They point out that "individual solutions are created, communicated and assembled into a social product that represents the group." But the group should not be endowed with personal qualities, for the group product in problem solving is actually the outcome of collective and collaborative individual inputs. The single result is a blending of the multiple ingredients of the members in interaction, a process of checks and balances. Therefore, Thibaut and Kelly postulate that "in pooling judgments the greater the number of competent judges, the greater the validity of their combined judgments." They also found as a result of their research that if there was a difference in members, the more confident members carried more influence and contributed more heavily to the decision. Thus what might appear to be group problem solving might be a reinforcement of the views of one or two, or a small minority of members.

When a group is in deliberation and attempting to arrive at a group solution to a problem, alternatives are presented and there emerges a process of decision making in which various alternatives are rejected until one alternative is finally selected. Unless there is some provision for minority expression, opinions that differ from the final alternative selected may get lost in the final group decision. But according to Collins and Guetzkow [46] group products may be superior because of the pooling of individual judgments which eliminate random error. The group, because of the several judgments, is more apt to discover alternative judgments not available to the single individual working alone. Thus the general quality of the group product may be improved. The interaction of members tends to provide a corrective in judgment, unless the more influential members have erroneous judgment and pull the group away from clarity and accuracy of thinking.

Group problem solving, therefore, has its benefits and its disadvantages. Whether the group process is superior to individual problem solving depends to some degree on the nature of the problem and the desired outcome. If a single individual has the necessary information he will probably take less time and do as well or

[46] Collins and Guetzkow, *A Social Psychology of Group Processes.*

better. If, on the other hand, the problem necessitates the incorporation of knowledge, information, and judgments which are beyond what any one person has, the group product may be superior, but take longer. Another factor of the decision regarding group or individual is, who will be responsible for implementing the outcomes or putting the suggested solution into effect. If the solution is going to affect the group and implies changes in procedures, the engagement of those who will be affected by the solution may ensure greater acceptance if the members determine the solution. Associations may be drawn for the uses of groups in administration, community organization and planning, coordination of services, and other task-focused groups in social work practice.

Change in System in Which the Group Exists

The group can be used as a means for changing social structures and institutions in which it exists. The organization of groups or the use of groups in this way suggests social or political action. The theory suggests that strength from numbers of people in collective action has effect on a target institution or organization. That is, in the political processes, many people speaking and acting collectively, or in an organized fashion, may have greater influence than individuals speaking separately.

Some of the political science theory of organization and power is relevant to this group use. Bennis, Benne, and Chin [47] refer to this group functioning "as an action on policy and program building group." They say that such groups need to give attention to social organizations appropriate to the goals which they are designed to serve.

The group which exists for external change, or for the specific purpose of affecting some wider system in which it exists will have to give some attention to its own organization. In order for the group to become an entity, members will need to work together and be able to give and take in the group deliberative system. Fur-

[47] Warren G. Bennis, Kenneth Benne, and Robert Chin, eds., *The Planning of Change* (New York, Holt, Rinehart & Winston, Inc., 1961), p. 698.

thermore, the development of the group must be encouraged enough to provide the cohesion of unified opinion on how to modify the external system.

While considerable research has been done on the internal workings of groups and the group as instrument for growth and change in individuals, and while social scientists have stated that the group is the link between the individual and the wider society, there seems to have been very little theory building or research on the group as an instrument for modification of the wider society.

Some of the principles to be considered in the use of the group for change of a wider social system as indicated by Bennis, Benne, and Chin are as follows:

1. The members must be able to function well enough as individuals and collectively to constitute a group that provides a unified force for action.

2. The group must be synthesized enough to support its members against the external resistance to change that generally appears as a reaction.

3. The group must provide rewards for the members from within the group if their proposed change means deviance from the wider social system and the possibility of negative social sanctions in the wider society or external system.

4. In order to change a system, the group must have access to strategic people or subgroups in it.

5. Resources (both financial and informational) must be available for the group to take the necessary action to be forceful and effective in moving toward its target for action.

6. Generally, it is thought to be essential for exerting influence to change a system, to have access to the news media and other channels of communication and information, in order to gain recognition and support.

It is recognized in the political arena that well-organized numbers of people with a unified outlook do carry political influence especially if they give evidence of being representative of others.[48]

[48] David B. Truman, *The Governmental Process* (New York, Alfred A. Knopf, Inc., 1951).

In other words, the power of organization and representation is well accepted. The inclusion of people who have prestige as group members whose eminence derives from sources outside the group, use of bloc voting, the organization of minority groups, and the use of mechanisms, such as demonstrations, work stoppages, engaging the public media to gain public recognition or make an administration's position uncomfortable, are measures to gain or exercise influence that may be used by an organized group. The target for change may be formal organizations or institutions, such as schools, police, agencies, or governmental structures, or, in contrast, less-organized structures, such as neighborhoods, apartment houses, or communities.

Some of the most pertinent research to guide use of the group to change the system comes from organizational theory emerging from studies of industry and the military. Berelson and Steiner [49] note that as a society becomes more complex and heterogeneous, more organizations and associations appear in it. Such differentiation within society provides the necessity for internal organization, from small informal groups, to formal or organized groups, to organizations and highly specified structures. Furthermore, as people organize on one side of an issue, their opponents organize on the other side,[50] so that an action-reaction phenomenon sets in.

Just as task-centered groups may evolve into personally satisfying social groups, so formal organizations formed for purposes of action outside the group may tend to lose sight of their original goals. People may gain more satisfaction from belonging to the group than in getting the job done. Thus, one might say the structure of the organization may come to outweigh the goals for which it was created. Selznick [51] in studying some of the operations of citizen groups around the Tennessee Valley Authority discovered that in order to get things done people must be organized and as soon as they are, they use their own initiative and begin to suggest means and methods other than those which the organizer had in

[49] Berelson, and Steiner, *Human Behavior.*
[50] Truman, *The Governmental Process.*
[51] P. S. Selznick, *T.V.A. and the Grass Roots* (Berkeley, University of California Press, 1949).

mind. The result may mean also a shift from the original goal of the organizers. This is one distinctive feature of group methods for external change.

When a group is sufficiently organized to take action and has achieved its goals, it is likely not to want to dissolve but rather to go on to new goals. The effectiveness of the organization and the morale achieved by group accomplishment give momentum to further activity. As Peter Blau [52] indicates, "new goals often emerge in organization as old ones have been reached." Furthermore, in working together on their problems, the members may form strong attachments to each other and to the group. Selznick [53] in his analysis of citizen organizations came to this conclusion. He stated, "decisions relevant to the actual problems met in translation of policy into action create precedents, alliances, symbols, and personal loyalties which transform the organization from a profane, manipulate instrument into something having sacred status and thus resistant to treatment simply as a means to some external goal."

The small group organized for purposes of external action may become formally organized in order to achieve the action. The result is the creation of an organization within an organization, system, or institution.

It has been suggested, however, that "the efficiency of a large formal organization is sizably enhanced when . . . [its operations] are tied into the informal network of groups within [it] so that this network can be used to support the organization goals." [54] Berelson and Steiner theorize further that "members are often tied to an organization by their membership in primary groups that mediate between the individual and the organization." In other words, the small group can be the bridge from the person to the larger organization, as well as the means by which the larger organization operates or is changed.

The operation of informal groups in a large system works two

---

[52] Peter Blau, *Bureaucracy in Modern Society* (New York, Random House, Inc., 1956), p. 95.

[53] Selznick, *T.V.A. and the Grass Roots.*

[54] Berelson, and Steiner, *Human Behavior*, p. 370.

ways. While on the one hand the groups may come into being to bring about change in their surroundings, to affect the system and the wider organization, they may in turn be used by the system to modify the participants and to acculturate them to the pressures and goals of the wider system. Thus state Berelson and Steiner,[55] "the informal group is extremely effective in translating, interpreting, and supporting the organization's norms and practices." Leighton [56] noted that "communication from a central authority to a community works much better if conducted through the informally selected leaders of the basic social units set up by the residents."

Most of the research and line of reasoning about small groups for purposes of social action and social change seems to focus on the internal workings of the group and the effect of the system on modifying the group, rather than on the processes by which the small group, when organized, may change society, or the wider social system. Berelson and Steiner,[57] nevertheless, conclude that "the broad effects of voluntary associations within society are usually considered to be . . . to promote social change by increasing pressures from particular organized segments of society. . . ."

Blumer,[58] in viewing "society as symbolic interaction," has noted this deficiency in theory. He suggests that any group taking action formulates its action on the basis of an interpretation and assessment of the situation in which it plans to act. People perceive a current situation in light of their previous life experiences. Members of a group composed of people of diverse backgrounds will be inclined to define the situation differently according to their various frames of reference resulting in considerable strain. Blumer suggests that society then becomes the framework within which the social action takes place but not the determinant of this action, and further that changes in the organization are the product of the activity of these internally organized groups, not the influence over

[55] *Ibid.*, p. 371.
[56] Alexander H. Leighton, *The Governing of Men* (Princeton, N.J., Princeton University Press, 1945).
[57] Berelson, and Steiner, *Human Behavior.*
[58] Herbert Blumer, "Society as Symbolic Interaction," in Arnold Rose, ed., *Human Behavior and Social Process* (Boston, Houghton Mifflin Co., 1962).

them. Although there are theoretical differences between the social science theorists about whether the social situation is the cause, the effect, or the setting of social change, they agree that the people in the small group who wish to effect change in their social conditions must be closely related to their target for change, that is, they must have positions in the system they wish to change.

If the group is to be effective in bringing about some change in the system or organization in which it exists, or if it is to have any effect on some other institutions, the group members themselves must be engaged in the process and committed to the purposes for which the group exists. Sometimes leadership, either staff or organizational, recognizes the existence of a problem or a situation which needs to be remedied. They then organize committees or task forces to work on a solution. However, the leadership may have already decided on procedures and solutions or expected outcomes. Their expectations of the newly organized group is that it will give carte blanche endorsements and support of the plans, procedures, and goals set by the organizer. This procedure, while it has been widely practiced in many settings, becomes an illegitimate and subversive use of the group. In fact, it is no use of the group itself. If people are to be involved in their own behalf or in activity to achieve some specific end, then they need to be legitimately engaged in deliberation and decisions about the direction of the activity, and their decisions and recommended outcomes must be respected.

Similarly, Thelen,[59] in his work in depressed neighborhoods, organized block clubs to train their own leadership. People in interaction with each other developed mutuality of feeling where there had been alienation and anomie. They also reduced the differences of ways people looked at some problems and came to some agreements on solution, and engaged more people in working on the solution, thus removing some of the external depression.

Riecken and Homans [60] state that "the imposition of a plan upon

[59] Herbert Thelen, *Dynamics of Groups at Work* (Chicago, University of Chicago Press, Phoenix Books, 1954).

[60] H. W. Riecken, and George C. Homans, "Psychological Aspects of Social Structure," in Lindzey, ed., *Handbook*.

members of a group from without can cause dissatisfaction among members," which in turn reduces effectiveness and efficiency. Thus the use of groups as the means to change the system within which the group exists, or to change a wider social system, must rest not only on the engagement of people in the goals and the tasks, but an open and honest commitment to use the work, the content, and the recommendations that emerge from the group, as the method and content of the means of change.

The Use of Group for Collaboration, Planning, and Production

In the administrative procedures of a social work agency, as well as for the administration, planning, and coordination of services between agencies, groups or group structures are used frequently. Groups are also used for collaboration of services in teams or interdisciplinary practices. Some of the social science studies should be useful in application to these types of group uses.

In administrative organization, it is obvious that persons in positions of authority must bear the ultimate responsibility for the actions and activity of the total operations. However, no administrator nor subadministrator can totally control the behaviors, beliefs, thoughts, and informal functioning of other staff members. Formal procedures can be established so that there are limits on behavior, but the informal behaviors of individuals and subgroups will still operate, either within the formal organization or outside and subversively around it. Peter Blau [61] in his studies of bureaucracies found the informal subgroups operating extensively and spontaneously within the formal systems. They affected both individual and systemic behavior. Even where people were instructed only to use formal channels of administration for their relationships and for conversations and consultation about their work, they met at the water coolers and over lunch to talk over their work and seek advice in working on problems. Since such is true, the concept of

[61] Blau, *Bureaucracy in Modern Society.*

substructures and engagement may just as well be put to use in engagement of staff in planning and carrying out procedures. Small informal groups may be used to plan and facilitate certain of the functions.

Hollander,[62] speaking of participation, says that people will feel more security, and more actively responsible for their work group, if they see that their views and assistance are needed and recognized as being important to the organization. The experience gives them a sense of mastery over their environment. He says further, "People should not be treated as means, but ends, accordingly the function of the social institution should be judged by its service to the development of each person. Any social policy decisions or solution to a problem is more likely to achieve its purposes if it represents a composite of unique views, experience and needs of person and groups involved." He says further that "participation will never work so long as it is contrived merely as a device to get somebody else to do what you want him to." In other words, people should be involved in a decision only if they are working on a legitimate problem and the intention is to follow their recommendations.

Supporting this position, Coch and French [63] in their studies of a factory cite the example of the experiment where a decision was made to change procedures. In one instance, workers were told of the decision and given no chance to plan ways in which they could work together in adapting to the new procedures. They learned their tasks slowly, displayed frustration and hostility. Another group, given an opportunity to discuss the changes, developed procedures to adapt their working operations to changing production methods, learned more rapidly and achieved higher production rates than they had had previously.

Some of the sociometric findings of Moreno and Jennings [64]

[62] E. P. Hollander, *Leaders, Groups, and Influence* (New York, Oxford University Press, 1964), pp. 38–41.

[63] Coch, and French, Jr., "Overcoming Resistance to Change," *Human Relations,* I (1948).

[64] J. L. Moreno, *Who Shall Survive?* (Washington, D.C., Nervous and Mental Disease Publishing Co., 1934). Helen Hall Jennings, *Leadership and Isolation* (2d ed., New York, Longmans Green, 1950).

would also be appropriate for staffs of large enough size. Where people choose their associates they tend to work more cooperatively and productively if they are clear on their task and goals and face deadlines of production. Groups of friends working together can enjoy each other so much that they can spend their time socializing if they are not forced to keep to the task of producing results.

Summary and Conclusions

In conclusion, then, theory and research in the social sciences has produced some hunches regarding the effectiveness of groups for certain conditions and individuals. These findings are suggestive, at least, that groups may affect some change in individual's values, behaviors, conceptions of self, and learning. They also suggest that for certain types of problems, groups may be more effective in finding solutions than individuals working alone.

In social structures, systems, and organizations, groups of people totally and legitimately involved in groups may be more effective in bringing about changes and reinforcing changes. The implications, then, of these findings need to be drawn over to some classification of the deliberate creation and use of groups for service delivery in social work.

The findings of social science research and theory formulation on the uses of small groups would suggest that groups are an effective means for socialization of the individual, for inducting him into new experiences, for anchoring the individual in the social system and society, for educating the individual, and for changing the individual's personality, self-image, attitudes, and behaviors. Groups also are useful for collective action between and among people for problem solving, system change, and societal change. There has been a mystique about group use which needs to be dispelled. Groups are not useful for all things and may not only be useless but also harmful. They may be more time-consuming and less efficient than individuals working alone in some instances. While they may stimulate creativity, they may also stifle it. But one way to dispel some of the mystique and to move toward more appropriate group usage is to have as thorough as possible understanding of group processes and to use groups deliberately when certain ends are desired. The remainder of this book continues examination of findings from studies and observations of groups, for the purpose of developing a clearer understanding of the factors in making groups a useful instrument for social work service delivery.

PHASES
IN GROUP DEVELOPMENT

Social scientists and social work practitioners who have worked closely with groups have noted for some time a sequence of phases of development through which all groups pass. Several such phases may occur during a single session or may appear over a longer time in a group which has several meetings. With the possibility of predictable group phases in mind, a social worker might act with an aggregate to facilitate the formation process or intervene with a group in particular ways to speed or to slow the phasing process or certain aspects of it. If, for example, the social worker has a set of criteria for assessing the level of group development, he might offer recommendations about group composition and size to facilitate its formation, or he might engage the members in particular activities of decision making, planning, goal setting, and goal achievement, to precipitate their movement into a functioning and maintenance phase of group development.

Phases of group development have been considered by several

social work writers who have attempted to link social work interventions to them. Sarri and Galinsky [1] have developed a seven-
phase scheme including (1) origin; (2) formation; (3) intermediate
I; (4) revision; (5) intermediate II; (6) maturation; and (7) termination. Garland, Jones, and Kolodny [2] have developed a five-
phase scheme of (1) preaffiliation; (2) power and control; (3) intimacy; (4) differentiation; and (5) separation. Northen [3] adopted a
five-phase modality: (1) "preparatory" including planning and intake; (2) initial orientation; (3) exploring and testing the group;
(4) problem solving and stabilization; and (5) termination. Many
workers have adopted a three-phase approach of beginning, middle, and termination. Northen notes in an analysis of the literature
on phases and stages of group development that there were at least
130 articles, of which she analyzed 45 that seemed most pertinent
to social work practice. She indicates that the number of phases
range from two to eleven with four as the modal number. The writings of these social workers would suggest that knowledge of the
phasing process in groups as established within social science research is useful for understanding and working with groups. The
Group Work Practice Commission of the National Association of
Social Workers developed a scheme that referred to pregroup intake and composition, group formation, group-in-session with
worker, maintenance aspects and activities, termination and post-
termination.[4]

Within the social sciences, Bales and Strodtbeck [5] have pioneered primarily with phasing in task groups through the *Interaction Process Analysis*. This system divided group sessions into

[1] Rosemary Sarri, and Maeda Galinsky, "A Conceptual Framework for
Teaching Group Development in Social Group Work," in *Faculty Day Conference Proceedings*, 1964 (New York, Council on Social Work Education, 1964).

[2] James Garland, Hubert Jones, and Ralph Kolodny, "A Model for Stages in
the Development of Social Work Groups," in Saul Bernstein, ed., *Explorations
of Group Work* (Boston, Boston University, 1965).

[3] Helen Northen, *Social Work with Groups* (New York, Columbia University
Press, 1969).

[4] Mary M. Seguin, ed., *Working Paper on the Nature of Social Work Practice in Groups*. National Association of Social Workers Commission on Social
Group Work (New York, 1967).

[5] R. F. Bales, and F. Strodtbeck, "Phases in Group Problem Solving," *Journal of Abnormal and Social Psychology*, XLVI (1951), 485–95.

three equal time periods and made a content analysis of the verbal contributions of participants in the deliberative process. They found in a first phase that group members were generally becoming oriented to the content of the group or collecting information; in a second phase members were generally evaluating the information, and in a third phase they attempted to make decisions, but also they were putting more energy into supporting each other. Having found this phasing process in experimental groups, Bales's scheme has been tested with many other types of group meetings, including jury deliberations, labor negotiations, classes, and therapy groups. Other social scientists who have done research on phasing include Bennis and Shepherd [6] from the standpoint of system change, Schutz [7] from the standpoint of compatibility of membership, and Thelen [8] from the standpoint of educational groups. Group psychotherapists have also observed phases in the development of therapy groups. Some research shows phases similar for all types of groups, while other inquiries suggest that the preoccupation of individuals with themselves in therapy groups precludes a phase process. Tuckman's [9] exhaustive survey of research on phases in experimental groups, natural groups, and therapy groups produced a model for group phases including both interpersonal and task aspects of group behavior. He developed a four-phase scheme: forming, storming, norming, and performing.

The phases of families as small groups have been dealt with in a different body of literature covering family life cycle over a period of years beginning with courtship and engagement, and including beginning marriage, the advent of the first child, through the middle age of parents and adolescence of children, to the separation of adult children and old age and widowhood.[10] While these phases

[6] Warren G. Bennis, and Herbert A. Shepherd, "A Theory of Group Development," *Human Relations,* IX (1956), 415–37.

[7] William Schutz, *Interpersonal Underworld* (Palo Alto, Calif., Science and Behavior Books, Inc., 1966).

[8] Herbert Thelen, and Watson Dickerman, "The Growth of a Group," *Educational Leadership,* VI (1949).

[9] Bruce W. Tuckman, "Developmental Sequence in Small Groups," *Psychological Bulletin,* LXIII (1965).

[10] Reuben Hill, "Methodological Issues in Family Development Research," *Family Process,* III (March, 1964).

are different in respect to family function, they have within them
some of the elements of small group life. In each of these stages the
family as a group may go through some of the small group aspects
of reformation around the addition of members, facing disintegration because of internal or external conflict and crisis, and reintegration following, sometimes facing, termination in process through
early death or separation of a member, and concluding with old
age and widowhood. It would appear to be too simple to make a
direct association between the very extensive and complex research
on family life cycle and the phasing process in small groups. Suf-
fice to say there may well be some similarities, and social workers
who intervene in families as total units may well want to consider
the phasing aspects of the group formation process in the family.[11]

Each writer, regardless of his professional discipline, who has
considered phasing has developed a somewhat different model.
Those who perceive groups as instruments for social work service
delivery see additional stages relevant to the initial contact and
contract and also phases related to post-termination planning because of the additional element of the worker in the role of affecting the group processes and development. They would see also different phases in collectivities which exist before they are affiliated
with agency or with worker, such as street corner gangs or neighborhood groups or teen-age cliques which arrive at an agency requesting the service of a worker and the use of facilities. Such
groups have some degree of formation already, but go through a
reformation process when a worker joins with them within the
agency context. It is apparent that all social work groups do not
pass through all possible phases. Their experience will depend on
the given situation, the people in their social milieu, the problem
addressed by the collective, the purpose of the service, the circumstances of the group, as well as the deliberate interventions of the
worker.

[11] Various schemes of the family life cycle have been developed by: Reuben
Hill, and Donald Hansen, "The Identification of Conceptual Framework Utilized in Family Research, *Marriage and Family Living*, XXII (November,
1960), 299–314; Evelyn M. Duvall, *Family Development* (Philadelphia, J. B.
Lippincott Co., 1967); and Roy Rodgers, *Improvements in the Construction
and Analysis of Family Life Cycle Categrories* (Kalamazoo, Mich., Western
Michigan University, 1962).

I have developed a five-phase scheme from an examination of social work practice groups and an analysis of social science research.[12] These phases are related not just to the normal life cycle of the group, but to the activity of the worker and the potential members as they begin to encounter each other with the intent of forming a group, and through a process until they terminate or plan for post-termination. This scheme, while developed independently from observation of groups, and records of groups kept by students, and emerging as the result of a question in my own research on group formation, resembles in many aspects the formulations developed by Northen, Galinsky, Sarri, Garland, Kolodny, and Jones. The scheme is as follows:

I. Pregroup Phases
    A. Private Pregroup Phase
    B. Public Pregroup Phase
    C. Convening Phase
II. Group Formation Phase
III. Integration, Disintegration and Conflict,
    Reintegration or Reorganization Synthesis Phase
IV. Group Functioning and Maintenance Phase
V. Termination Phases
    A. Pretermination Phase
    B. Termination
    C. Post-termination Phase

The Pregroup Phases

Prior to the existence of any new group, an idea occurs to someone that it might be useful, helpful, or appropriate to develop a group for some purpose. Whether a group is spontaneous or autonomous by the people who become its members, or is deliberately established for a particular purpose, someone has the idea about form-

[12] My thinking about these phases was tested out in discussions of them with the Group Work Practice Commission of the National Association of Social Workers in 1965 and in a paper delivered at the National Conference of Social Welfare, 1970.

ing a group. Coyle [13] refers to this phenomenon as follows: "Within the intricate web of the community, associations form, dissolve, combine and separate in a complicated and ever-changing pattern. If one attempts to discern at close range the process by which such organizations come into being, their beginnings are usually to be found in some moment when there is precipitated in the minds of a number of persons the recognition of the mutual value of collective action for fulfillment of individual interest." Within the context of social work, the idea to develop a group may occur to a worker, the staff of an agency, a neighbor to a settlement house, a youngster who wants to belong but does not know anybody because of his newness to the school or the community; the principal or teachers of a school; the director of an institution; the administrative physician of a hospital ward; a group of people who somehow are drawn together and then decide it would be good to repeat their meeting together and thus form a group.

The history of many groups which have grown and compounded over time is similar. Two or more people joined together for some purpose and got others to go along resulting in the formation of a new group. Over a period of years I have collected histories of beginnings of groups of many types as reported in news items, scientific journals, popular literature, and student reports of groups of which they have been a part. For example, Alcoholics Anonymous, as reported in the Annals, began with two people who had problems with excessive drinking who wished to break the habit. They got together with a third and began to form a group to work on control of their problem. It is reported that two young lawyers from small towns met and decided others like themselves might like to meet once a week for lunch to combat their sense of isolation and loneliness and thus the Rotary Club was formed. Histories of groups, whether within social work settings or in the general society, exhibit similarities in their beginnings. The reasons for considering formation of a group vary with the circumstances. Sometimes groups may be seen as a quicker way to reach more people around a particular problem or issue. Groups may be seen

[13] Grace Coyle, *Social Process in Organized Groups* (New York, Richard R. Smith, 1930), p. 28.

as the method of choice for working on particular kinds of problems, such as socialization, resocialization, social control, motivation, the way to help members gain a sense of attachment or belonging, a means for satisfying people's interest in each other, or some activity which people would like to do but which cannot be done alone may bring a group together. Groups may also be seen as a way to organize numbers of people for power or influence in social action and to coordinate pressure for system change. But for whatever purpose, someone or some collection of people have an idea that it would be useful to attempt to form a group of selected people around a particular problem or purpose. This period in the life cycle of any group occurs before the group exists, thus it is *pregroup*, and before the intention is generally known. It is private, but it is an important aspect of group development often ignored in the analysis of group phases.

Pregroup Private Phase

The pregroup private phase Eric Berne [14] suggests is the period when the group exists in the mind of the organizer. It may be a period in which staff are reviewing intake or registration materials and trying to determine potential group composition. It may be the period in which staff are observing indigenous groups or cliques of residents in an institution or are assigning particular individuals to dorms or cottages or wards or camp units. It may be the time when a community organization staff worker and a layman are considering the composition of a new committee on a newly recognized problem. It may be the period when the street corner gang is becoming conspicuous by acting out behavior, but has not been reached by an agency or worker. It may be when a problem is recognized, for example, isolated older adults living alone in their own homes who need some social contact or for whom there is no social substitute family or institution to help. Or, it may be the time of the recognition that parents of young children who are not prepared for parental roles could use some help in parent education through a group established by an agency. It may be the pe-

[14] Eric Berne, *The Structure and Dynamics of Organizations and Groups* (Philadelphia, J. B. Lippincott Co., 1963).

riod of recognition that a particular collection of unwed mothers who keep their babies need help in learning to cope with the problems that they are facing in common. It may be the time of recognition that parents of mentally retarded children need not only services for their children but also help in handling their own feelings about having such children. It may be the time of recognition by agency staff of the problems of a neighborhood which has disintegrated or become disorganized, due to transiency, rapid population mobility and the development of anomie, and their subsequent discussions about developing some organizational scheme to deal with the problem.

In all of these instances an agency, a social worker, or a group of concerned citizens may consider confronting the problem through the organization of a group service. The projection of some type of group to meet the problem, the consideration of potential group membership, the deliberation regarding the effectiveness of group methods exist in the mind of one or more people in or outside of an agency, but the blueprint does not yet exist, thus the pregroup and private aspect of this group phasing.

This phase is referred to as pregroup and private because there really is no group, not even an aggregate, and only the organizer has a notion that a group may come into being. Actually, what happens at this initial time, who makes the decision to have a group, the suggested purposes of the projected group, decisions about who should be informed that there might be a group, and how they are to be informed, or selected, and by whom, has a great deal of effect on what happens later when an actual group comes into being.

Very few social scientists give any cognizance to any of the aspects of the pregroup phase as a phenomenon of group development. When the researcher is designing his prospectus, however, and deciding where to select his sample and subjects for experimental groups, he could be said to be going through a pregroup private phase.

Within the social work literature, Northen mentions this phase in her preparatory category, Kolodny in preaffiliation. Otherwise, this phase, in spite of its importance to group origin and later group development, gets very little attention on practice literature and none in social sciences.

Pregroup Public Phase

The second stage of this scheme, labeled the "pregroup public phase," is the period in which the decision to have a group is made known to others, beyond the originator. Two or three people may decide that there are others like themselves who would like to meet for a particular purpose and begin to recruit such persons. Many social clubs, such as poker clubs, bowling clubs, young couples' groups, began just this way, as well as social work service groups like parents of handicapped children, residents of a tenement house where services are inadequate, or citizens concerned about their schools.

Within the social agency context, this is the phase when a potential group service is made known to the possible participants. Individuals, who have applied for counseling service, economic help, or health care, may be notified to come at a particular time or place for a group session. The staff of the group service agency may send out fliers announcing their schedule of clubs and classes. They make announcements to the participants of other institutions, such as schools, churches, or neighborhood gatherings, that a group program is about to begin and request recruits. They may contact patients to be released from a psychiatric hospital to let them know about a group to facilitate their re-entry to the community. Sometimes this phase is characterized by individual recruitment wherein potential participants are contacted personally by agency staff or the person who plans to be group leader. These people are told about the projected creation of a new group for specified purposes and asked to indicate their interest by coming to a meeting. Sometimes a "third party" becomes involved in recruitment at this time. A teacher may suggest students in her class who could benefit by a group. A minister may suggest parishioners who are aged and isolated who might be invited to a senior citizens group.

Those who are interested are asked to state their preference on such matters as meeting time, location, duration, size, other people who might be interested, etc. Sometimes they are asked to indicate what they would like to see such a group accomplish. Thus, prior to group formation, as the possibility of a group is planned and is made known, the potential members have a part in the group formation that may follow when the public stage of the pregroup phase will be entered.

Autonomous groups coming to the agency to seek resources, facilities, and leadership may be invited to organize within the agency. The street corner gang, however nebulous, may become aware of a worker trying to meet them. They must make a decision as individuals or as a group whether or not to respond to the worker's offer of help, when the intention is made public.

This may be called recruitment, intake, or the preformation period in which some selecting and notifying of particular candidates for the group takes place, and people decide whether or not they wish to become a part of a group with the stated purposes.

Berne [15] says that at this time the person who is organizing the group "selects candidates from . . . those who are eligible and makes known to them the proposed group activity." In this phase the knowledge of the potential group begins to build expectations in those who know about it and they face the decision of whether or not to participate and thus to arrive at the designated time and place. Such decisions are also made by those who are virtually captive to the group, like those in corrections who are asked to participate in a group as the condition of their probation, or residents of an institution where the group seems semicompulsory.

While this aspect of preformation receives very little attention within the social sciences, several social workers have observed this phenomenon and written about it. Northen [16] notes, for instance, that within the social work context this is a "phase of origin in which the focus is mainly on the social worker's action in the determination of group purpose and composition, the establishment of a contract with individual members about the service to be provided."

[15] *Ibid.*   [16] Northern, *Social Work with Groups*, p. 86.

Garland, Jones, and Kolodny [17] refer to this period as preaffiliation and characterize it as "approach and avoidance," terms reflecting the individual's ambivalence about becoming involved. Ambivalence toward belonging or joining may not be dispelled by a decision to attend, but may recur periodically as long as a person belongs.

Galinsky and Sarri [18] suggest that what is said to the potential member at this period will affect considerably what follows. While decisions are made by someone at this point on potential composition, size, membership characteristics, and location, the original orientation that is given to the potential member as the public phase is entered will affect his expectations and the procedures that follow. What people are told about who will be there, what the content and tasks will be, the proposed goals and purpose of the group, and the procedures to be undertaken will condition the way in which they begin in the group and at least how they behave initially. Thus, the pregroup public phase becomes an important one for both workers and members and sets the climate and style for what may follow.

Knowledge about group composition, or who fits together for particular purposes, or the effect of composition on task achievement, will affect who may be recruited for a particular group at this phase. If the group is deliberately composed, certain people may be asked and others avoided. Criteria for a particular group may be established in the pregroup private phase and acted upon in the public phase.

In community development process this pregroup public phase may occur when the neighborhood worker first begins his contacts to learn how many people in the community have recognized a particular problem or need, and indicate a willingness to meet with others to work together on it. Thus people are alerted to the nature of need and the possibility of working on it.

[17] Garland, Jones, and Kolodny, "A Model for Stages in the Development of Social Work Groups," in Bernstein, ed., *Explorations*.

[18] Sarri, and Galinsky, "Conceptual Framework," *Faculty Day Conference Proceedings*.

In the coordination and planning aspects of community organization, the pregroup public phase may be the period in which organizations are asked to elect delegates or select representatives who will serve on a task force or committee to deal with a particular problem. The projected group and its work are, therefore, made known, and a process is engaged to begin the composition of the group.

In an association governed by an elected board of the members, which in itself becomes a small group with specified tasks, the pregroup public phase is an election. It is sometimes preceded by a pregroup private phase when a nominating committee is meeting and considering the matter of composition of the board and considering names of people to put on a ballot. This process becomes public when nominees are asked and agree to run for office and their names are placed on a ballot for the electorate.

Pregroup Convening Phase

The beginning of the first meeting of the individuals with the worker still precedes group formation. At this time the potential members, or some of them, meet face to face, bringing their expectations of the group, of each other, and of themselves in the situation. This collection is an aggregate and there is no "groupness," yet, at the convening phase, the potential for group begins to materialize.

Berne [19] refers to this as a preliminary phase in which people are assembled without group-related roles. They lack internal organization, and they engage in social rituals and pastimes, such as introductions, stereotyped conversations about the weather, and attempt to locate each other by status and role while they strive to establish a favorable image of themselves. The members attempt to locate mutual interests in time, places, people, materials, events, and activities. They are also seeking someone interesting, looking for complementary interests or attitudes, and perhaps beginning some preliminary or transitory pairing. Berne also suggests that at this time individuals are testing out whether their expectations are going to be met and are comparing their expectations with those of

[19] Berne, *Structure and Dynamics.*

others. He characterizes this period as one of restlessness, tension, talkativeness, laughter, and sometimes withdrawal.

In groups in social agencies these signs are frequently seen as the group gathers and before there is any formal interaction. Usually this is a very important time for the worker to observe the interactions and activities, to listen to informal conversations while he is at the same time helping the members to make connection with each other if they are not already acquainted. He should not, however, minimize the importance of both the content and the process of this informal activity, for it may give significant clues about individual's needs, interests, and capacities, and also to the group process that follows in a more formal way. The informal chatter during the convening period may give clues as to what is on people's minds, their concerns, hopes and expectations, or resistances to the group that is to follow.

Garland, Jones, and Kolodny [20] also note this phase. They not only speak of the stereotyped behavior of the interaction, but comment on the parallel versus interactive behavior that frequently occurs, and the accepting or not accepting behaviors of the members, as some people keep their distance from others. In this initial period people may speak without listening, ask questions but not listen to answers, display ideas and personality in the presence of others without really attending to the feedback or reaction of others. There may be some or no connections of people with each other. People may be judging each other's dress, style, or appearance, or they may be merely preoccupied with themselves.

Similarly, Schutz [21] includes this phase, and describes the process whereby people confront each other to find where they fit in and to size up the others.

The group convener, social worker, or person responsible for the first group meeting, being aware of this phase, may facilitate its passage toward group formation and functioning if he knows as much as possible about the potential members in order to connect with them and help them to connect with each other. He may

---

[20] Garland, Jones, and Kolodny, "A Model for Stages in the Development of Social Work Groups," in Bernstein, ed., *Explorations.*
[21] Schutz, *Interpersonal Underworld.*

short-cut this phase by mentioning the areas in which all present share concerns, or he may use some introductory means of connecting people with each other and focusing on the purpose for which the people have come, such as by having them introduce themselves and state their expectations. But only the members can actually connect with each other, given some orientation to one another. They must develop trust, reach out to each other, respond to each other before the group can move into the formation stage.

Actually, this particular phase may be observed in almost any collection of people regardless of age or nature of problem, interest or motivation, and it cannot be bypassed in the informal convening process. It can be facilitated and it can be hastened generally as the group moves on toward some formation. Apparently some aggregates which do not move on to formation have not been facilitated in the process of defining roles and selves in relation to others, and defining others in relation to group purpose. Thus, people have not really connected with each other in the convening process. Sometimes an assumption may be erroneously made, that all people present know each other because they live in the same block or the same ward, or are in the same grade of school, or are members of the same staff, or have children in the same classroom. In the formation of new committees of people who know each other, time needs to be taken to form into the new configuration and sets of relationships, and to become used to each other's way of working or interacting with others. Failure to get people oriented to each other may slow the movement toward group formation.

In the convening state, in order to deal with some of the personal ambivalence about belonging and also to set the group direction, the group purposes as indicated in recruitment need to be restated. Members may be asked to interpret why they are present and to state their understanding and expectations for the group. Thus as the group convenes, it begins to set its direction toward a common course of activity.

In treatment groups or person-centered groups, the convening phase is an important time for people to become well enough acquainted with each other and anchored in the group that they can begin to share their concerns and trust each other as the group formation phase begins.

In task groups, such as committees or councils, where the focus is more clearly on a job to be done and less of the personality is to be invested, the convening phase may be spent on orientation. This includes clarifying the purpose for which the group is convened, making sure all of the participants are introduced and made aware of the frame of reference of other participants, including their points of view or what they represent in the group.

In the convening phase it may be helpful for the collection of people to have some simple task to consider which is only vaguely related to the ultimate outcomes of the group. Since a characteristic of this initial phase may be "the dance," where there is a good bit of activity, irrelevant conversation, debating of issues not centrally important, or testing out of selves and each other, the organizer may need to introduce some idea, task, or process around which the individuals can engage in this orientation and testing. If an effort is made to move the people too soon to begin to act as a group, to address and focus on a subject or a task while they are getting used to each other and their own presence in the group, and while they are dealing with their ambivalence about being there, they may lose motion and direction on the real issues. Once they have worked through this phase and have a little more comfort with each other they are ready to form a group and begin to work together. Sometimes an intermission in the convening session will provide an opportunity to end "the dance" and begin the regular activity.

Group Formation Phase

Once the people who have been convened begin to take on significance for each other, begin to discern common purposes or goals as a group, and to work on the tasks to achieve these goals, begin to define themselves in the group, and to see the particular group as an entity apart from other groups, begin to set some expectations of behavior for themselves and others in the group, establish role system and some patterns of behavior, they may be said to have engaged in the process of formation.[22] Formation may occur during one session or the process may take many encounters and interactions, depending on the people, their capacity, and the purpose of the group. Thus, short-term groups may form in a single session, open-ended groups with changing composition may re-form at each session.[23] Longer term groups may not coalesce for several sessions and both worker and members may feel no need to precipitate themselves into a formation process. Groups of persons with little social skills or capacities due to age, background, state of health may take considerably longer to find any sense of entity.

Bennis and Shepherd,[24] who derive most of their data from sensitivity training groups and research or experimental groups, consider formation to be the first phase in group development. This position they share with many small group authors, according to Tuckman's review of fifty articles on phasing. They characterize the period as one in which the member is establishing his dependence on leaders, other group members, and the group as a whole, while he is also experiencing counterdependence and the resolution of conflict in power relations. Bion referred to this phenomenon as "flight-fight," [25] wherein members are resolving their ambivalence about attaching themselves to the leader and to other members, whether to stay and struggle or run away from the group.

Berne [26] refers to this as the organizational phase of the group. At this time, he says, there begins to be a separation of leadership-membership categories, where people begin to function in their roles.

The appropriate worker activity is to facilitate this process by which members test out themselves, find their roles, come clear on group purposes, participate in the direction of the group, and de-

[22] M. E. Hartford, "The Social Group Worker in the Process of Group Formation" (unpublished Ph.D. dissertation, University of Chicago, 1962).

[23] Robert Ziller, "Toward a Theory of Open and Closed Groups," *Psychological Bulletin*, LXIII (September, 1965).

[24] Bennis, and Shepherd, "Theory of Group Development," *Human Relations.*

[25] W. R. Bion, *Experiences in Groups* (New York, Basic Books, Inc., 1961).

[26] Berne, *Structure and Dynamics.*

cide whether it will meet their expectations or satisfy the purpose for which they think they are participating. This process occurs in both person-centered and task-centered groups and is, therefore, equally applicable for personal involvement groups or social change and action groups.

Hare [27] sees this as a phase for the evolution of group goals and norms, as well as the development of role system. He also sees the beginning of affectional ties at this time. Thus, people notice each other, take on meaning for each other, become important to each other, whether in a positive or negative sense, and begin to be influenced or attempt to influence each other. They begin to establish group roles for themselves, that is, expected behaviors, such as initiator, synthesizer, mediator, antagonist, supporter, attacker, clown or jester, teacher, helper, or many others. Each person's behavior styles repeat so that group members begin to take on specific roles expect each other to perform similar roles, and as these roles become patterned, the group begins to form.

Thelen [28] sees these emerging roles as existing in a hierarchy of relationships as each individual is attempting to locate and keep or change his place in it. In this place-finding, Thelen suggests that there may be a restraint on expressing hostility or what may be thought to be unacceptable behavior. In other words, during the group-formation phase, the participants may put their best foot forward and control their impulses until they are more sure of their place in the group, their relationships with others, and their attachment to the group objective.

Tuckman [29] refers to this as the "forming" stage and along with the characteristics already noted of orientation, testing, identifying boundaries of expected interpersonal and task behaviors, he also comments on the establishment of dependency relationships. The capacity on the part of the person to be able to risk becoming appropriately dependent on others and at the same time permitting others to depend on him is one of the major aspects of any rela-

[27] A. Paul Hare, *Handbook of Small Group Research* (New York, The Free Press, 1962), pp. 73–80.

[28] Thelen, and Dickerman, "Growth of a Group," *Educational Leadership*.

[29] Bruce W. Tuckman, "Developmental Sequence," *Psychological Bulletin*, pp. 384–99.

tionship. It is compounded in a group where the potential relations are many, unless a person moves only in dyadic or triadic affiliations or remains an isolate. Thus, during the formation phase, each individual is testing out this relationship capacity with the other individuals who happen to be part of the grouping. This is, in part, the phenomenon of conflict and conflict resolution at a fairly superficial level in the formation phase.

Another characteristic of the formation period, if it extends over several meetings, is the stabilization of attendance. I [30] observed this in a study of the group formation process in certain latency age groups. In these instances, if groups formed, the irregularity of attendance ceased after the second or third meeting.

The formation phase is, therefore, essential; without it, the collectivity remains an aggregate, if it continues to convene at all. Without it, people may regularly convene, but they have very little meaning for each other and are unable to influence each other significantly and unable to establish any common purposes to achieve meaningful task.

To facilitate the formation process within the group, the social worker needs to take into account aspects of group functioning that lead to formation, including helping people become attached to some degree to the worker, but also facilitating their becoming attached to each other. The worker can encourage the members to clarify their reasons for participating and their expectations for the group. He may want to facilitate any emergent hierarchy of leadership and reinforce roles that seem helpful or productive to the group development. He may wish to help members find a safety in belonging, in sharing, in depending upon and being depended upon, in the group's work. He may do what he can to stabilize attendance. He will need to help the group to establish meaningful goals and objectives and then to find the way to achieve them.

The Phase of Integration, Disintegration,
or Reintegration

Just when the group seems to be forming, a radical change may take place. There may be a strong forward thrust toward integra-

[30] Hartford, *Social Group Worker in the Process of Group Formation.*

tion, or there may be conflict and disintegration followed by rapid termination or reintegration. In a one-session group this appears shortly after the group seems to have settled on its direction. In a group of several sessions this phenomenon seems typically to occur in the third or fourth meeting. In a week-long institute group, it may fall at about the mid-point, in a camp session, the middle of the first week.

In a study of phasing of four-session groups, Bales found a rise in negative social and emotional behavior in the second session.[31] It is risky to predict when the apparent disintegration will appear in a group, for in some groups it never occurs. This phenomenon has been observed in groups for therapy, for education, for social purposes, for tasks, or groups for deliberation or problem-solving, according to Tuckman,[32] who calls this phase "storming," the appearance of conflict around "interpersonal issues, and expressed resistance to group influence and task requirements." Bennis and Shepherd [33] also note the personal aspect of this phenomenon in what they call enchantment-disenchantment.

Thus, just after the group seems to form and settle down to its business, a period of testing seems to occur. In everyday language, the honeymoon is over. Upon further acquaintance, people do not always seem as interesting or pleasant or helpful as they appeared at first, nor can an individual remain on his good behavior. Defenses begin to lower and people may become disenchanted with each other, the group, its tasks, and the amount of autonomy that may have been given up in becoming a part of the group. The individual may not like the demands made by the group on his time, energies, or the fact that he must share some of himself to be a part of this collection of people. The discomfort emerging from the participants' reaction to belonging may show itself in hostilities, resistances, anger, striking out, or withdrawal. It may also show in confusion. There may be denial of having heard or participated in any preliminary development of group purposes and tasks. In

[31] C. Heinicke, and R. F. Bales, "Developmental Trends in the Structure of Small Groups, *Sociometry*, XVI (1953), 7–23.

[32] Tuckman, "Developmental Sequence," *Psychological Bulletin.*

[33] Bennis, and Shepherd, "Theory of Group Development," *Human Relations.*

discussion or problem-solving groups, it may show by the introduction of extraneous questions, ideas, or information. It may take the
form of scapegoating a particular member or even the worker or
indigenous leader. Issues which have been decided upon in previous deliberation may be reopened for further consideration, or
decisions may be reversed.

Berne [34] suggests that this process may become so important that
the group is delayed in its work on task and may find it necessary
to focus entirely on its own development and maintenance. In
other words, the members may have to focus their attention on
what is happening to their interpersonal relationships, their development as a group, their capacity to work together, before they
can proceed with their problem-solving tasks, or they may merely
have to go back over previous content and rework it again.

Frequently, according to Hare,[35] groups spend a great deal of
time at this period attempting to establish rules for their operations, to establish appropriate behavior for their members, and to
redefine the task for themselves.

Schutz [36] suggests that part of the struggle in this phase may be
related to a redistribution of power, control, and the competition
for a redefinition of leadership. The leadership and hierarchy that
appears to occur in the initial formation frequently shifts after the
members have begun to feel their way and new leadership may
begin to emerge.

Another occasional aspect of the struggle in this phase is that
members discover this group is not like other groups they know,
according to Thelen.[37] Furthermore, members frequently do not
have the same roles and status that they have elsewhere, and go
through a readjustment to establish their positions and identities in
the new group. This may be particularly evident among inexperi-
enced members of therapy groups, task groups, or discussion
groups who expect such groups to function like social clubs, their
work organizations, or their families. People accustomed to high

[34] Berne, *Structure and Dynamics.*
[35] Hare, *Handbook.*
[36] Schutz, *Interpersonal Underworld.*
[37] Thelen, and Dickerman, "Growth of a Group," *Educational Leadership.*

status in other groups may be surprised or made uncomfortable by having to establish themselves in the new group. This may cause enough discomfort to precipitate negative behavior. Particularly in community-organization committees composed of community leaders or people with high status jobs, some members will be disturbed at occupying membership roles rather than leadership roles, and may have to go through a process of adjusting to new ways of functioning. This readjustment to new roles is also seen in sensitivity groups or T groups and in therapy groups where the focus is on person rather than task. In the latter type of groups, people may wish to keep the focus away from themselves, and introduce irrelevant or abstract material as avoidance in beginning to work toward the purpose for which the group was established.

So after the period of the initial formation, there occurs a period of disintegration, reintegration, or integration. Sometimes the disintegration is slight and after briefly focusing on its own functioning, the group realigns its structure, restates its goals, and moves ahead to do its business. In other instances, the conflict goes unresolved and the group disintegrates. The social worker must be prepared for this phase. He may confront the members with the nature of their conflicts, or explain the naturalness of this phenomenon and attempt to get them to rework their organizational structure and restate their purposes so that they can get back to work on their tasks. The task itself may need to be redefined. In some instances where the group and the worker have had an initial contract, there may be a renegotiation of the contract.

If uninformed about it, workers sometimes become alarmed when this phenomenon occurs. They do not understand the symptoms which they observe, of members striking out against each other or the group as a whole, or the worker, of extensive absenteeism, lack of work or getting to business, of bickering, questioning the work, or even belittling. In therapy groups there may be an expression that the group is not helpful, in the committee an expression that they are not accomplishing anything, in the class that people are too competitive or they are not learning anything new. Morale is low and cohesion has not yet developed. The worker's options for positive interventions include getting members to look at the group and themselves and their expectations and to refocus their attention. He may also attempt to bring conflict to the surface for confrontation and resolution. He may find some small or attractive task which members can complete together to achieve a sense of accomplishment.

Sometimes this phase points up clearly that the aggregate cannot and will not become a group. There may have been mistakes in composition and selection of members. The members may not fit together, or there may be individuals who cannot work in a group, whether it be on personal problems or on some task. The worker should consider in such cases whether the interpersonal conflicts can be resolved with time, and whether the group can coalesce in spite of the conflicts. He can consider whether individuals who seem to have difficulty in being part of a group may be able to learn through this experience or should for everyone's sake be encouraged to leave. The social worker probably will need to engage the group members in these decisions and considerations, and in taking appropriate action about its development as a group. The worker may follow up on dropouts or absentees or ask other group members to find out why others are not coming and encourage them to return.

The disintegration phase may provide leadership clues for the social worker. If he can hold firmly to the stated purposes and help group members to face the conflict, and get them to work through their task or to redefine it, the group may be able to move through the phase to a higher level of integration, better able to move forward in its work. Hopefully, the group can weather this phase and move on toward reintegration so that it can get back to the work that it began in the formation stage. Many groups do!

Group Functioning
and Maintenance Phase

After these preliminaries, the group may settle in to accomplish its task, whether this be examining and working on the personal problems of the members, or defining a job or action and making plans to achieve it.

In this period the group culture, style, way of doing things, and norms of group behavior are established and become observable. Members refer to the group as "we" and seek agreement on issues and approval from each other in their activity. There usually is some willingness to give. In Bales's [38] terms, the social emotional qualities of giving support and helping appear. Clearly the "way we do things in this group" is expressed in behavior if not in language. In some groups there may appear imitative behavior in dress, vocabulary, objects carried and used. There may also be established a time and style of arrival and a patterned way of seating by the participants in the session. Both Berne [39] and Coyle [40] call this the emergence of culture—the establishment of an ethical system, artifacts, etiquette, and social contract.

The group is preoccupied with finding and carrying out ways and means of achieving its goals. Berne [41] says that in this phase "the group is at work in the fulfillment of purposes even though the work may lead to change in structure and activity." In therapy groups the "members are dealing with individual anxieties and needs." Hare [42] suggests that "organized interaction arrives after the members agree on direction." Hearn [43] refers to goal setting and achieving as the "means the group devises to meet its needs which become institutionalized and are the fabric of culture called 'groupness.'"

The interpersonal relationship patterns usually stabilize at this point. Alignments become clearer in the subgroup patterns of dyads and triads based on personal affection, interests, or other attractive forces. Having resolved the conflict, people settle in to the group. There is an intensification of personal involvement, a willingness to share self, a concern about the group and effort to carry

---

[38] Heinicke, and Bales, "Developmental Trends," *Sociometry.*
[39] Berne, *Structure and Dynamics.*
[40] Grace L. Coyle, *Group Work with American Youth* (New York, Harper & Row, 1948).
[41] Berne, *Structure and Dynamics.*
[42] Hare, *Handbook.*
[43] Gordon Hearn, "The Process of Group Development," *Autonomous Groups Bulletin,* XIII (1957).

out activities of the group. People begin to acknowledge each other's uniqueness and find their own particular contribution.

Schutz [44] also emphasizes the emotional aspects of this phase. He says this is a period of affection, of emotional integration of members with each other. There is a lowering of defenses and an increase in sharing. Pairing behavior may be observed, he says. Thus, there is more intensity of people's investment in the group at this time.

High group cohesion develops out of members working together and the importance that the group has assumed for its members. Thelen [45] refers to this aspect as consolidation and group harmony. Roles appear for members that are supportive, conciliating, leading, integrative, and may focus on making the group functional and viable in working on the goal. At this time one may see the emergence of firm plans to carry out the goals and a clearer direction.

Similarly, Tuckman [46] sees the phenomenon in his phases of "norming" and "performing." He sees one aspect of the phase as the development of in-group feeling, establishment of cohesion, new standards and new roles which are adopted, and more intimate personal opinions expressed. This could appear as the reintegration aspect following his "storming" phase. But it follows in his "performing" phase that he suggests that the new emergent interpersonal structure becomes the tool for task activities, as roles become more flexible and functional and group energy is now channeled into the task. With the structural issues resolved, that is, with resolution of the conflicts in the emergence of leadership, the structure then becomes supportive of the group activity.

Emergent structure or the stabilization of leader-follower patterns and the firming of the status hierarchy based on skills appropriate for the purpose of the group is one of the observable aspects of this phase. Even in groups of young children or of adults with fairly fragile capacities there seems to occur some initiation and supportive roles among the participants. The social worker, by

[44] Schutz, *Interpersonal Underworld.*
[45] Thelen, and Dickerman, "Growth of a Group," *Educational Leadership.*
[46] Tuckman, "Developmental Sequence," *Psychological Bulletin.*

supporting such patterns if they are in the best interests of the group and all of the members, can help the group do its own work. In fact, the worker's activity during this phase in encouraging the emergent group leadership may well move the worker into a less central role, and maximize the group's functioning in its own behalf.

There may be periodic reintegration phases if the group loses or adds members, if members face crises that are brought into group content, if the group has failures or special successes in its operations, if some external factors change the group's status in the hierarchy of groups within which it exists. But if the group has formed finally, becomes integrated and moved on to maintaining itself and functioning to carry out its tasks, then it can usually work through any crises.

Termination Phases

Most groups end. Some merely drift away. Some go on for years with addition of new members to make up for losses and a shift in focus and purpose and some periodic reintegration. But most groups encountered in social work services have an ending as well as a beginning.

In social work perspective, the termination phase can be said to have three parts: pretermination or the period of preparation for the actual ending; the termination itself—the recognized ending; and post-termination, the plan for follow-up, if any, of the group and the service. Pretermination includes acknowledgment that the group is actually about to end. This period may also include planning for the ending, enumerating and evaluating the group accomplishments and failures, planning for recognition of individual members and leaders, and a period for working through the difficulties that some members may feel in breaking the ties. The pretermination period may also include planning some ritual for ending.

Even though the end of group may be scheduled from the beginning, as some are, members may need to be reminded prior to the last session in a pretermination that the group is about to stop. If a group has been struggling to organize and has failed to become integrated, the members must be confronted with the possible termination if they cannot synthesize. This would probably consist of a hasty and precipitous pretermination period combined with actual termination. Many groups which are completing their tasks will need to be reminded that with the completion the members will end the experience together. If the experience in working together has been particularly satisfying, members may attempt to find reasons to continue the group.

Termination itself takes place in the actual last session of the group. Sometimes the plans for this meeting include a summary, sometimes a ritual like a closing ceremony, a party or a special event, tending to wind up the activity of the group and formalize the breaking of ties. Plans for the last meeting of a group do not always work out, as we will consider later, but in good termination planning, the ending is acknowledged and formally anticipated.

In social work groups, depending on their composition and purpose, plans for a post-termination phase may be appropriate. Members may wish to have the security of knowing that some other type of service will follow. This would be post-termination for individuals rather than for the group. Some groups, however, plan for reunion of the entire group or of subgroups. Plans for post-termination may be made in the pretermination sessions or in the final session itself. It may be useful for the group and the leadership to be clear as to the purpose and content of any post-termination meeting of the group. On the other hand, if the group has terminated well (with a good integration of content and an appropriate severing of interpersonal ties), a postgroup session may be awkward and unnecessary.

Some groups in social work function for a program year and then reconvene in the next program year. This is frequent for groups in youth service, group service, neighborhood agencies, or in school-related groups. Groups also may recess while there is a change in worker, or while staff have vacations. In these cases the groups, for all intents and purposes, may terminate and reconvene as a slightly different or new group, especially if there is change of worker, new members, or loss of members. When this is foreseen, plans may be made to acknowledge the ending or the intermission. If the dates of reconvening are known, if there is to be a change of leadership, or membership shift, these factors can be considered at the last session in some plan for post-termination renewal.

Groups may end in any of the following circumstances: when the group has reached the time limit set in the beginning; when the group has completed its tasks; when the members no longer need the group; when the group does not coalesce, or when it seems to fall apart having coalesced; when it suffers extensive loss of membership or loss of leadership, including, in social work groups, loss of worker.

The termination point for some groups is determined at their outset, that is, the number of sessions, or the length of time that the group will exist is stated before the group begins. Six-, ten-, or fifteen-session groups may be established. Other groups may be established to last a weekend (a conference or institute), two weeks, a month (a camp session), or a semester (an interest group). Although the duration of the group is known initially, members may forget or deny and reject the ending. They may need to be reminded in the pretermination period that the last session is approaching.

The end point of some groups is expected upon completion of a particular task. For instance, a committee or task force may exist to do a particular kind of job and should, therefore, go out of existence when its job is done. Groups whose members are having a particularly satisfying experience may resist completion of their goal if the group seems more gratifying than achievement of the goal. They may delay commencing or completing their work in order to prolong the group. Leaders of such a group may confront the group with the importance of finishing the task, since it is their reason for existence.

Bales suggests that the "tendency for groups to shift from task groups to friendship groups is so strong that some groups attempt to persist on a friendship basis after the task that originally brought them together is completed."[47] Task groups whose members decide to shift the focus to personally satisfying action may hereafter find less impetus to remain together and too few subjects for conversation or interaction. In pretermination, such groups can consider on what basis they might continue.

Groups which exist as a contingent to some other condition in the lives of the members cease to exist when the condition is met or members leave. For instance, motivational and counseling groups for people in job-training programs cease to be necessary once their members are on regular full-time jobs. Groups dealing with the condition of unwed pregnant girls lose members as soon as the girls deliver and re-enter the community. Predischarge groups are no longer needed when the member leaves the hospital or institution in which he has been living. People undergoing treatments, such as shock therapy or certain types of surgery or series of shots, no longer need the supportive treatment group when they have concluded their treatment. Often these services are offered in "open-ended" groups in which some members enter and others leave almost constantly so that some members of the group are beginning and terminating at all times. On the other hand, some groups of this sort are composed of people who are beginning and ending the treatment at about the same time. Theoretically the purpose of the group which is to orient members to treatment, or support them in it, has been fulfilled with the completion of the treatment. However, human needs for support after the experience is concluded may suggest post-termination plans for another type of group or another type of service.

When a group does not coalesce, once through the initial formation state and some disintegration and reintegration, then it terminates. This may happen abortively and spontaneously, or some of the members may need assistance in this termination, ones who hang on, guiltily feeling fault that the group did not work out. Reasons for failure of a group to coalesce are varied: poor composition or incompatibility of members; member's lack of interest in the groups' purposes; too few potential members; poor timing or

[47] Heinicke, and Bales, "Developmental Trends," *Sociometry*.

location of meetings; or lack of leadership. Sometimes unresolved interpersonal conflict also causes precipitous group disintegration.

Groups which suffer heavy loss of members may terminate because so many breaks in interpersonal ties are more than the remaining members can absorb, or because there are too few people left to maintain a group. A group may survive loss of members if enough people remain to have a satisfying experience, or if new members can be added to enrich the group and reorganize it. Generally, however, loss of members is a reason for termination. Addition of new members may mean the formation of a new group.

Loss of leaders, either indigenous or staff leaders (in social work groups), may cause termination if the leader has been particularly central to the group existence. The resultant floundering may provide the opportunity for new leaders to emerge, but it sometimes results in disintegration of the group. Where the staff function or role performance has provided the central group leadership and the staff member leaves, the group may be temporarily terminated by the social worker or the agency while new staff is sought. In some such cases, members feel such a sense of loss or desertion that they will not continue, or they may not relate to a new worker.

Many writers have observed striking behaviors in groups facing termination. Bennis and Shepherd [48] refer to the "ways of avoiding or denying the reality of ending." They and other researchers report an upsurge of clinging together, getting to work more enthusiastically on the group task, rejecting the work of the group altogether, rejecting leadership, projecting group faults and failures on the group leadership or staff, individual depression, lowering of group morale, abdication of responsibility, excessive absenteeism, regression to previous states of group disorganization.

Schutz [49] states that groups that are terminating find ways to reduce their interactions such as increasing their lateness or absenteeism; they come late or not at all, forget to bring things they had offered, and generally decrease their involvement. He notes that

[48] Bennis, and Shepherd, "Theory of Group Development," *Human Relations.*
[49] Schutz, *Interpersonal Underworld.*

members' departure from the group depends on their individual needs which the group has satisfied for them and also their capacity to cope.

Several writers refer to a process of evaluation or the recollection of previous experiences. This evaluation or recollection may not necessarily be accurate but may in fact appear in opposites. Fairly good experiences may be minimized and refuted while poor experiences will be given glowing positive recollection. Schutz speaks of the group experience of working over past events that were not resolved in the group.

Mann [50] describes the process of evaluating by the instructor, trainer, or staff leadership. He recalled that members abdicated responsibility in the terminal review, expecting that the leader would produce the work to express the group evaluation.

The phenomenon of "separation anxiety" may appear in the group, members blaming each other for bad behavior or lack of contribution and calling this the reason for termination.[51] There also may be expressions of personal guilt, "I didn't do all that I could." These kinds of expressions may occur even in groups whose end was scheduled from the beginning. In task groups that have completed their assignments, one can sometimes hear the expression that "we might do a little better if we took a little longer," or "maybe we could start over." Mann [52] suggests that the final separation may reactivate feelings of loss and abandonment from other life experiences and an expectation that the leader will somehow hold the group together. He also states that termination stirs up feelings of incompetence, that members may berate themselves for having gotten or given less than they should have in the group.

After the pretermination evaluations, positive and negative, some resumé of experiences, dealing with their good and bad feelings about the groups, the members seem better able to accept separation and to resolve their relationships and dissolve the group. They release control over each other, and work on their relations to each other individually rather than on group or task problems.

[50] Richard Mann, *Interpersonal Styles and Group Development* (New York, John Wiley & Sons, Inc., 1967).

[51] Schutz, *Interpersonal Underworld.*

[52] Mann, *Interpersonal Styles and Group Development.*

Termination in social work groups may be examined in four respects: the meaning to the individual members; the meaning to the worker; the relation to group purposes; and the group aspects. First it should be recognized that termination may be an important aspect of normal life, and to be helped in facing endings appropriately and in a healthy way may prepare the individual for other terminations that will confront him throughout life and may prepare him to move on to other experiences. Appropriate dealing with separations lead on to the next aspects of life, help people to learn to sever ties and break the dependencies created in cohesive groups. Thus, despite feelings of grief and sadness upon the ending of a group, the experience may benefit the members in the long run if the termination is well handled.

Understanding of group phases as a natural and expected aspect of group development and functioning from beginning to end should enhance the social worker's activity with groups. He may act more purposefully and feel more secure as he recognizes the appearance of predictable phenomena. Mastery of this kind of knowledge in practice should improve his skill in all group experience both as worker and member, but particularly where he is attempting to help the group to become the viable instrument of service, whether in the member-directed group for help or change of the person, or in the task-directed group for problem solving or community action.

GROUP COMPOSITION
AND MEMBERSHIP

Group composition and membership includes styles of grouping, methods of recruitment, convening, and decisions which bring people together as well as the source of membership. In social science theory and research, composition has been considered from the standpoint of social factors, such as age, sex, ethnicity, race, and socioeconomic class. Personality factors such as capacity of people to relate to others or to use the group experience and the compatibility of members have been studied. The subject of composition has been considered in social work practice and group therapy on the basis of problem orientation, similarity of needs, and interests or concerns of individuals which they hold in common, or problems which they share in their social situation.

Those people who actually become members compose the group, and participate in its development are determined by a set of criteria which may be overt and clearly stated or subtle and informal. Guidelines are established by those who offer and organize the group, or by the people who are the members and set expectations for others who join them. Factors for group membership are related to the purposes for which a group exists but are usually further delineated by certain social factors, by personality characteristics and capacities, and the common problems or similar interests of potential members.

Groups vary in the degree to which membership is open or closed, depending upon the purpose of the group, the sponsoring auspices, the members themselves, and those who have the final authority in determining who may belong. The terms "open" and "closed" refer to groups which do or do not add members once the group has convened in its initial session. The open group may add members from time to time, sometimes at every session, and may have members leave fairly frequently. Ziller defines open group as "an interacting set of persons in a continuous state of membership flux." [1] The closed group has set criteria for inclusion of members. Once these people are convened, no others are admitted.

Two terms, "autonomous groups" and "convened groups," which will be used in this chapter, need definition. Autonomous is used to refer to groups which are formed spontaneously by the people who become members of the group. These groups are variously referred to in the literature as "natural" groups and "self-formed" or "member-formed" groups.

The dictionary definition of autonomous is self-governing or without outside control.[2] Examples of autonomous groups which form themselves and are later served within social work are street clubs, gangs, small cliques of boys and girls, and citizen-action associations. Sometimes within institutions small cliques of residents or patients will organize themselves in autonomous fashion. Families are also defined as small autonomous groups in that they are self-formed and self-directed. In the social sciences, study of this type of group is referred to as "natural state" groups and sometimes as "field" study.

[1] Robert Ziller, "Toward a Theory of Open and Closed Groups," *Psychological Bulletin,* LXIII (1965), 164–82.

[2] *Webster's New International Dictionary of the English Language* (2d ed., unabridged, Springfield, Mass., G. & C. Merriam Co., 1950), p. 188.

In contrast to self-formed groups are those convened for a specific purpose by someone who may be a leader or researcher but not a member of the group as a participant. Theoretically, such groups should be labeled "allonomous" or "not self-governing or self-determining" or "influenced by outside forces"[3] by Webster definition, that is, the opposite of autonomous. In social work literature this type of group is usually referred to as "agency-formed or worker-initiated." Actually, of course, such groups are agency- or worker-convened since the formation process depends upon the interaction of the members. In the social science literature, these groups may be referred to as experimental groups, or people convened for purposes of study.

Social Factors as a Basis for Grouping

Examining the social factors which may be considered in composition, Hare says that "it is possible to control the pattern and outcome of interaction by selecting members with certain combinations of social characteristics. Some of these characteristics, such as age and sex, are easily identified, and others, such as social class, ethnicity, or friendship group, can be discovered with relatively little investigation."[4] He goes on to say that most of the research on group composition comes from field studies rather than experimental studies since experimental studies tend to "hold constant" the variable of composition by employing subjects who are relatively homogeneous on social characteristics.

A review of social work and group psychotherapy literature reveals that most practitioners also consider grouping by the social factors of age, sex, ethnicity, race, or socioeconomic level. Depending on whether the desired objective is heterogeneity in order to have social diversity or homogeneity in order to have some social

---

[3] *Ibid.*, p. 186. Also for discussion of autonomous and allonomous groups, see Norma C. Lang, "A Broad Range Model of Practice in the Social Work Group" (paper delivered at the National Conference of Social Welfare, Chicago, 1970). [To be published in *Social Service Review* (in press)].

[4] A. Paul Hare, *Handbook of Small Group Research* (New York, The Free Press, 1962), p. 206.

similarity. Wilson, for instance, says, "The worker should take into account in grouping the following factors: age range, intellectual range, educational background, social experience, occupational experience, social class and sex." [5]

Northen [6] notes that "there are many opinions about criteria for group composition, [but] there has been little systematic study of who should be together in groups." She refers to Redl's [7] "law of optimum distance" that groups should be homogeneous enough to ensure stability and heterogeneous enough to ensure vitality. She continues that "some balance is necessary so that no single member represents an extreme difference from other members, for this usually makes integration into the group unlikely."

A crucial matter in the consideration of the questions of homogeneity and heterogeneity of social factors in grouping is the purpose for which the group is organized. For example, if the focus is on the effect of the group experience on the participants, especially if they have personal problems to be dealt with in the group, similarity in social factors might lead to more intimacy and sharing of personal problems. If the focus is on attitude change about racial, ethnic, and socioeconomic values through experience in the group, a more heterogeneous group would provide greater exposure. A task-centered group of representatives from various organizations may well include people of different ages, sexes, races, and socioeconomic backgrounds drawn together by their common interest in the problem under consideration, and convened on the basis of their group of origin regardless of social factors.

Age Factors as Criteria

Several observers of behavior in both research and practice have commented on the differences at various ages in social ability and

[5] Gertrude Wilson, and Gladys Ryland, *Social Group Work Practice* (Boston, Houghton Mifflin Co., 1948).

[6] Helen Northen, *Social Work with Groups* (New York, Columbia University Press, 1969), p. 95.

[7] Fritz Redl, "Art of Group Composition," in Suzanne Shulze, ed., *Creative Group Living in a Children's Institution* (New York, Association Press, 1951), pp. 76–96.

capacity to relate to others in groups. Preschool or nursery age children engage primarily in self-centered or isolated play even in the presence of others. They communicate with others by verbal and nonverbal means, showing each other objects or performing for others as audiences, but they show very little cooperative or sharing activities.[8] Although some therapists and nursery school teachers report observations of groups of preschool children, by and large, they actually are observing aggregates or individuals in the presence of others, carrying on parallel play or interpersonal encounters that are not sustained or developed.[9] In guidance centers, mental health clinics where preschool groups have been used for diagnostic purposes, the evidence suggests that the focus of service must be primarily on the individual as his behavior is observed in reaction and response to his peers and to adults.

At ages four and five, children begin to notice others more; while their play and social contact still tends to be egocentric, they have greater capacity to participate with others, to share, to engage in low-demand group games and other social activities. Irene Josselyn [10] says "healthy relationship with one's peers requires a capacity to accept loss of identity as an individual and to find gratification in a new identity as part of a group." She continues, "a child of six should not be expected to lose himself in identification with the group."

Piaget [11] noted that latency age children evidence the capacity to share, to belong, to move into larger groups, to relate to more people, to give and to take, to lead and to follow. If they are proceeding through usual social and personal relationships in other aspects of their lives with parents and siblings or other family members, peers, school groups, they will have capacity to participate in groups. As they develop a sense of themselves and a trust

[8] Susan Isaacs, *Social Development in Young Children* (New York, Harcourt Brace Jovanovich, Inc., 1933), pp. 247–72.

[9] Mildred Parten, "Social Play Among Preschool Children," *Journal of Abnormal and Social Psychology*, XXVIII (1933), 136–47.

[10] Irene Josselyn, *Psychosocial Development of Children* (New York, Family Service Association of America, 1948), pp. 84–85.

[11] Jean Piaget, *The Moral Judgments of the Child* (New York, Harcourt Brace Jovanovich, Inc., 1932).

of themselves and others, they begin to share with others, thus the capacity to belong and participate in groups of one's peers becomes strong at the ages of seven, eight, and nine, and may be firmly and well set by early adolescence.[12] Irene Josselyn [13] says that if a child is unsure of himself as a person in his own right, the threat to his identity (of belonging to a group) is too great, and he may, therefore, withdraw from the group, attempting to maintain his own sense of security by avoiding the hazards of group participation. With some strength he may remain in the group, asserting his right to protect himself against the demands of the group.

Writers from both sociological and psychological viewpoints describe a strong tendency toward the formation of peer group cliques, secret societies or gangs in the adolescent period. Hollingshead [14] observed the social organization of the high school in *Elmtown's Youth* characterized by strong peer cliques. Parsons [15] described the sociological phenomenon of the adolescent peer society, a network of small groups. Buxbaum [16] wrote of psychological aspects of the gang phenomenon wherein the adolescent transfers his identification with adults to an identification with peers in the formation of the ego and finding identity in adolescents. Erikson [17] also described the emerging adolescent ego as one moving to peer group affiliation.

S. N. Eisenstadt,[18] observing the grouping among adolescents, has written that groups of people of the same age "have an inherent tendency toward solidarity" because they share the same emotional strains and experiences in growing through a period of tran-

[12] Erik Erikson, *Childhood and Society* (New York, W. W. Norton & Co., Inc., 1963).

[13] Irene Josselyn, *Psychosocial Development of Children.*

[14] Augustus Hollingshead, *Elmtown's Youth* (New York, John Wiley & Sons, Inc., 1949).

[15] Talcott Parsons, "The School Class as a Social System," *Harvard Education Review*, XXIX (1959), 297–318.

[16] Edith Buxbaum, "Transference and Gang Formation in Adolescence," in *Psychoanalytic Study of the Child*, Vol. I (New York International Universities Press, 1945).

[17] Erik Erikson, *Insight and Responsibility* (New York, W. W. Norton & Co., Inc., 1964).

[18] S. N. Eisenstadt, *From Generation to Generation* (New York, The Free Press, 1964), p. 46.

sition and are at the same place in life in facing their destiny. They have similar needs, strivings, and fears, and feel uncertainties regarding their future roles so that they are drawn together by their shared or common need to find themselves and form an identity.

Authors who have considered the phenomenon of adult socialization have indicated that the group has strong influence on teaching adults skills, values, and defining adult roles.[19] These authors give firm credence to the important capacity to participate in groups as adults. While the adolescent groups serve to help the emerging personality to develop internally as well as socially, groups in adulthood tend toward defining roles of citizen, family member, worker, and social participant in associations. In other words, the usual adult groupings found in society are task- and achievement-oriented or around some special interest. Thus, the tendency for group participation among adults, at least in this culture, is oriented toward activities with clearly defined goals that may be educational, recreational, or social, or employing physical skills. This is not to say adults do not participate in mutual support groups where the focus is on themselves and their own development. The success of adult study groups, sensitivity groups or T groups, and adult social clubs with fairly normal, well-adjusted people gives evidence that many adults recognize that they may be enhanced by learning to use group experiences better. Jane Howard describes the popularity and the proliferation of self-actualization groups in her book on sensitivity groups, *Please Touch.*[20] There is the recognition that many people have missed out somewhere along the way on the usual life, interpersonal experiences which necessitate their correction in adult groups which are not focused on task or activity but rather on improving interpersonal social relationships. In addition, there are adults who, because of some current crisis, internal or external, may benefit from a group experience with others facing similar crises. Again, in these groups the focus is on person and problem rather than adult tasks of citizen responsibility and concern for others.

[19] Orville G. Brim, Jr. and Stanton Wheeler, *Socialization after Childhood* (New York, John Wiley & Sons, Inc., 1966).

[20] Jane Howard, *Please Touch* (New York, McGraw-Hill Book Co., 1970).

But, according to Erikson's developmental tasks of adults, emo-tional energy would tend to go toward groups in which the focus is either on recreation or on taking action for society. It is, of course, in adulthood also that the pairing phenomenon leading to the for-mation of new families occurs.

In aging there may be a renewed need for groups that are fo-cused on personal support and self-gratification, as well as facilitat-ing new role definition and induction and the creation of new social networks. Brim [21] notes the factors of loss and crisis faced by the older person who finds himself upon retirement separated from former associates and confronted with a loss of role status derived from his occupation. Furthermore, his frequently limited income may restrict his social participation from the types of community and recreational activities he had when he was employed. This phenomenon was noted by Wright and Hyman.[22] Rosow [23] speaks of the contracting social world of the older adult noting that var-ious studies show that with increase in age there is a decrease in memberships in organizations and less participation. On the other hand, he notes that a greater importance is attached to friendships and primary group ties. A part of the decrease in social participa-tion noted by several studies is related also to physical capacity and mobility, characterized by some loss of energy, the necessity to give up driving, and some feeling of insecurity about walking or travel on public transportation in the urban community. Thus, per-sonal and social forces influence the older adult's capacity for group participation while his need for interpersonal and social as-sociations may be increased. Impairment of hearing and vision, memory and physical stamina may lessen capacity for group par-ticipation.[24] The aged person's need for group experience to induct

[21] Orville Brim, Jr. "Adult Socialization," in John Clausen, ed., *Socialization and Society* (Boston, Little Brown & Co., 1968).

[22] Charles Wright, and Herbert Hyman, "Voluntary Association Member-ships of American Adults: Evidence from National Sample Surveys," *American Sociological Review*, XXIII (1958), 284–94.

[23] Irving Rosow, *Social Integration of the Aged* (New York, The Free Press, 1967).

[24] Mary M. Seguin, "The Small Group as Agent of Socialization: A Model for Social Work Practice with Older Adults" (unpublished paper delivered at the National Conference of Social Work, Chicago, 1970. Mimeographed).

him to new roles, to provide ego support while he becomes accustomed to physical and social changes has been likened by some authors to the development of the peer society in adolescence. Therefore, group composition may be facilitated with older adults. Rosow [25] has stated, "despite youthful self-images and their public dissociation from other old people, viable friendships do not spontaneously develop between age groups, but are confined almost exclusively within them." In a study by Aukes of a low-income housing project in Chicago, she found that relationships between the generations were colored by "lack of mutual interest and understanding." In Detroit in a similar study of a housing project with residents of all ages, the old people living alone had no significant contact with young or middle-aged neighbors. In middle-income trailer park communities in Florida, including young and middle-aged residents, friendships and informal associations developed strictly within age groups. From that Rosow concludes "there is an effective social barrier between the generations which propinquity and contact apparently do not dispel." The implication that may be drawn is that since autonomous groups do not seem to occur across generational lines, it may also be difficult to compose groups across these lines.

The age factor in group composition is also relevant to family groups where there is usually a range of ages depending on how many generations are present within the close and intimate interaction of the particular family. While the nuclear family of two generations has been described by Parsons [26] and others, it would appear that there is increasing evidence that extended families even where they are dispersed across vast geographical distances are very close and influential on each other.[27] Thus the age range within family groups who interact together may range from infancy to old age with subgroupings in a single family on a single age level or across age groupings. For instance, the children and par-

[25] Rosow, *Social Integration of the Aged*, pp. 33–35.
[26] Talcott Parsons, "Age and Sex in the Social Structure," *American Sociological Review*, VIII (1942), 604–16.
[27] Eugene Litwak, "Geographical Mobility and Extended Family Cohesion," *American Sociological Review*, XXV (1960), 385–94; and Marvin Sussman, "Isolated Nuclear Family: Fact or Fiction," *Social Problems*, VI (1959), 333–40.

ents may form two subgroups. On the other hand, small children and adolescent or young adult children may form subgroups. Sometimes there are subgroup alliances of children and grandparents.

The cross age factor of grouping, similar to family patterns, has been utilized in the group composition of some multiple family treatment groups and some residential treatment institutions. Multiple age groupings have also been employed in some planning bodies and community committees organized to work with specific social problems. Generally the bottom level for participation in these groups is adolescence, and they may range to old age.

The social research on characteristic social functioning that may be expected at given ages gives clues and cues about group composition on an age basis. It may be concluded, for instance, that any grouping of preschool children will merely be aggregational, characterized by parallel activity although transitory interaction can take place. Several young children can be gathered together to do individual type activities or may even respond to a single presentation, either by each other or by a central leader.

School-age children, on the other hand, can affiliate with groups, be concerned about each other, follow leadership, take some responsibility, and pursue tasks. The strongest group cohesion could be expected, then, from preadolescence through mid-adolescence where the group phenomenon is the strongest, but where the age range in the group may tend to narrow.

While older adolescents can be expected to have the capacity to participate in groups, their natural tendency may be away from the group toward pairing with persons of the same and opposite sex. The group has been utilized widely by young adults as a means of meeting others, particularly in the urban communities where there is high transiency. Young adults are probably preoccupied with establishing their own families, but may also have interest in types of groups that have task and interest focus. But the capacity to participate in groups on an age basis is probably most fully developed in adulthood. Older adults or the elderly, while they may have an increased need for groups, may have decreasing capacity for participation. In family groups or in groups that someway replicate family, such as group homes, groupings of people of various ages can function together.

These generalizations about age in group composition must also be viewed with notation that some individuals, because of current or past experiences of social or personal deprivation, illness, or catastrophe, may appear in latency, adolescence, adulthood, or old age without the capacity for interpersonal sharing in a group. Thus age by itself cannot be seen as a single variable in grouping. Age is, however, one indicator of probable capacity for group participation which can be considered in group composition.

Given the age-related differences in development of motivation and capacity to participate in groups, and the age ranges across which people participate by their own choosing, special consideration would need to be given in practice where the group might be composed of various ages. It has already been noted that families include various ages, but it also should be noted that family members have different functions and roles within the family group to which age is associated. Observations in social work practice suggest that certain other factors may provide a leveling factor across age. For instance in a pediatrics ward the children are from infancy to adolescence. The fact that they are ill, all confined to the same place, and all away from home and their usual associations seem to draw them together. Albee [28] noted that they could be brought together for group sessions and in some activities children assumed different roles according to age and in others they separated into subgroups on an age basis.

Chavers and O'Rourke [29] established a group in the home for unwed mothers from an autonomous clique of girls who grouped on the basis of their arrival date at the home. This group included girls in early adolescence, some in their twenties, thirties, and one in her forties. Their common bond was their similar physical and social condition, regardless of the wide age span. I also observed the grouping of patients on a psychiatric floor of a hospital where

[28] Constance I. Albee, "Group Work with Hospitalized Children," *Children*, II (1955).
[29] Faye Chavers, and Helen O'Rourke, "The Use of Groups with Unmarried Mothers to Facilitate Casework," Mimeographed. Cleveland, Child Welfare League Regional Meeting, 1967.

the ages ranged from adolescence to late middle age. These people could act as a group around ward management and handling of some of their personal problems, but they tended to separate for their recreational activities on close age-related lines. The younger patients drifted toward the piano for singing and dancing, the middle adults engaged in various crafts and skills, and the older group wanted to sit and watch television.

Sex Factors in Composition

There is very little research on the actual factor of sex differentials in group functioning as such; however, examination of some of the studies of sex role behavior may give clues as to the effect of sex on group composition. For instance, the child development literature [30] that notes separation into subgroupings of boys and girls in latency, and the group dating of boys and girls in adolescence is useful for the consideration of composition. Furthermore, the use of single sex peer groups in adolescence for ego supportive purposes, for sharing intimacies and testing out ideas, philosophies, and identity as noted by Eisenstadt [31] is also applicable. These observations lead to the conclusion that children's and adolescents' therapy groups, where the focus is on the person, might well be single sex, while task groups where an action is being addressed could well be composed of both sexes, especially in adolescence.

From the socialization literature and cultural studies it is noted that early in life boys and girls are inducted into differing sex roles that affect how they behave in groups. Berry, Bacon, and Child [32] studied the differing socializing process of boys and girls in a number of cultures and concluded that boys are taught to strive for achievement, self-reliance, and independence. Girls are trained to be obedient, responsible, and to nurture others. Parsons [33] noted a

[30] Martin L. Hoffman, and Lois Hoffman, eds., *Review of Child Development Research*, Vol. I (New York, Russell Sage Foundation, 1964).

[31] Eisenstadt, *From Generation to Generation*.

[32] H. Berry, III, Margaret Bacon, and I. L. Child, "A Cross-Cultural Survey of Sex Differences in Socialization," *Journal of Abnormal and Social Psychology*, LV (1957), 323–32.

[33] Parsons, "Age and Sex," *American Sociological Review*.

similar phenomenon, that is, that girls are expected to assume socioemotional and affective roles, while boys are encouraged to take on instrumental or action-oriented roles. If the socialization process takes effect then, it would follow that boys and girls, together or apart in groups, would function differently from each other. It could be predicted that girls would tend to hold back their opinions and expressions in groups with boys, while they would be freer in their expressions of aggression and initiative in one-sex groups.

Strodtbeck,[34] attempting to determine if there was difference in participation of men and women, used simulated jury deliberations. He discovered that men tended to initiate action directed toward the solution of the task problems, while the women tended to react to their contribution. In mixed committees, Carey [35] noted that women engaged in more personal tasks while men dealt with more abstract ideas, and that the women indicated awareness of this behavioral difference. Lois Hoffman, engaged in a review of the research on the motivation of women toward achievement, especially in light of the women's liberation movement, indicates that current studies still reveal that women tend to underestimate their achievement potential especially in arenas where men are predominant.[36]

The conclusions that may be drawn from these studies is that while women may not make instrumental contributions in mixed task groups, committees, or community-change activities, the mix of sexes may be important for the division of labor. Hoffman concludes, in fact, that girls who were socialized early by their mothers to be independent or who were left without mothers may tend to be aggressive, instrumental, and contribute more initiating functions. So there may be some differentials. Parsons also noted that some men showed capacity to carry affective and social emotional roles.

[34] Fred L. Strodtbeck, and R. D. Mann, "Sex Role Differentiation in Jury Deliberations," *Sociometry*, XIX (1956), 3–11.

[35] Gloria Carey, "Sex Differences in Problem-Solving Performance as a Function of Attitude Difference," *Journal of Abnormal and Social Psychology*, LVI (1958), 256–60.

[36] Lois Hoffman in lecture to the faculty of the School of Applied Social Sciences, Case Western Reserve University, December, 1970.

Ethnicity and Socioeconomic Status in Group Composition

Social class, race, and ethnicity are factors which may draw people together or set them apart depending on the social context of the group, the purposes for which the group exists, and the general social attitudes of the community at the time. For instance, there have been periods in the past twenty years when it was popular in many communities, but not all, for people to associate in groups with others of different racial, ethnic, and socioeconomic backgrounds. In the establishment of groups, therapeutic or personal growth groups as well as task-focused groups, special efforts were made to ensure the inclusion of persons from various social strata of the community.[37] There followed a period of separatism where identity with "one's own kind" became a more popular issue, and group composition focused on single race, single ethnic, and, to some degree, narrow range of socioeconomic levels. Obviously customs vary regionally and within different contexts and in different times in our social history. Housing patterns and living arrangements may also influence attitudes [38] and willingness to associate in the same group.

Studies of the social life of the community have produced evidence that people of different socioeconomic or social class levels develop differences in life styles, language, methods of expression, and ways of relating to others within their own reference group and those outside of it.[39] These differences are more distinct where

---

[37] Dorothy Height, *Step by Step in Interracial Groups* (rev., New York, National Board of the YWCA, 1954).

[38] Morton Deutsch, and Mary Collins, *Interracial Housing: A Psychological Evaluation of a Social Experiment* (Minneapolis, University of Minnesota Press, 1951).

[39] W. Lloyd Warner, *American Life* (Chicago, University of Chicago Press, 1953); Allison Davis, Burleigh Gardner, and Mary Gardner, *Deep South* (Chicago, University of Chicago Press, 1941); Hollingshead, *Elmtown's Youth;* John Dollard, *Caste and Class in a Southern Town* (New York, Harper & Row, 1949); and St. Clair Drake and Horace R. Cayton, *Black Metropolis* (New York, Harcourt Brace Jovanovich, Inc., 1945).

a rigid pattern of segregation or separation exists and where there is less casual and informal association. Catherine Richards [40] found a different style of problem solving between people of the middle class and those of the lower class. These findings could well affect the functioning of groups of people of mixed socioeconomic backgrounds.

Within the stratified levels of society people are also acculturated to a sense of identity which designates their position and role and those of others according to Inkeles.[41] Evidences of the racial awareness of children in the studies by Goodman [42] and Clark [43] support this position. Clark showed further that children were aware of differential treatment accorded to black and white children. Warner and Srole [44] noted the sense of separation and differences in nationality groupings, a phenomenon which seems to be evident in a resurgence in social and political areas in the 1970's. Their findings have been well documented in the growing body of literature, both biographical and fictional about Jews, Italians, Irish, Armenians, and Japanese in America. New organizations of American Indians, Chicanos, and black Americans give evidence of growing racial and ethnic awareness which makes for group cohesion on a homogeneous basis and separation on a heterogeneous basis.

Inkeles cites as example the low esteem associated with certain occupations demanding little or no skill or education, particularly related to service and sanitation jobs. He cites a study that shows that these occupations and the people in them were ranked low or

[40] Catherine V. Richards, and Norman Polansky, "Reaching Working Class Youth Leaders," *Social Work*, IV (1959), 31–39; and Catherine V. Richards, "A Study of Class Differences in Women's Participation" (unpublished D.S.W. dissertation, Cleveland, Western Reserve University, 1958).

[41] Alex Inkeles, "Society, Social Structure, and Child Socialization," in Clausen, ed., *Socialization and Society*, pp. 73–130.

[42] Mary Ellen Goodman, *Race Awareness in Young Children* (Cambridge, Mass., Addison-Wesley Publishing Co., Inc., 1952).

[43] Kenneth B. Clark, *Prejudice and Your Child* (Boston, Beacon Press, 1955).

[44] W. Lloyd Warner, and Leo Srole, *American Ethnic Groups* (New Haven, Yale University Press, 1945).

undesirable by both the people in them and by others.[45] Inkeles also refers to a study by Almond and Verba [46] on civic competence of the individual, feeling that he understands and can influence the political process. They found that the competence rose with increasing education. Gurin's [47] study is also cited to illustrate that the sense of positive image of self increased with education and with social class position.

A study done some time ago, but apparently still substantiated by current observations, was the work of Neugarten [48] on latency age children. She found that children ages ten to twelve, of both middle and lower class, "had negative images of lower-class children as being poorly dressed, not good-looking, unpopular, agressive, dirty, bad mannered, unfair, and not having a good time." Thus within the same group these children feel considerable social distance, at least initially.

The problem in group composition that emerges then is to what degree and for what purposes people of differing socioeconomic status, race, or ethnicity can be associated within the same groups. There is social research in field studies and experimental studies where the central factor under examination is change in racial attitudes through a mixed group experience.[49] For instance Mann [50] composed racially mixed, six-person groups of graduate students. He found from a measure taken after the third and eleventh sessions that there was some change in ethnic attitudes but not other attitudinal changes. However, there are mixed findings on the ef-

[45] Inkeles, "Society, Social Structure, and Child Socialization," in Clausen, ed., *Socialization and Society.*

[46] G. Almond, and S. Verba, *The Civic Culture: Political Attitudes and Democracy* (Princeton, N.J., Princeton University Press, 1963).

[47] G. Gurin, J. Veroff, and Sheila Feld, *Americans View Their Mental Health: A Nationwide Interview Survey* (New York, Basic Books, Inc., 1960).

[48] Bernice Neugarten, "Social Class and Friendship Among School Children," *American Journal of Sociology*, LI (1946), 305–13.

[49] John Harding, Harold Proshansky, Bernard Kutner, and Isidor Chein, "Prejudice and Ethnic Relations," in Gardner Lindzey and Elliot Aronson, eds., *The Handbook of Social Psychology* (2d ed., Reading, Mass., Addison-Wesley Publishing Co., Inc., 1969).

[50] J. H. Mann, "The Differential Nature of Prejudice Reduction," *Journal of Social Psychology*, LII (1960), 339–43.

fect of association and attitude change. Yarrow [51] and associates studied eight-to-thirteen-year-old white and Negro boys and girls during a two-week summer camp. It was found that radical shifts in long standing interracial orientation did not occur, but social distance between the two groups was reduced and race as a criterion of friendship exerted less influence at the end of the two-week period. Mussen [52] found that there were no changes in attitude after a two-week camp session. Yarrow [53] found that crossracial friendships occurred primarily between and among cabin mates and were confined to cabin activities. When the children participated in wider camp activities, such as swimming, games, dramatics, they separated into racially segregated cliques.

Deutsch and Collins [54] found in studies of residential contact between different ethnic groups in noncompetitive equal status situations, integrated in housing projects, that 56% of the residents favored the interracial living, as well as work and social associations. Hunt [55] on the other hand found that although 65% of the residents liked the neighborhood, only 20% of whites and 46% of Negroes favored the racially mixed neighborhood.

Judging from the observations of social workers, including my own work in this area for many years, when the group composition anticipated is racially, ethnically, or socioeconomically mixed, it is well to have a clear purpose, preferably focused on task. But it may be anticipated that heterogeneous groups are not as easily composed as groups where the members have fewer differences. The other conclusion to be drawn is that recognizing some of the strain of social distance, the worker will need to provide stronger guidance in the formation of diverse groups. When subcultural differences are noticeable in life style, values, expectations, material

[51] Marion R. Yarrow, ed., "Interpersonal Dynamics in a Desegregation Process," *Journal of Social Issues*, XIV (1958).

[52] P. H. Mussen, "Some Personality and Social Factors Related to Changes in Children's Attitudes," *Journal of Abnormal and Social Psychology*, XLV (1950), 423–41.

[53] Yarrow, "Interpersonal Dynamics," *Journal of Social Issues.*

[54] Deutsch and Collins, *Interracial Housing.*

[55] C. L. Hunt, "Negro-White Perceptions of Interracial Housing," *Journal of Social Issues*, XV (1959), 24–29.

possessions, language, and nonverbal expression, tensions and feelings of strangeness or distance may be noticeable when people of different groupings attempt to associate. These feelings of strangeness will need to be dealt with in the group.

In some institutional settings, particularly the medical, and sometimes mental health, homes for unwed mothers, handicapped and retarded, and in some social agency camps, there may be socioeconomic or ethnic and social and racial diversity. Usually common or similar problems provide a ground for interpersonal relations across status, language, or life-style diversity. Task-oriented groups also provide participants with a target outside of themselves and each other and therefore a basis for interaction regardless of social distance. Some research shows, however, that people who come to a group with higher social status derived from their life outside the group tend to participate more and take more aggressive roles.[56] This would give some clues to a social worker staffing a group of people of mixed socioeconomic backgrounds, whether it be in a therapy group or a committee. The objective would be to make sure that the structure and operation of the group gives opportunity for all to participate freely and equally.

If values, life styles, and status are components of socioeconomic, social class, ethnic, and racial reference groups, then it would follow that people of the same background would more easily form groups. Heider and Newcomb [57] have proposed that a person will tend to be attracted to another if he believes that the other's attitudes and values are similar to his own. Moreover, this attraction will be stronger the more important the attitudes or values are to the person.

Berelson and Steiner [58] hypothesize that the more alike "mem-

---

[56] Hare, *Handbook.*

[57] F. Heider, *The Psychology of Interpersonal Relations* (New York, John Wiley & Sons, Inc., 1958), and Theodore Newcomb, *The Acquaintance Process* (New York, Holt, Rinehart & Winston, Inc., 1961) referred to in D. Cartwright and A. Zander, eds., *Group Dynamics*, Chapter III, "Groups and Group Membership," Introduction (3d ed., New York, Harper & Row, 1968), p. 55.

[58] Bernard Berelson and Gary A. Steiner, *Human Behavior* (New York, Harcourt Brace Jovanovich, Inc., 1964), p. 353.

bers are in norms, skills, personality status, et cetera, the more the procedures of the group are accepted and understood, the more effective and satisfying is the performance of the group in its task." They support this hypothesis with the finding from Klein in which she suggests that "a group with status conflict resembles a competitive group; the attainment of aims by one member hinders other members in the performance of their own work; members withhold information from one another; members communicate hostile feelings and criticism and members communicate a great deal of material unrelated to the task." [59] Depending upon the purpose for which the group is established and the potential use of resolution of internal group conflict, the composition may reflect homogeneity or heterogeneity in sociocultural factors.

Sociocultural factors, then, of age, sex, ethnicity, race, religion, socioeconomic position and their attendant role expectations may be given some consideration in group composition if care is taken not to stereotype the individual by his sociocultural attributes. Although each person must be seen within his categorical framework, his individual uniqueness must also be recognized. Leland Bradford [60] has succinctly stated, "each member brings many differences, different past experiences and present problems, different fears and anxieties about possible consequences of membership, different pressures to learn and change, different degrees of paying in the process, different assumptions, values and perceptual screens, different self-concepts, different patterns of relationships to others and to authority, different approaches to learning; all of these differences must be accommodated if a learning association is to be created."

Personality Variables

Various kinds of personality variables have been examined with regard to group composition and group functioning. Based on assess-

[59] Josephine P. Klein, *The Study of Groups* (London, Routledge and Kegan Paul, Ltd., 1956).

[60] Leland Bradford, "Membership in the Learning Process," in Leland Bradford, Jack R. Gibb, and Kenneth Benne, *T Group Theory and Laboratory Method* (New York, John Wiley & Sons, Inc., 1964), pp. 193–94.

ment of individual characteristics, such as intellectual capacity, adjustment, extroversion and introversion, masculinity and femininity, and like factors, attempts have been made to predict how a person will behave in a group. The behavior tendencies which a person may show on an individual basis when tested alone may be different from his actual behavior when he is in the presence of others or interacting with them. Hare [61] warns that "all intended behavior is modified to some extent before it becomes overt so that the relative strength of basic tendencies can only be inferred by considering the force exerted in the situation to modify them." The Murphys' [62] study of children substantiates this. She showed that children took special notice of who was present and tended to behave in a manner that responded to what the child thought was expected of him by others. In other words, some people who may show tendencies to behave one way as individuals alone may find themselves inhibited or stimulated to act out in a group situation, or in the presence of others with different or similar behavioral tendencies. A person who tends to be aggressive and has leadership qualities which enable him to assume responsibility for any group may restrain himself in a situation where he is in the presence of high status people whom he wishes to impress with his affability, or who may be more competitive than himself.

Schutz,[63] in an effort to predict compatibility of people in group functioning, developed some measures of personality on predictable interactional qualities. His test, called FIRO (Fundamental Interpersonal Relations Orientation), measured three dimensions of an individual's potential behavior with others: personalness, power, and assertiveness. Personalness or counterpersonalness refers to the individual's capacity to move into close personal relationships, getting people to like him, being a "good guy" and treating people differentially as opposed to keeping people removed and at a distance, remaining aloof, appearing indifferent. The power orienta-

[61] Hare, *Handbook.*

[62] Lois Murphy, and G. Murphy, "The Influence of Social Situations upon the Behavior of Children," in C. Murcheson, ed., *A Handbook of Social Psychology* (Worcester, Mass., Clark University Press, 1935).

[63] William C. Schutz, *F.I.R.O.: A Three-Dimensional Theory of Interpersonal Orientation* (New York, Holt, Rinehart & Winston, Inc., 1958).

tion refers to ways of relating to authority, or taking on authority, following rules, following the leader, conforming to manipulation or controlling the power structure. The assertiveness orientation refers to the predisposition to express one's self openly in interpersonal relations or to withhold expression. On the basis of a test of these qualities, profiles are constructed for each individual, and people are grouped with similar profiles. These groupings are referred to as compatible. People grouped on the basis of mixed profiles were referred to as incompatible. It was found that people with similar profiles were more compatible than people with widely diverse profiles. For instance, people who were considered personable grouped together created a more compatible group, and people who were considered counterpersonable were more compatible and operated better together than the mixture of both personable/counterpersonable. Groups composed of people with similar interpersonal qualities attained higher cohesion, maintained a more permissive and supportive group atmosphere, and their members were more strongly attracted to the group and to each other. Incompatible groups, composed of people with dissimilar traits, lacked focus, shifted leadership and frequently gave up.

William Shalinsky [64] used Schutz's scheme for the composition of living group units in a social agency camp, and found that the instruments did predict interpersonal group behavior in the units. The children were administered the FIRO test when they registered for camp, and they were assigned to living groups on the basis of their ratings. Several of each of the incompatible and compatible units were composed of children on the basis of their ratings. Shalinsky found that the compatible groups participated well together in activities, housekeeping duties, decision making, and general camp living. The incompatible units, on the other hand could not seem to get organized, could not make decisions, had trouble and conflict in activities and camp living. The counselors responsible for these children, while they knew a study was under-

[64] William Shalinsky, "The Effect of Group Composition on Aspects of Group Functioning" (unpublished D.S.W. dissertation, Cleveland, Western Reserve University, 1967).

way, did not know its nature. Those with incompatible groups found that regardless of their leadership and interventions they could not help their groups to resolve their conflicts and get organized.

On the other end of the spectrum, the composition of groups for task achievement, Collins and Guetzkow [65] have developed some criteria based on the Schutz formulation. They say on the basis of their research in planning for a conference group that increased heterogeneity of personality within a group will increase the problem-solving potential, but it will also increase the difficulty in building interpersonal relations. Greater variations in personality increase the chance of incompatibility. Participants motivated by personal and self-centered needs decrease the group's effectiveness because of the disruptive nature of competitive individualistic behaviors which lead to high conflict, low participant satisfaction, low group solidarity, and low productivity. Thus, one may conclude from Collins and Guetzkow's findings that if a person needs a therapy group or tends to use groups for his own therapeutic satisfaction he may act out in the committee or conference group in an effort to gratify his own needs. When he finds that he cannot gain this satisfaction in such a group he is therefore frustrated but also may inhibit the group from getting to work on its task. The interpersonal orientations necessary and important for group task participation can be stated as questions: Does he work within the power structure, that is, follow rules, follow the leader? Does he work through close personal relations? Does he respond to people and get them to respond to them?

Another personality rating scheme is the test of authoritarianism by the F Scale developed by Adorno, Frenkel-Brunswick, Levinson, and Sanford.[66] The person who rates high on authoritarianism is comfortable with a rigid set of rules, is totally submissive to those in power without raising any question, generally is preoccupied with power and authority, and wants to punish anyone who does

[65] Barry Collins, and Harold Guetzkow, *A Social Psychology of Group Process for Decision Making* (New York, John Wiley & Sons, Inc., 1964).
[66] T. W. Adorno, Else Frenkel-Brunswick, D. J. Levinson, and R. N. Sanford, *The Authoritarian Personality* (New York, Harper & Row, 1950).

not adhere to the rules. He generally shows strong opinions of likes and dislikes to the point of being prejudiced. In an experiment conducted by Scodel and Freedman,[67] persons who tested high on authoritarianism thought the others were high also, but those who tested low thought the others middle or high. In another experiment people who rated high on authoritarianism were found to be most suggestible to changes in opinions from others in the group.

In another test using the authoritarian personality scale [68] the behaviors of group members were observed as they worked on a creative and cooperative task. It was observed that people who had low authoritarian scores were rated higher on effective intelligence, demonstrated more leadership skills, showed greater sensitivity to others, equalitarian behavior, goal striving and greater security in the experiment, and showed less desire to elicit friendly relationships from others. Those ranking high on authoritarianism were more dissatisfied with the group achievement, thought their groups lacked cooperation, thought their groups were less competitive, and had less differences of opinion.

In a study of personality factors in therapy groups, Taylor [69] found that affection was the most important personality dimension. People who were affectionate or hostile to the group thought that they aroused the same feelings in others, and assumed their feelings were reciprocated.

Cattell [70] developed a sixteen-factor personality test to show the presence of such characteristics as vigor, dominance, adventuresomeness, suspiciousness, nervous tension, emotional immaturity, and many others. Experiments were performed composing groups of persons with various ratings on Cattell's tests in order to determine

[67] A. Scodel, and Maria L. Freedman, "Additional Observations on the Social Perceptions of Authoritarians and Non-Authoritarians," *Journal of Abnormal and Social Psychology*, LII (1956), 92–95.

[68] W. Haythorn, A. Couch, D. Haefner, P. Langhorn, and L. F. Carter, "The Behavior of Authoritarian and Equalitarian Personalities in Groups," *Human Relations*, IX (1956), 57–74.

[69] F. K. Taylor, "The Three-Dimensional Basis of Emotional Interactions in Small Groups," *Human Relations*, VII (1954), 441–71.

[70] R. B. Cattell, "Concepts and Methods in the Measurement of Group Syntality," *Psychological Review*, LV (1948), 48–63.

whether the combination of people with similarity or variance of ratings on these tests might predict to group performance. Cattell and associates introduced the concept of group syntality, meaning the internal synthesis of a group or the group's functioning as an entity which produced the capacity of the group members to perform together. Since no two persons would probably have identical personality profiles, they used group means on each personality variable rather than a combined rating. They also made combinations of variables related to certain group synergy states. They found, for instance, that groups that showed task performance at a high level of coordination, such as doing things together, which was preferred over discussion, resulted from a group in which there were high group means on vigor, dominance, adventuresomeness, purposefulness, orderliness, self-determination, and freedom from anxiety. Groups where there were high group means on suspiciousness, tension, immaturity, anxiety, and lack of self-sufficiency showed high frustration, lack of leadership, lack of order, and "we feeling," low motivation, and little organization and interdependence.

When members showed high group means on friendliness, intelligence, level of radicalism, along with variances on such factors of talkativeness, enjoying carefree excitement, and fast repartee and variance on social norms, their groups showed a high level of accuracy on tasks requring a judgment of facts from inferences. They also showed a controlled group atmosphere. Groups where there was considerable uniformity in emotional maturity were characterized as being optimistic and having confidence in their achievement aspirations.[71]

Cattell's research is noted because reference to it appears in much of the literature on small group, and while it is unlikely that the Cattell personality inventory might be used in social work, it is possible that social workers could observe certain personality traits that are similar to Cattell's classification which could be predictive of group functioning. The trait factor is as applicable for task groups as it is for therapeutically oriented groups.

[71] For a further discussion of the application of Cattell's work, see Hare, *Handbook*, 191–93.

Hare [72] says that "in selecting members with personality or social characteristics which will result in a productive group, the requirements of the task must be kept in mind." He suggests further
that it is best to select members who do not have too much internal conflict if the group is established to consider problems of control or affection. Furthermore, he contends that if the group task is
a cognitive one of problem solving with the need to analyze and
propose action, it is wiser to choose people who have those capacities and fairly equal skills.

Groups in which members are compatible with each other seem
to be more productive, organize quicker, and have greater satisfactions. Determination of member compatibility can be achieved by
observations of people's relationships with each other in other situations, by using a sociometric choice, or by some of the personality
tests, such as the Schutz, the test for authoritarianism or others
which predict individual behavior in groups. While the question
arises regarding the administration of tests in social work practice,
it should be recognized that this is not a totally new phenomenon.
The intake process itself, developing the client's eligibility, and the
diagnostic process in determining the nature of the problem have
some of the qualities of a test. Furthermore, in some clinical settings clients are given a variety of psychological and affective tests.
Therefore, to suggest a Schutz FIRO test, an F Scale test, or a Cattell's personality inventory as prerequisite to inclusion in a group
might provide a better group composition on the long haul. But
short of administering the tests, if a social worker wanted to chart
out certain personality characteristics of people based on observations of their behavior in interpersonal relations, such as an intake
interview in an open lounge or an intake or orientation group session, it might be possible by simple observation to note people
who are personable or counterpersonable, who seek control or to
be controlled or who reject control, or who appear to be authoritarian, or who are optimistic and talkative, or depressed and with-
drawn. Using the grouping conclusions of some of the studies indicated above, it would be possible to combine therapeutic groups
with compatibility for working together or for conflict in order to

[72] Hare, *Handbook*, p. 379.

surface particular types of problems. In task groups it might be desirable to have a harmonious group that would begin quickly to get a job done, or a more diverse group that would bring in a range of ideas and solutions. The important application of some of the research on personality factors in composition is that it may provide some guidelines beyond the hit-and-miss collections of group members, if the organizer has a choice. Another useful derivative from this research may be help in understanding composition factors which may be functioning to cause some groups to be harmonious and productive while others are not, in situations where the worker has had no hand in composition. For instance, some autonomous groups may have formed themselves and become riddled with conflict, dissention, and incapable of working together. A worker who intervenes with such a group might explore the composition along with other factors which might cause conflict. A task group composed by gathering together people who have a particular interest in common or who represent separate segments of a larger organization might not necessarily be able to function. The worker responsible might look at the personality factors and compatibility of members. It might become apparent that any work that gets done by this group would have to be carried on in small subgroups of compatible dyads or triads, or individual work that is finally pooled. But understanding some of the findings of research on composition should give clues to facilitating group functioning.

Problem Orientation

Earlier we noted that there seems to be little research on group composition based on problems of members or common concerns about problems within the social sciences. Since grouping in some of social work practice tends to be by classification of problem, we searched the literature to determine those criteria for group composition which have been used in social work. While classification by types of problem, such as delinquency or mental illness, appeared in social work literature, other factors appeared in a few articles. These are noted here.

In the literature on social work and group psychotherapy, many schemes of grouping or group composition are in use, though none is definitive and most are based on problem classification. Maloney and Mudgett [73] speaking of the formation of groups of delinquent children and adolescents referred by school, police, or court set the following criteria for grouping: "problem homogeneity, degree of internal controls, amenability to external controls, social age, school grade, and socioeconomic backgrounds." Sloan,[74] in composing treatment groups of former psychiatric patients, considered the following criteria: "the individual's ways of reacting to the present situation, potential strength in interpersonal relations, factors of similarity or difference that would affect his capacity to relate to others and they to him." What Sloan does not develop is what she means by "way of reacting to present situation." No doubt she has some scheme for classifying the behaviors in the present situation in order to determine which fit together and which do not. Neither does she state how to assess the potential strength in interpersonal relations. These generalized classifications could be developed in more detail.

Redl [75] suggests for grouping of children who reside in an institution for emotionally disturbed a scheme, somewhat more refined, of "toughness, shyness, developmental phase, tastes, use of adult relationships, sex, language sophistication and need for security." His criteria seem to require some assessment of personality or behavior.

A general scheme for grouping is suggested by Vinter,[76] "similarity in interests, potential for attraction, adequacy to participate in activity and structure and capacity to form relationships."

---

[73] Sara Maloney, and Margaret Mudgett, "Group Work and Casework: Their Similarities and Differences," *Social Work*, IV (1959), 31.

[74] Marion Sloan, "Factors in Forming Treatment Groups," in *Use of Groups in Psychiatric Settings* (New York, National Association of Social Workers, 1960).

[75] Fritz Redl, "The Art of Group Composition," in Suzanne Schulze, ed., *Creative Group Living in a Children's Institution* (New York, Association Press, 1953).

[76] Robert Vinter, "Components of Social Group Work Practice," in *Readings in Group Work-Practice* (Ann Arbor, Campus Publishers, 1967).

Taking a somewhat different tack, Louise Shoemaker [77] in speaking of groups of welfare recipients lists type of clients who cannot use groups. She includes the person who is so upset that he is heading for a breakdown, could not tolerate a group, and might even damage the group because his behavior would be so threatening; the client who is so overwhelmed by his own problems that he projects everything on the agency, refuses to see his own responsibility and tends to withdraw from the group; the person whose problems are so overwhelming that he cannot talk about them in a group or in the presence of others; the person whose close proximity to his neighbors may make sharing of intimate problems difficult or impossible because he does not want his neighbor to know his troubles.

The literature of group psychotherapy contains many equally developed but not very definitive statements regarding the composition of groups coming out of practice experience. Typical of the reporting is a statement by Kirzenbaum, Panzer, and Gordon [78] for a mental health center where most patients are served in groups. These staff compose groups of children, adolescents, and adults on the basis of similar age, same sex, without consideration of diagnostic categories except for the following. Regressed schizophrenics and mentally retarded are not served, nor are children whose primary symptoms were sexual acting out, homosexuality or promiscuity (they were put into individual treatment), and school phobic children (who were seen individually on an emergency basis).

Speaking of ways to establish methods of selection for therapy groups, Luchins [79] lists the following criteria: "diagnosis, symptoms, ego defenses, nature of problems, age, sex, socioeconomic background, education, and interests." He adds the following comments, "a psychopath will stir up a group, a depressed patient will

[77] Louise Shoemaker, "Uses of Groups in A.D.C.," in M. Montelius, ed., *Helping People in Groups* (Washington, D.C., U. S. Department of Health, Education, and Welfare, 1964), pp. 17 ff.

[78] Minna Kirzenbaum, Edward Panzer, and Sol Gordon, "Group Psychotherapy as the Treatment of Choice for the Majority of Patients in a Community Mental Health Clinic." Mimeographed. Orthopsychiatric Conference, 1963.

[79] Abraham Luchins, *Group Therapy: A Guide* (New York, Random House, Inc., 1967).

quiet it down." He suggests that in composing groups certain other qualities might be sought, such as "an individual to lend intellectual spark to the discussion, individuals to furnish certain experiences or problems or personality patterns for the group or to create certain relationships."

From experience in a general out-patient mental hygiene clinic, one staff of therapists worked out an elaborate scheme for selecting patients for group psychotherapy and for grouping them. The groups were established as the helping instrument. The therapist limits his interventions to clarifying and interpreting material, rarely educating or reassuring, but instead remaining relatively silent and permitting the group to move in its choice of topics while the members are encouraged in relationships with each other and to deal with their interpersonal and personal emotional problems. For these types of groups, therefore, the staff has developed the following categories of patients who respond to groups: [80] persons who gain from permissive atmosphere, who cannot use individual therapy because they are inarticulate and lack social aptitudes, but who can participate nonverbally in the group; others who are fearful of intimate relationships but can have satisfactions and rewards from social and emotional interchanges in the group; patients whose transference involvements with the therapist become unmanageable in individual treatment but whose relations are diffused in a group; exceptionally dependent types who were severely deprived in childhood and who may not regress to such helplessness in a group; persons who feel guilty when they receive individual help are relieved of this pressure in the group; the person who cannot express hostility against authority but receives support to do so in the group. Other types of people whom these authors think can use groups are those who tend to defend away their symptoms but can become aware of their problems through group members' reaction to them; and, patients who have difficulty in facing reality of the results of their behavior until challenged by

[80] J. E. Neighbor, Margaret Beach, Donald Brown, David Kevin, and John Visher, "An Approach to the Selection of Patients for Group Psychotherapy," in Max Rosenbaum and M. Berger, eds., *Group Psychotherapy and Group Function* (New York, Basic Books, Inc., 1963), pp. 413–23.

the group. The same staff also established categories of patients who could not use groups, including persons who have such intense social anxiety that they cannot consider participation; patients with imminent or active psychosis; patients whose defenses are so rigid that they are too threatened by mild probing; and persons so deprived that they cannot tolerate sharing a therapist with a group.[81]

This staff suggests the following group composition: "An effective group must include some individuals who have an awareness of their anxiety and an ability to express it through a discussion of conflictual material. There must also be patients with a relatively high degree of perception and of sensitivity to the psychological problems and maneuvers of others. They are able to make interpretations that might be unacceptable if they came from the therapist. There must also exist a variety of social experience, defensive structures and presenting problems (to provide an opportunity for contrast, comparison and self-evaluation)." [82] While this classification of problems and composition comes from the clinic where all potential group members have symptoms or diagnosed illnesses, the principles may be adaptable to various types of grouping. Besides social criteria, personal criteria, or problem orientation, three other factors may determine group composition: availability of potential members who meet the membership criteria; the structural properties of size, time, and location; and, the attractiveness of the group to potential members or their willingness to belong.

Availability of Potential Members

There must be enough people available who meet the criteria set by the organizers to make a viable group or there is no reason to have the criteria. Criteria may have to be modified in order to attract more members. An example was a group planned by a worker who decided he wanted only patients with a given clinical diagno-

[81] *Ibid.*, p. 419.
[82] *Ibid.*, pp. 419–420.

sis, only to discover that there were not enough such patients in the hospital. He therefore had to establish broader criteria. In a youth counseling agency after several staff consultations to set qualification for the boys who would fit together on the basis of age, socioeconomic level, and nature of problems, compromises had to be made on all of these scores in order to find eight boys who could be included in a counseling group and no more than five of these ever attended at one time because of their individual reasons. In an effort to establish an indigenous advisory committee to a youth program in the inner city, it was difficult to find enough residents who had either the social skills or the emotional and physical energy to invest in the committee process. Thus, criteria must be flexible enough and broad enough to provide a reasonable category of potential membership.

Influence of Size, Time, and Location

There may be a relationship between size, the purpose of the group, and the nature of possible participants. Sometimes more people are qualified than can be absorbed in a single group so that it may be necessary to create more than one group. The composition of each group will be determined in part by the limitation of size. The various studies of the effect of group size on group functioning will be considered later, but for instance, if the purpose of the group is to provide for close and intimate face-to-face contact, the group must be small enough for all people to interact with each other.

When and where the group is convened may also affect who will be available to belong or who will be willing to attend. Conditions of travel, of socially and psychologically desirable or undesirable locations may also influence who participates. Size of available space may also be a factor. Hours of the day or night, duration and frequency of sessions may also affect composition. These factors will be discussed more fully later.

Attractiveness of Group
for Potential Members

There are usually personal reasons why individuals may seek out, desire, and agree to participate in a group. People will be motivated to belong to a particular group, according to Cartwright and Zander,[83] because (1) they like the other members; (2) they are interested in the activity; (3) they are attracted to or identified with the purpose; (4) they see the group as a means of reaching some goal which may be external to the group; or (5) they may feel that the group offers some means of protection from a threatening environment. We would add one additional motive, and that is, that people may see in the group the possibility of personal gratification or help for themselves in some discomfort or problem. Group composition will ultimately be determined by those who choose to participate, from those who have the opportunity to belong.

Styles of Group Composition
in Social Work

In social work practice, groups are composed by at least four styles or combinations of these. They include: (1) membership by individual choice and self-selection by the individuals who join the group by their own initiation of interests; (2) selection of members by the group itself through some system of establishment of criteria, recruitment of members, and agreement on the inclusion and incorporation of these members into the group; (3) grouping on the basis of a specific characteristic, need, or problem of people who happen to be in a given location at a given time; and (4) worker- or agency-determined composition.

Although the individual person practically always may choose whether he will or will not participate in a group, there are groups

[83] Dorwin Cartwright, and Ronald Lippitt, "Group Dynamics and the Individual," in Warren G. Bennis, Kenneth D. Benne, and Robert Chin, eds., *The Planning of Change* (New York, Holt, Rinehart & Winston, 1961), p. 264.

composed entirely of persons who have chosen to belong, attracted by the purpose or the task of the group or by the other people in the group. For instance, some groups consist of any people within a given area who choose to arrive at an announced time and place to concern themselves with a given subject and thereafter form themselves into a group. Examples of this type of group are the typical children and youth groups and some groups of older adults found in group services settings of Y's, scouts, community centers and settlement houses, parent-education groups, and informal education clubs and classes, or the people who happen to register for a particular session of camp. Many young adult singleton social clubs are composed of individual members who choose to join an already established group. People who volunteer to serve on a committee to work on a specific community or social problem may also form a self-selected group. In all of these instances the general purpose for which the group is established by someone, and a time and place are set, but the specific composition of the group depends on who arrives and avows interest in belonging. Perhaps the composition ultimately is the result of who returns the second time and the third. Where open-ended groups exist in a particular setting, a person may have the chance to visit existing groups to determine which he would like to join. This method of individual selection is used in some psychotherapy groups, as well as youth and adult group services.

The second style of membership determination is where members select each other and decide on their own composition—street gangs, street corner clubs, neighborhood family clubs, friends' discussion and social groups wherein members must be invited by those who form or those who belong. Studies have indicated that most societies are organized into networks of autonomous groups of this type that form within neighborhood living areas or around vocational interests, family background, age, sex, taste, religious or philosophical beliefs, or interpersonal attraction. Some of these groups are loose aggregates, but others are highly organized systems. Periodically, such groups arrive at social work agencies, requesting facilities, equipment, and staff service. These groups have determined their own membership and intend to continue to do so, though they may permit a worker to become a part of their group as a needed resource.

In a number of settings, social workers have attached themselves to autonomous groups as a means of providing service. One such type of group is the street corner or teenage gang of socially acting-out or delinquent youth. Composition is totally self-determined and continues to be, and the social worker works with the group as it is even when the composition seems to be detrimental for all of the parties concerned. As the members of the group with the worker begin to work on their problems, they may at some time confront the nature of the composition, if the group is too large, or if the composition is not conducive to healthy development for all participants.[84]

When social workers have worked with total families, either nuclear (the parents and the children) or the extended three- or four-generation family, they relate to an autonomous group composition. The family composition depends upon additions by marriage, birth, or adoption which are to some extent based on individual member's choices. Family composition frequently reflects group pressures, especially from parents and siblings on those choosing marital partners, in inclusion or exclusion. Additions also depend upn the chance of birth. The social worker who works with the family as a whole enters an autonomous group where he usually has little role in the composition, initially. He may, of course, affect composition if he encourages separation or dissolution of a marriage, placement of children or older parents, or if he encourages certain additions. Adoption workers have more influence on composition.

In some instances, particularly in group service settings, social workers may suggest to persons who wish to belong to groups that they should recruit additional members; in other words, that they form groups autonomously. This may be particularly true when the social worker knows that the group members have better contact with others like themselves and know who would be acceptable group members. Block clubs, parent-education discussion groups,

[84] Irving Spergel, *Street Gang Work* (Reading, Mass., Addison-Wesley Publishing Co., Inc., 1966).

tenant councils, teenage social clubs, and children's groups may be composed this way with fairly good success.

In an early period of the development of social group work, emphasis was placed on encouraging people to form their own groups which would then use agency facilities and use staff service of social workers.[85] This principle of formation was supported by the notion that people worked better in groups of their own choosing. Findings from studies by Newstetter,[86] Jennings,[87] and Moreno [88] supported the action.

In some group psychotherapy situations, particularly hospitals and clinics, groups have been permitted to establish themselves and choose their members and vote in new members. One therapist describing such a procedure suggests that it has the advantage of reducing resentment toward newcomers, since group members made the decision to include them and it gives the group the power to control its membership, but may also lead not to democracy but to oligarchy, that is, to promoting exclusive and prejudicial attitudes of discrimination toward others who are different and are therefore excluded. This may not be a helpful procedure and may not be therapeutically helpful to the group member in finding his place in a mobile society.

Situationally Determined Groups

The type of composition by the situation most frequently occurs in the institution but may also occur in the community when people who have a particular problem are associated with others like themselves. For instance, all of the children on a pediatrics ward,

[85] Grace L. Coyle, *Group Work with American Youth* (New York, Harper & Row, 1948).

[86] Wilbur I. Newstetter, Marc C. Feldstein, and Theodore Newcomb, *Group Adjustment* (Cleveland, School of Applied Social Sciences, Western Reserve University, 1938).

[87] Helen Hall Jennings, *Leadership and Isolation* (New York, Longmans Green, 1950).

[88] Jacob L. Moreno, *Who Shall Survive?* (rev. ed., Beacon, N.Y., Beacon House, 1953).

all of the patients facing discharge from a mental hospital, parents of children in treatment for hearing problems, wives of alcoholics, the girls who arrive in one month at the home for unwed mothers, the members of the caseload of a particular probation officer, all of the residents of an apartment building or block of the ghetto, are examples in which the composition is generally determined by the situation. In some counseling and adoption services, groups are composed by the ten or twelve persons who appear in intake during a given period of time. Thus, the composition is random but based on the arrival of people requesting service at a given time. Such composition is based not on personal or social characteristics, but on problem or need characteristics by virtue of the chance that the particular people with the problem are in the same place at the same time. Even in such "captive" situations, however, the individual usually has some choice to attend or not attend the group session, and as the aggregate becomes a group, the group itself may through subtle or not so subtle ways determine who attends or skips the group.

Agency or Worker Determined Groups

The fourth method of composition by agency or worker is a result of some calculated plan for membership. Selective intake and group placement on the basis of specific social, personal, or problem criteria is done by a single worker or by staff deliberation and decision making in case conference or by some referring agent who suggests people for the group. This process produces what has been called agency-formed or agency-initiated groups. Actually, the term is more accurately "agency-convened" groups, since the worker may bring people together, but only the members can form themselves into a group.

The relative merits or uses of different methods of composing groups for social work practice have not been definitively determined and in some instances, there may be little alternative. The early writings on social group work practice emphasize the use of member-formed or autonomous groups. This emphasis was based on the belief that people function better in groups of their own choosing and that such groups were more democratic. Actually, of course, the question arises "better for what" depending on the purpose of the group. People who strongly attract each other and who already know each other may have worked through the activities related to getting acquainted and be able to get to the achievement of the group task if the task is related to something external to the group or away from an intimate view of themselves. Group maintenance tasks in this instance may be at a minimum because the interpersonal ties are already established. Perhaps the main interpersonal tension is the admission of the worker to the already formed group. If the worker is to have an important role in an already composed group, he will of necessity be offering opportunities for change both in structure and in direction. Otherwise, there is no reason for his entrance into the group. These offerings may be resisted by the group which established itself without him originally.

Some scientific data is available on the intervention in autonomous groups by professional workers as the instrument of service. Moreno [89] has said that the "psychological re-equilibrium is better achieved when members are allowed to group themselves in accordance with spontaneous choices." This apparently refers to the use of autonomous groups for therapy. Here the objective is personal and behavioral change and the members assume roles in changing each other as well as themselves. Their knowledge of each other comes from association in the therapeutic or educational situation.

On the other hand, in some instances, individuals who sought out counseling service from a social agency and were placed in groups with people whom they knew previously indicated that they could not talk freely about their problems with their friends and neighbors present. Shoemaker [90] cites an example of welfare recipients who did not wish to be identified as such and did not wish to join with others whom they knew to be "labeled."

---

[89] Moreno quoted in Edward Shils in Daniel Lerner and Harold Lasswell, *The Policy Sciences* (Stanford, Calif., Stanford University Press, 1951).

[90] Louise Shoemaker, "Uses of Groups in A.D.C.," in Montelius, ed., *Helping People in Groups.*

Hare [91] cites several studies of groups of friends with reference
to composition and the results in group life. He says "since friendship is based upon common social characteristics, values, and personality, persons who choose each other for friends may well be
the same age, sex, social class and ethnic group. In general, friends
tend to be more homogeneous in their behavior patterns. They
communicate to each other more and are more productive unless
they spend too much time in socioemotional activity or conspire to
slow down the job. They conform more to self-originated norms
and show more resistance to change from outside." Hare [92] states
further, "friendship, whatever its basis produces marked differences
in interaction; groups of friends usually have higher morale, exert
more influence on each other and are more productive." If the
objective of the group is to change behaviors or values, then on the
one hand friends in an autonomous group may have more influence
over each other, but they may be more resistant to changes suggested from the outside. Therefore, the interest and motivation to
change values would need to come from the group itself and not
outside influences of worker or agency. Furthermore, if one of the
objectives is exposure to differences and some conflict resulting
from polar views or personal differences, these probably would not
occur in an autonomous self-formed group unless it was a deliberate group target established by the members themselves in recruitment and in defining their goals. If on the other hand, the purpose
of the group is achievement of some task, people who know each
other may be able to work together more rapidly. The content and
level of interaction may determine whether or not an autonomous
or self-formed group is indicated.

Sometimes, also, when members are encouraged to recruit their
own groups they do not actually know enough people who would
be compatible members of the group in social terms.

If people do not know enough people well enough to invite them
to a group, they therefore latch onto anyone who will come and
the result is not necessarily a group of friends, but networks of ac-
quaintances and others who are tolerated because the group needs

[91] Hare, *Handbook*, p. 218.
[92] *Ibid.*, p. 220.

them to satisfy some number requirement. An example of this type of procedure was the instance of a pair of latency-aged friends who had a close and unhealthy sadistic-masochistic relationship. The agency offered to help them to form a group which they said they wanted. The worker met with them, not recognizing that their interpersonal involvement was in part related to personality problems which rendered them incapable of relating to their peers. He suggested that they recruit the additional club members, on the theory that normal boys this age should relate to peers and that self-recruited groups were more democratic. The boys recruited the brother of one, the only peer with whom they had contact, and he recruited his friends. Soon there was a well-functioning group, but the two original members were missing; they had disappeared again into their two-person world. For these two, the group, if it could work at all, would need to be carefully composed by a worker who could attract group members on the basis of interest and activity and who might be able to facilitate attachment of these two to new connections if their problems were being worked on simultaneously.

In another agency with an established policy that all groups must be self-recruited, a worker told a small nucleus of a group of Negro boys who had just moved into the area, a racially changing neighborhood, that if they wished to have a club in the agency it must include some white boys. Since the Negro boys were new to the area and considered invaders by the older residents, they were not successful in their invitations to any white boys whom they met at school to join the group. Since they were unable to meet the agency requirements that they recruit and maintain an interracial group, they left the agency, found an adviser, and formed a fraternity in the neighborhood. In this case, if the agency believed it was beneficial for groups to be racially integrated, the staff were in a higher status position to help compose such a group than the newcomers to the community. Autonomously formed groups in this instance tend not to be democratic in composition.

Autonomous, spontaneously member-formed groups tend not to be racially mixed even in communities where housing is racially mixed, in public schools which are racially integrated, or in occupational settings where people of different races work together in the same units. School clubs and cliques, self-formed club groups in national agencies tend to be racially separate. Neighborhood cliques, adults as well as children, tend to be racially separate and while people may work side by side, they tend to take their lunch breaks separately and associate separately outside of work. Generally, recreation groups which they form within the work situation are also racially segregated. Margaret Berry,[93] in discussing racially integrated groups within the social settlement, worked out a detailed plan for agency-composed integrated groups. The stimulus for her plan was the fact that in a mixed neighborhood where the settlement was a high status agency, groups were not racially mixed. The agency found it necessary to work out careful plans, policies, and procedures to have either task groups or social groups with any mixed racial composition, because the mixed groups did not occur.

Thus, one can see advantages and disadvantages of member- or group-composed groups, assuming that self-formed groups will tend toward homogeneity. Style of composition will, therefore, need to be weighed in light of group goals and objectives or the purposes for which the group is offered in social work services.

There are, however, circumstances and types of groups where it is more practical and feasible and appropriate for an agency or worker to form the group; and it is for these types of groups that consideration must be given to the criteria for composition or grouping.

Open and Closed Groups

Whether a group should be opened or closed is a decision that frequently confronts agency staff in the pregroup decisions about offering service. Assuming that an adequate number of people can be located to form a congenial group, is it more effective from the

---

[93] Margaret Berry, "Grouping Devices for Interpersonal Goals in Agency Initiated Groups," in *Social Work in the Current Scene*. Selected papers from the National Conference of Social Work. (New York, Columbia University Press, 1950).

standpoint of continuity, group development, and task achievement to have a constant group of members, or to have the additional inputs from turnover and new membership? The question is equally relevant to treatment groups and community action or social change groups. Ziller [94] in attempting to formulate "a theory of opened and closed groups" offers several ideas that may well be considered by social workers in the decision about open and closed groups. He discusses four dimensions for consideration: (1) time perspective; (2) the achievement and maintenance of equilibrium; (3) the expanded frame of reference; and (4) the changing membership. On the time dimension the members of a closed group are closely related for a given period of time while the "members of open groups are aware of the transitory nature of the relationships, the future dominates." For instance, if the "present membership is to benefit from a particular action, the action must be taken immediately." Obviously there is not time to delay or think through or plan over time. In the open group, members may also attach themselves more to the group than to each other. Instability is the basic shortcoming of the open group resulting from loss of leadership, turnover in personnel, exodus of members, loss of group identity. These may be minimized by an adequate size so that the group is not threatened by member loss. The possibility of increasing compatibility, by the possibility of matching of members, may result from increase in size in the open-ended group.

If turnover is rapid or in large blocks, it may deplete the group, or may disrupt the flow of work if a large new contingent enters. However, gradual turnover may be handled by the group depending on its task. On the other hand, lack of change in a group in time could deplete its strength because of the lack of new ideas. The advantage of open groups is the influx of new ideas, beliefs, or values. In fact, several studies are cited to demonstrate that open groups are more creative than closed groups. Another feature of the open group is that change in composition erases group history. A low-group image or morale may be obliterated by the arrival of new members who have not experienced the poor past. On the

[94] Robert Ziller, "Toward a Theory of Open and Closed Groups," *Psychological Bulletin*, LXIII (1965).

other hand, a successful group may want to hold onto its members and may feel threatened by loss of members.

The arrival of newcomers will threaten existing structure of subgroups and alliances and may set up competition among members. The newcomer in the open group is not subject to the same controls as the other members since he has not yet learned the rules and procedures. He may, therefore, have more power to do and say what he pleases, and have more control over others. This factor rearranges the power structures among those who remain in the group. In reverse, the person who is known to be leaving may lose power and influence because he is thought to be separating. The group may have less influence over him also.

Summary

Group composition, styles of grouping, open or closed membership, attraction of individuals to particular groups, criteria for selection, inclusion or exclusion of members are all important aspects of developing groups as instruments of service in social work practice. A review of the literature of the social sciences, social work practice, and group psychotherapy equips one to say that while there are no definitive conclusions about the basis on which membership may be selected to produce a viable group for particular purposes, there are some strands of knowledge which provide the practitioners with alternatives to consider in planning for particular types of group offerings.

The manner by which members are recruited and included in groups may rest with the voluntary choice of the group by the individual, may rest with the group decision and group activity on recruitment, and inclusion may depend almost entirely on the situation and the people who happen to be around with a particular condition in common, or groups may be composed by some procedure of intake, diagnostic assessment, testing, or deliberation on the part of the worker, a staff, case conference, or referring agent, or the administration comprising committee, or task groups. Criteria for matching people in groups may be based on sociocultural factors, as for example, age and stages of social development, sex role expectations, socioeconomic level, and ethnicity. Criteria for membership may also be related to some prediction of potential group functioning and interpersonal compatibility based on any of several measures of personality traits. Other possible criteria include classification by problem, similar or common problem, diagnosis, symptoms or circumstances, interests and motivations. Whatever the criteria used and whether by worker, staff, or group itself, the important point to see in consideration of group composition is that some scheme for determining composition may lead to more predictable outcomes in the uses of groups for specified goals.

GROUP GOALS

All groups have some reason for being, whether vague and unspecified or clearly stated and specific. The organizer has in mind and usually expresses his reasons and hopes for the group; and everyone who participates arrives with some expectations. But group goals are more than a composite of individual expectations for the group. They are the emergent product of the interaction of all of the participants together, the organizer and the members, as they express their ideas and feelings about the reasons for the existence of the group and its anticipated outcomes. Group goals include, therefore, rationale, expectations, and objectives toward which the group puts its collective efforts. Goals may be single or compound, simple or complex, one or many. They provide the incentive and direction for group activity.

In social work groups, distinction must be made among "service goals," "worker's goals," "individual goals," and "group goals" in developing a definition of group goals. Service goals actually are set at least tentatively by the agent offering the group service. That agent may be agency, staff, or individual worker. Usually the service goal for any group is expressed only generally, for example, education of foster parents, retraining of delinquents, organization of neighborhood residents for community improvement, preparation of patients for a specialized treatment, provision of socializing experiences for ten-year olds, or coordination and planning of services for the elderly. These purposes are set within the institutions in the pregroup private and preliminary stage by the administration or a staff member who may or may not be related to the specific group. The development of group goals remains for the members once they are convened and begin to develop their own new entity as a group. Once the social worker begins to be related to potential group members, he will develop more specific goals for the group. His goals will reflect the service goals which the agency has set for the group, plus his assessment of needs, capacities, and interests of the individual participants and the level of group development. The worker will also have the objective to facilitate the establishment of a group viable enough to achieve the desired ends, whether these be some effect upon the members, some task to be accomplished, or some action about the social situation. The worker's goals for the group, then, are multiple and are expressed through his relationship with the members and his participation in the group.

Individual's goals, on the other hand, are the hopes, expectations, and objectives of each member as he enters the group. These member's goals may be overt and openly expressed and usually consistent with the service goals as suggested by the organizer. While these expectations may be avowed, conscious, and stated, individual members sometimes have unavowed goals for the group experience of which they are fully aware, but which they may not express within the group or to others. They act upon these goals and may deliberately attempt to direct the group to the fulfillment of these objectives. Unavowed goals might include gaining prestige by being associated with the group while being unwilling to assume responsibility for the work, or belonging in order to be with one's friends or with the worker rather than being invested in the problem on which the group is working.

Individuals may have also unconscious and unavowed goals for the group, ones of which they are not even aware. Yet, an individual member's unconscious goals may motivate him to participate in such a way as to affect the group development. His unavowed and unconscious expectations for the group may include such things as seeking personal gratifications not satisfied elsewhere in life, fulfillment of unresolved family relations, seeking affection, gaining power by having a following in the group, being controlled externally when the ego is not strong enough for self-control, or being dependent on someone more powerful. These needs so affect his behavior in the group that he unknowingly attempts to manipulate the group for his own satisfaction, or his own goal achievement.

Golembiewski [1] has referred to these individual unavowed goals as "direct expression of impulse unmediated by conscious goal seeking." Regardless of the type of group, an agency staff, a committee, a social club or interest group, or a therapeutic group, any individual may bring to the group one or all three of these types of goals, avowed, unavowed, or unconscious, and behave accordingly.

Group goals come into being as the group convenes, and the members begin to think together about why the group exists, what they want it to accomplish, and how the objectives can be reached. Cartwright and Zander [2] show that "the formation of group goals requires that the various goals for the group held by the different members be somehow converted into a single goal capable of steering group activities."

Generally group goals are established during the organizing period of the group, but they may later be re-examined or assessed. They may be modified as the group changes focus, or as the group changes composition if it is an open-ended group. Although total group goals are generally avowed, expressed, and understood by all members, the "secret" expectations, held by individual members, organizers, or subgroups, may influence the direction of

[1] Robert Golembiewski, *The Small Group* (Chicago, University of Chicago Press, 1962), p. 187.

[2] Dorwin Cartwright, and Alvin Zander, *Group Dynamics* (3d ed., New York, Harper & Row, 1968), p. 406.

group goals. These have been labeled "hidden agenda" by some writers. A "hidden agenda" [3] may distort or redirect the planning or action of the group. Golembiewski [4] has emphasized that group goals may not always be consciously perceived by all group members and that the hidden agenda for the group held by the organizer or by some of the members may change the focus of the activities. "The hidden agendas are not necessarily malicious, or even conscious attempts to disrupt the group process," according to Gerald Phillips.[5] He says further that most of the time members are not even aware that they are acting on a hidden agenda. For instance, members may feel some physical discomfort and thus try to get the group to come to a quicker conclusion, or they may have conflicting loyalties with the work of other groups and may wish to divert the present group from its direction.

Mills [6] warns that group goals "are not the sum of personal goals of individual members, nor can they be directly inferred from them." He affirms that the group goals refer to a desirable state for the group and reside in the minds of the members, probably shared by most or all of the members and help to define the group as a unit. Goals can become a group product only as they are discussed, considered, and made fairly explicit by the group members together through some deliberative process. In the vernacular of some, this deliberative and decision-making process by which the group comes to some conclusion about the nature of its business and direction is referred to as "setting a contract." In social work groups where the worker engages with the members in the deliberative process in establishing group goals, he will interpret the service goal or reason for offering the service as part of his contribu-

---

[3] The idea of the "hidden agenda" was apparently first expressed by Leland Bradford in an article in *Adult Leadership* (September, 1952); however, the concept has been well recognized and come into common usage in small group literature in recent years.

[4] Golembiewski, *The Small Group*, p. 187.

[5] Gerald M. Phillips, *Communication and the Small Group* (Indianapolis, The Bobbs-Merrill Co., Inc., 1966), pp. 115–116.

[6] Theodore M. Mills, *The Sociology of Small Groups* (Englewood Cliffs, N.J., Prentice-Hall, Inc., 1967), pp. 17–21.

tion to the group. He will also engage with the group on the basis of his own goals for the group which he may be developing and changing as he knows the members better, and observes the group development process. For instance, a group created for marital couples in conflict to discuss their individual problems and to help each other in working on these problems would have the service objective introduced by the worker in notifying the members prior to the beginning of the group and reiterated as the members convene. The members themselves, however, need to state in their own words and with their own feelings in the collective session what they expect to accomplish together in the group. This discussion is the process by which the group goal emerges. From time to time throughout the group sessions, the group goals may be redefined and even modified.

Some social group work practitioners have tended to confuse service goals with worker's goals for the group and its members and with the group goals that emerge from the group interaction and decision-making process. Another error in practice has been a reluctance on the part of some social workers to share with the group the service goals and the worker's goals for individual members and group as a whole. Sometimes service goals for anticipated outcomes in task groups or planning groups for social change have been held by the worker, but not shared with group members. Some workers have behaved as if they had a secret expectation for the group which they assumed would be fulfilled by some subtle interventions which the members might not notice. Some workers have expressed the fear or concern that if the group members really knew why the group was being offered, for instance, "to modify members' attitudes," they would not participate. If the group is to be a viable instrument for the achievement of the agency, worker, and member expectations, the members must be engaged in a process of deliberation that includes formulation of goals and development of plans to achieve these goals. The worker's goals or the agency goals in offering service become part of this process as the members and worker together talk over their hopes and expectations for the group. Out of their work together the contract for the group is established. This procedure is applicable to task groups, coordinating and planning groups, as well as treatment-focused groups.

The engagement of all participants in the group goal setting should be emphasized. Rosenthal and Cofer [7] found that even one person present who displayed lack of interest or distaste for the task at hand undermined the entire group effort and also contributed to low-group productivity. Similarly, Fouriezos, Hatt, and Guetzkow [8] in another study concluded that "the presence of those who are committed to ends other than the group goal tends to undermine the effectiveness of the group as a whole and to impair the group productivity." Recognizing, then, the possibility of "hidden agenda" or unavowed individual goals which cause some group disintegration or redirection, it is well to attempt to have members bring to the surface these personal goals and to have the group consider them.

Members also must become aware that in group goal setting, some individual objectives may not be met. Riecken and Homans [9] observe that "it is plausible to assume that in most real life groups there is both identity and opposition between group goals and individual goals." The important principle for practice is to realize that while this conflict between individual goals and emergent group goals may exist, the opportunity for the members to engage in discussion of their hopes and expectations to make suggestions for direction and to participate in the final decision in setting group goals may provide for wider input toward group goal development and resolution of some of the conflict among individuals. Fouriezos, Hatt, and Guetzkow [10] state further that "members who

[7] D. Rosenthal, and C. N. Cofer, "The Effect on Group Performance of an Indifferent and Neglectful Attitude of One Group Member," *Journal of Experimental Psychology*, XXXVIII (1948), 568–77.

[8] N. T. Fouriezos, M. L. Hatt, and Harold Guetzkow, "Measurement of Self-Oriented Needs in Discussion Groups," *Journal of Abnormal and Social Psychology*, XLV (1950), 682–90.

[9] Henry W. Riecken, and George C. Homans, "Psychological Aspects of the Social Structure," in Gardner Lindzey, ed., *Handbook of Social Psychology*, Vol. II (Reading, Massachusetts, Addison-Wesley Publishing Co., Inc., 1954), p. 809.

[10] Fouriezos, Hatt, and Guetzkow, "Measurement of Self-Oriented Needs," *Journal of Abnormal and Social Psychology*.

agree on the goal for the group become aware that the benefits for all depend upon the efforts of each and the norm to help one another is aroused." Thus as a member feels that his own inputs are being considered by the group in the establishment of the group goal, and as he sees some gratification of his own needs while at the same time becoming motivated toward concern for group outcomes, he may feel more relevant and involved in pursuing the group goals.

Primary and Secondary Goals

Groups have primary and secondary goals.[11] As the abstract goals of the group are operationalized or made more concrete, they may be spelled out into those which are of greatest or of primary importance and those which are of lesser or secondary importance. Any group which exists over a period of time may in fact fulfill its primary goals and then pursue some of its secondary goals. This phenomenon is referred to in the literature as "goal displacement." Berelson and Steiner [12] say that "there is always a tendency for organizations to turn away at least partially from their original goals." They suggest that goal displacement may come from letting the means become the ends, or from getting a number of people into the group who wish to use the group to follow their own ends, or from the fulfillment of original goals and finding new ones in order to keep the group alive. Many task-oriented groups move toward becoming social or affectional groups in time. Committees, staffs, work groups, even therapy groups may move or be moved by some of the members to have social functions. Sometimes the social activities and personal enjoyment of the members may become more important than the task to be done, to the extent that there is no longer time nor interest in the primary objective. Then the group either abandons the primary goal, or shifts the primary

[11] Grace L. Coyle, *Social Process in Organized Groups* (New York, Richard R. Smith, 1930), pp. 36–63.
[12] Bernard Berelson, and Gary A. Steiner, *Human Behavior* (New York, Harcourt Brace Jovanovich, Inc., 1964), pp. 366–67.

to secondary and vice versa, or may in fact go out of existence because of lack of goal achievement. For example, an adult committee formed to study the interracial practices of agencies and to rec-
ommend changes where needed was composed of people of various
racial and nationality backgrounds, and from board, staff, and
participant levels in several agencies; soon after the group was
convened and had begun to make plans for the task, and had set
group goals to accomplish the assigned job, they decided that they
would like to meet over dinner and then do their work. One member offered her home and said she would serve a buffet supper.
Thereafter, the group held all of its meetings in each other's homes
and the suppers became more elaborate, featuring various ethnic
foods. Conversation turned increasingly to the members themselves, and their lack of association prior to the committee with
people of other races or nationality. These discussions became so
interesting and extended that there was little time left to carry out
the original charge to the committee. Confronted with the fact that
the primary goal was to produce a study and to make recommendations for change, and only secondarily were they to work on
their own understanding and relationships as part of the process,
they held a short business meeting. In the meeting they decided
that the study was a technical job and a professional worker
should be hired to carry it out. They constituted themselves as an
advisory group who would be able to help because of their increased understanding through their experiences together. They
then proceeded to have their regular dinner meetings and interpersonal encounters as their primary goal.

A shift in goals may be the result of changing membership in an
open-ended group. New members may join a group because of
their interest in secondary rather than primary goals. If these new
members become a majority, they may make secondary goals primary. As a result, some of the original members may no longer be
satisfied and may drop out. Thus a group of single parents may
join a parents-without-partners group ostensibly to find support in
the problems of parenting without a mate, dealing with their own
loneliness and frustration, and finding others who understand and
are willing to listen to their concerns because they share similar

problems. Individual expectations for the group and group purposes coincide with the service goal. It is scarcely a hidden agenda in such groups that some of the members are secondarily looking for another mate. If more members join the group whose true motivation is to find an acceptable mate, they may push for more social activities to learn to know each other. Party planning and arranging of social events or talking about themselves may become so important that there is not time to work on the parenting problems. Those members who are not primarily interested in another marriage may drop out as the secondary objective becomes primary in the group activities.

Setting Achievable Goals through Group Process

The importance of setting achievable group goals should be emphasized. Thibaut and Kelley, Mills, and Cartwright and Zander all point to the necessity of establishing group goals through a process of group decision making, some degree of consensus, or some level of agreement on the part of all of the members. Then, suggests Mills,[13] "members will be gratified as the group progresses toward its goal—some of the group members will attempt to assure the group's survival so that it may continue to gratify members through the pursuit of the goal; members will assess the effect of event on goal achievement or survival, take action or redirect the process toward the goal and counteract negative effects that might work against the goal."

According to Thibaut and Kelley,[14] "as long as group members are interdependent in attaining their goals there must be wide acceptance of the chosen means as well as the goals themselves. . . . participation in developing planning a means heightens understanding of it and commitment to it. The group problem-solving process may be more economical than one that begins with more

[13] Mills, *Sociology of Small Groups*, p. 18.
[14] John W. Thibaut, and Harold Kelley, *The Social Psychology of Groups* (New York, John Wiley & Sons, Inc., 1961), p. 270.

expert thought and advice because of the group effort toward achievement of the goal."

Cartwright and Zander [15] suggest that groups with no clearly identifiable goal have no criterion to evaluate alternative courses of action and find it difficult to organize a coherent program of activities and therefore lack any sense of satisfaction. A group that has clearly specified goals can plan a course of action and members are motivated to collaborate with each other to facilitate goal attainment. They, therefore, sense satisfaction with attainment and frustration with failure.

In the process of group development, the expression, discussion, and establishment of group goals may be one of the crucial aspects of formation. As initial agreement is reached, members have a direction which is unique for themselves in the particular group. The group takes shape and character around the process of arriving at goals and in formulating activities to achieve these goals. Participation in goal setting may not be of equal degree or strength for all participants however. Since goal setting comes early in the formation phase, some members may be more articulate than others, some more at ease in expressing their opinions, others reticent in expression because of their discomfort in the new group. Cartwright and Zander [16] suggest that individual participation in goal setting may be influenced by "difference in the amount of participation of members and the difference in the amount of influence exerted by certain individuals." Group goals, then, may actually be set by a few of the most assertive members in the early formation period with others merely acquiescing. The worker may, in fact, need to be on the alert to this matter and attempt to facilitate the widest possible participation in goal setting. Those who are not initially articulate may feel dissatisfied with the goals, as established, if they have not been helped to express their opinions in the group development process.

[15] Cartwright and Zander, *Group Dynamics*, p. 401.
[16] *Ibid.*, p. 406.

Common and Similar Individual Goals
for the Group

In some groups members have common goals, that is, they have the same interest, problem, or concern which can be worked on better collectively than individually. For instance, parents of school-aged children may hold in common their concern about the school, the educational program, the facilities, the playground. Although each individually has the concern, it is also a common concern. Coyle [17] defines the common interest where "a number of individuals pursue one single comprehensive concern of all, the attainment of which will bring fulfillment to the individual interests of the members." The patients on a ward in the hospital may have the common concern about the management of the ward or even the quality of medical care. Individually these are problems but collectively they are common and can be worked on together. The tenants of public housing have common concern about the admission policies of the housing authority. The common objectives or goals for a group organization contain a mutuality. The achievement of goals, such as change in the system, accomplishing a task that one cannot do alone, leads to common goals. For instance, playing team sports or a string ensemble, playing card games, engaging in interracial or biracial dialogue requires multiples of persons sharing common purposes. Secondarily, individuals may have other individual goals that they wish to achieve by engaging in these groups, such as to belong, to socialize, to meet others, to change things, but primarily, their investment in group is for the achievement of common goals with other people.

Similar goals are expressed when members have interests, problems, concerns, or objectives for the group that are somewhat alike. Parents of preschool children have similar concerns or needs to learn parenting, different for each family, but with some similari-

[17] Coyle, *Social Process in Organized Groups*, p. 37.

ties. Their hopes for the group experience are that they will learn similar things about being parents. Patients on the ward all share the anxiety of the unknowns of their own medical treatment, or the social isolation from their family and friends during their hospitalization. A group can help them to talk about the feelings which they share alike and relieve some of their anxiety. Group activities for working toward these similar goals may include some parallel activity or mutually shared activity, to talk and to listen, to learn individually by studying together in a collective setting; other individual pursued interests in group situations might include such things as listening to music, watching TV together, or engaging in individual sports, such as swimming and bowling—sports where each person functions individually but in sequence as a member of a team and the group accumulates collective score. These group activities are different from team sports in which there are differentiated and interdependent roles, such as in baseball or basketball. Phillips [18] in drawing a distinction between common and similar objectives in groups compares problem-solving groups where the "individual tends to subordinate his personal goals to the group. The member becomes part of a totality, and temporarily surrenders part of his identity as he interacts with others to achieve a common goal." On the other hand, in some therapy groups where the "objective is to bring about intrapsychic changes in the patient, to revise some attitude or inculcate a behavior change, it is difficult . . . for the patient to give up his identity to the group . . . therefore there may be no common goal in the therapy group." Obviously, the members of the latter type of group hold in common the objective of creating a group atmosphere that is helpful and supportive but they are seeking similar goals rather than common goals through the group.

In achieving both common and like interest goals there is a sharing but in the achievement of common goals, demands for higher interaction and interdependency are required while individuals may achieve similar goals in the group by loss of interdependency although there is interaction and support.

[18] Phillips, *Communication and the Small Group*, p. 57.

The establishment of goals, then, gives the framework for the development and assessment of group activity that becomes the means for goal achievement. Goals do not establish means but they provide the desirable or ideal ends toward which the means can be directed, assessed, and reassessed as the group progresses through a single session or from session to session.

Frequently in group sessions when the discussion or the action may become diffuse or go astray, members may question: "What are we here for?" "What are we supposed to be doing?" "Where are we getting with this discussion?" "Why aren't we doing anything?" These are questions that signify a need for reorientation and clarification of direction. Members are clearly seeking to establish, reestablish, or assess direction in relation to goals, or desiring to renegotiate the contract. At this point in group development, goals may be discarded and new ones established.

Goals and Composition

The anticipated goals of a group influence composition. For instance, the service goals, as established by the agency or worker in offering the possibility of the group, will affect who will be recruited, interested, eligible, or asked to attend. Once the members are organized and establish their own goals, these group goals will condition whether or not the group may appropriately be closed or open to additional membership. Some people who were attracted to the service goal of the group when it was announced may not go along with group goals once they are developed and may leave thereafter. An open membership group will be conditioned in the goals it sets by who will be eligible, interested, qualified, willing to participate in the group. People will probably not choose to join a group or stay with it if the goals are not compatible with their interests.

Nature of Group and Personal Investment

A group whose primary purpose is a task to be achieved at a cognitive or action level may ask less investment of the person than a group where the purpose is effect on the members. Although there may be commitment of the person to the goal as translated in the task, there may be less investment by the person of himself and his emotions and personality. In a committee, for instance, or an action group, the attachment is to the task but the person's self may remain somewhat anonymous so long as he performs his function. In therapy groups, however, where the participant's behaviors, feelings, actions, and reactions become the content of the group, his personality is more exposed. A great deal of the person may be invested, since the goal of both the service and the group is to effect the individual members.

Jennings [19] has labeled these two types of groups "psyche" and "socio" groups. Psyche groups are those in which the members are seeking personal gratification and satisfaction, maintain intimate relationships, and invest themselves in each other in the activity of the group. These are exemplified in friendship or social clubs or therapy groups. The members' individual goals and group goals are consistently to gratify members. Socio groups are essentially tasks groups. They are formed to achieve some action. Members may invest less of themselves but give of their thought and activity. If socio groups achieve a high level of coalescence and morale, they may take on a psyche group quality and people may attempt to find personal gratification and social experience from a group such as a staff, a committee, or a study group. Such a shift may be appropriate only if the group as a group and not just a few of the members have re-examined their goals and agreed that the shift in focus will fulfill their collective hopes and expectations, and if the work is completed or abandoned.

Effect of Surrounding Environment on Goals

Group goals are frequently influenced by their surrounding culture. The pervasive values and norms of the society, the community or the institutional context within which the group is established will

[19] Helen Hall Jennings, *Leadership and Isolation* (New York, Longmans Green, 1950).

frequently condition the group goals and objectives.[20] For instance, a group such as a gang may establish itself as a protective device against a hostile community.[21] Similarly, an ethnic group may organize as support or protection in a hostile community when values and behaviors may be different or where there is discrimination against the members individually because of their backgrounds, nationality, or races. In social work, protective and supportive groups have been established in a rejecting culture for people with certain types of handicaps, nonconformists, low achievers, et cetera, where the group members in some way deviate from prevailing values and cultures, and where they find support in joining with each other against the external pressures.

According to Thompson and McEwen [22] when a group embarks on goal setting it is in part establishing a desired relationship between the group and its social environment. Cartwright and Zander suggest that "Members may be influenced in selecting group goals at least partially by anticipated reactions from the social environment of the groups." [23]

In carrying out goals that have been established for the group, the members may find themselves trying to convince those outside the group that their goals have merit. For instance, there may be those who believe that a group is too social, or too work-oriented, or too self-oriented. The group may need either the moral, financial, or social support of others. It may need the alliance of other groups or its sponsoring body to support its goals. This is particularly true of social action groups like civil rights promoters or welfare rights groups who need legislators to help in their goal achievement. But it is equally true for groups of offenders, alcoholics, parents of mentally retarded who need understanding, support, and not criticism from their society.

[20] Coyle, *Social Process in Organized Groups.*

[21] George C. Homans, *The Human Group* (New York, Harcourt Brace Jovanovich, Inc., 1950), discusses the external system of the group referring to the reaction of the group in its system of society. He cites the study of *Street Corner Society* by W. F. Whyte as an example.

[22] J. Thompson, and W. J. McEwen, "Organizational Goals and Environment: Goal Setting as an Interaction Process," *American Sociological Review,* XXIII (1958), 23–31.

[23] Cartwright, and Zander, *Group Dynamics,* p. 405.

According to Cartwright and Zander, [24] "It is not uncommon for groups to spend considerable energy and talent in convincing the significant elements of their social environment that their goals should be accepted by society." They also point out that sometimes segments of society may attempt to invent ways to curb or destroy a group whose goals are viewed as threatening. This factor is well to remember in a time when nonconforming groups, or those created for institutional change or social change, are prevalent and are at the same time the brunt of considerable attack from the organized and established society. Even social agencies may resist the goals and objectives of some of the groups developed within their sponsorship. The question to be confronted is how much freedom and autonomy a group can have to establish its own goals and directions within the agency and under the agency purposes, and how much effort, time, and energy must the group spend convincing the board, staff, and other groups that its purposes are worthwhile and consistent with the culture of the agency.

The group that attempts to make its goals, and thereby its composition and program, interracial in an area of high racial prejudice or works for integration of itself where segregation is the prevalent custom may have a job larger than its own goal setting in convincing those outside that the objectives are worthwhile. Those who are opposed may resort to labeling or name-calling in order to avoid facing the demands of the group. Although the example given is a social action one where the issue is striking, this concept of cultural influence and control over autonomous goal setting could well apply to a therapeutic group in a hospital, clinic, or couseling agency, a social or interest group in a community center or neighborhood agency. For example, the socialization group of patients in the nursing home that attempts to suggest that patients who are able to be in wheelchairs or are up and dressed should be served meals in a common dining room in the company of others rather than being fed on trays in their own rooms may find that their objective of system change is not popular. The nursing staff whose routines are interrupted and the maintenance staff who have to clean up may not only be opposed to the suggested

[24] *Ibid.*, p. 406.

change in the system, but may also suggest that the group should not exist because it only makes trouble for the management when you get sick people together. The nursing staff maintains that moving the patients in wheelchairs to a dining room takes them away from patients who need them more. Furthermore, they believe that patients are senile or sick enough that they do not need to eat with others. Group members themselves, regardless of the power of the worker, may not have the strength to counteract such pressure, and furthermore, may feel totally dependent on the nursing staff for other services, such as delivery of medicine, baths, et cetera, so that they do not wish to raise questions. Only staff and patients who are not so dependent may be able to push for system change.

Group Maintenance As A Goal

Obviously, in order to function, a group must form, go through its initial struggles, and then get to work on its defined task. Therefore, regardless of the long-range or short-range goals related to the task which the group intends to perform, there always is some goal of group development and maintenance. Without the creation and functioning of a state of synthesis, no task-related goals can be accomplished. However, sometimes when groups fulfill their tasks and reach their termination point because of time, function, or goal achievement, the members are unwilling to terminate because the group has taken on so much meaning for the members. The maintenance and perpetuation of the group then becomes a goal in itself.

One such group, an interracial dialogue group of an equal number of couples of two races, was created to meet for three sessions in the homes of some members to consider some of the racial problems each encountered in daily life in a segregated society. After they had completed their series and had discussed the subject rather thoroughly they were supposed to terminate. Some of the couples decided that they were enjoying each other so much that they would like to continue as a supper club. With some struggle in readjustment of roles and leadership, such an event was planned and finally carried out. Several of the couples dropped out because they did not have time or interest in such a function. Those who did arrive found themselves uncomfortable and virtually without purpose. There was some struggle for leadership because the dialogue leadership no longer functioned. After one uncomfortable attempt at a social event, the group no longer attempted to reconvene, although many members expressed an interest in coming together again. The original goal having been achieved, the time limitation having been reached, the goal of group maintenance was too difficult and inappropriate for the members so the group dissolved informally as it had dissolved formally at its last official meeting.

The goal of group maintenance [25] may also become a preoccupying force at any point in the course of group functioning if there is some struggle going on for power, direction, interpersonal adjustment, or other conflict. Especially in the aspects of the struggle or crises of the group, the members may want to confront the difficulties they are having in getting their work done. Where there is a social worker he may need to face the group with the struggles the members were having in getting to work on their avowed goals, so that the conflict can be resolved and the group move on about its work.

Application of Concept of Group Goals to Autonomous Groups

Groups which exist prior to their association with agency and worker will have established goals for themselves from their inception. Since goal development is one of the crucial aspects of group formation, it would follow that autonomous groups could not exist without some goals, however nebulous or covert. A worker who approaches an autonomous group with a service objective must also work quickly to assess the nature of already existing goals. Whether the autonomous group is a gang, a friendship club that has requested service, a block club, or a family seeking counseling,

[25] Berelson, and Steiner, *Human Behavior*, p. 367.

the worker will need to observe and listen to the indicators regarding individual and group expectations for themselves. The worker's own goal for the group and even the service goal may be modified as the group and worker establish a working contract. If the group's goals are antisocial, as might be true of a street gang, or harmful to individual members, as might be true in some families, there may eventually be goal modification on the part of the group as well as the worker.

Abstractly, the group goals of families are perpetuation of the family, gratification of the individual needs and drives of the members, provision of emotional, social, economic, and political supports, education and socialization for all members at all ages. Some of these goals reflect the expectations which society has established for families; however, the operationalizing of these goals, the development of ways and means for carrying them out rests within each specific family group. All that has been said about the development of group goals, the participation of all of the family members as they are chronologically able in goal development and re-development, selection of primary and secondary goals, the influence of goals on composition whether addition by birth, adoption, or marriage have pertinence in understanding the family as a group. The surrounding environment also influences family group goal setting, not only by the community and changing social norms about the family in society, but also the influence internally of generational differences, and externally of the extended family, expectations of in-laws, grandparents, and spouses of adult children. Therefore, a social worker concerned with practice with the family as a unit would need to examine the existing group goals and the process by which goals are established within the particular family.

Summary

No group exists then without goals, whether they are avowed or unavowed. Within social work practice there is a service goal or an expectation set by the agency in deciding to offer service through a group, provide a worker and facilities. The agency service goal is usually fairly abstract. The group goals emerge from the interaction of the group members, and the social worker in a prescribed role participates in group deliberation around group goal setting. The worker has his own hopes and expectations for the individuals and the group but these cannot be achieved by the group if they are not expressed and made part of the group content. Individual members bring to the group three types of goal expectations—avowed, unavowed but conscious, and unconscious. All are expressed through behavior of the individuals as they become part of the group. Group goals then emerge from the interaction process in the group, from discussion, planning, and decision making, and this may be called negotiating the contract. They are only truly group goals when all members participate in the decision making. Although the group goals reflect individual goals, they are more than a sum of individual goals. They are the product of the unique condition of each group and the particular combination of individuals.

No group can proceed to work deliberately on its ascribed or prescribed task until its goals have been determined. Group activity is truly the product of the group when the members are conscious of the purposes toward which the activity is aimed. The group goal will reflect to some extent the surrounding milieu in which the group exists and some of the time and energy of the members may need to be spent in convincing those outside of the group that the goals of the group are worth being pursued.

SIZE, SPACE, AND TIME

The structural elements of size, time, and space, while related to each other, also affect and are affected by other elements and processes such as group purpose, composition, deliberation and decision making, interpersonal ties, cohesion, and goal achievement. For instance, the variable of size must be viewed in light of purposes because some research shows that larger groups are more productive for certain problem-solving functions, while smaller groups provide a better individual involvement and satisfaction. Furthermore, the maturity or social skills of members will determine the number of relationships that can be encompassed in certain groups. Other research shows an association between size of group and duration of session in arriving at decisions. However, in spite of the dependency of the variables, let us attempt to look at some of the findings for each of the elements of size, time, and space recognizing that there is an interrelationship among them. We shall begin with size.

Group Size

Simmel, one of the first group theorists to give attention to the effects of group size, wrote in 1902, ". . . a group upon reaching a certain size must develop forms . . . which serve its maintenance and promotion, but which a smaller group does not need. On the other hand . . . smaller groups have qualities, including types of interaction among their members which inevitably disappear when groups grow larger." [1]

Research and theory building have followed Simmel's hypothesis based on experimental and natural-state groups. Observing the natural phenomenon of group size, John James [2] recorded groupings observed of pedestrians, people on a playground, shoppers, and work groups. On the basis of about 9,000 instances, he made the following observations: 71% of all groupings were two people; 21% were three people; 6% were four people; and 2% were groupings of five or more people. He concluded that the size of informal groups tends to be small. One might suggest here that group size might have been affected by the nature of the activity, and that if he had observed college bull sessions, picnics in a park, parties in a home, his averages might have increased. However, there seems to be very little other research on size of cliques.

Thrasher's observations of street gangs showed larger groupings. He noted gangs ranging in size from three to 2,000. However, in a tabulation which he made of 895 gangs, 22.1% consisted of six to ten members, 21.5% consisted of eleven to fifteen members, and 16% consisted of sixteen to twenty members. Most of the groups had memberships under fifty and the median size was close to fifteen. Thrasher notes that the "necessities of maintaining face-to-face relationships set definite limits to the magnitude to which a gang can grow. . . . The size of the group was determined by the

---

[1] George Simmel, "The Significance of Numbers for Social Life," in Hare, Borgatta, and Bales, eds., Small Groups (rev. ed., New York, Alfred A. Knopf, Inc., 1965), pp. 9–10.

[2] John James, "A Preliminary Study of the Size Determinant in Small Group Interaction," American Sociological Review, XVI (1951), 474–77.

number of boys readily able to meet together on the street or within the limited space of their hangout." [3]

Theoretically, Hare [4] suggests "there is no definite limit of a 'small' group. A group is usually defined as small if each member has the opportunity for face-to-face interaction with all others." Homans [5] says a group must be small enough for all members to get around it. Berelson and Steiner [6] also conclude that "it is impossible to specify a strict upper limit . . . except . . . by the requirement that all members be able to engage in direct personal relations at one time—roughly 15 to 20," and the personally most satisfying size seems to be five, because of the ease of movement within.

But Slater [7] found that groups of four to six were most satisfying to members, while groups larger than six were felt to encourage too much aggression, competition, and inconsideration.

Moving to an even smaller size, Shepherd [8] says "groups of two or three persons possess characteristics due to their size which are sharply modified or tend to disappear in groups of four or more." He states further "in a two person group sentiments and feelings tend to be more emphasized than in larger groups, in a three person group coalitions of two against one tend to be so potent that a small group may not be developed." He also concludes that when there are only "two or three people the power of their relationships may become more important than the task."

Golembiewski [9] found that groups of fewer than four exposed

[3] Frederic M. Thrasher, *The Gang* (Chicago, University of Chicago Press, 1927).

[4] A. Paul Hare, *Handbook of Small Group Research* (New York, The Free Press, 1962), p. 21.

[5] George C. Homans, *The Human Group* (New York, Harcourt Brace Jovanovich, Inc., 1950).

[6] Bernard Berelson, and Gary A. Steiner, *Human Behavior* (New York, Harcourt Brace Jovanovich, Inc., 1964).

[7] Philip E. Slater, "Contrasting Correlates by Group Size," *Sociometry,* XXI (June, 1958), 129–39.

[8] Clovis Shepherd, *Small Groups* (San Francisco, Chandler Publishing Co., 1964), pp. 3–4.

[9] Robert Golembiewski, *The Small Group* (Chicago, University of Chicago Press, 1962), p. 146.

their members too much. They felt tense and too constrained to express their attitudes and feelings freely. Thomas and Fink [10] found that "smaller groups inhibit expression of disagreement and dissatisfaction more than larger groups."

Emphasizing the communication factors, Phillips [11] concluded that the group discussion "process becomes unwieldy when members can no longer sit around a table facing each other." As size increases, he observes "voice level must be raised," and it is more "difficult for members to look at each other." Hare [12] adds that as the amount and quality of communication are affected by size, "the character of interpersonal orientations" are also affected.

It could be concluded that if individual participation, satisfaction, and engagement of the group members in a process that will bring about change in themselves is the aim of the group, obviously it must be small enough for each person to be heard and to contribute, and also to feel the impact of the group upon his beliefs and behavior. However, groups should not be so small as to overexpose members or to provide too little stimulation.

Increase in Size

Studies have been made on the effects of interpersonal relationships as groups increase in size. Bossard,[13] using the family as his example, showed that as numbers of members increased, the numbers of relationships multiplied. Thus between two people there is one relationship, among three there are three, among four there are six, among five there are ten, among six there are fifteen, and so on. But Bossard discovered that as soon as a group moves beyond two there exists the potential of a subgroup of two plus one. Therefore, the number of relationships is compounded beyond the relation-

[10] Edwin Thomas, and Clinton Fink, "Effects of Group Size," *Psychological Bulletin*, LX (1963), 371–84.

[11] Gerald M. Phillips, *Communication and the Small Group* (Indianapolis, The Bobbs-Merrill Co., Inc., 1966), p. 42.

[12] Hare, *Handbook*, p. 224.

[13] J. H. Bossard, "Law of Family Interaction," *American Journal of Sociology*, L (1945), 292–94.

ships among individuals to include relationships of individuals to subgroups and subgroups to each other. Kephart,[14] using this formulation noted that when the eldest child of a family of five marries and adds one in-law, or when a grandparent comes to live in a family of five, parents and three children, a total of 211 possible relationships have been added. The same might be concluded for the addition of a social worker to a family of five, if the worker is to relate to each person, each subgroup, and form alliances with individuals in subgroups.

In considering the optimum group size, then, for discussion, social association, support, therapy, problem solving, or coordination, planning, or action, the desired nature and quality of relationships should be taken into account in planning for the group. If the worker intervenes in already formed autonomous groups, he needs to be aware also of the numbers of relationships he is taking on, and how his inclusion by the group will increase the interpersonal relationships.

With increase in group size some changes take place in the group which affect not only the individuals but group processes as well. For instance, as the number of potential relationships increase rapidly, placing greater emotional demand on the member, the need is created for greater coordination of the group. Each member not only has more individuals to respond to, but he also finds himself responding to the dyadic and triadic relationships of others, their coalitions, however fleeting, in any group action or interaction. There is not only an emotional responsive demand but also a cognitive demand to ideas, thoughts, deliberations, and decisions. It may engage him in empathetic, sympathetic giving and receiving demands at a complex level. The increase in size increases these interactions up to a point that the group is large enough to subdivide. Fischer [15] observed that the "frequency, duration and intimacy of contacts among members are found to decrease as the

[14] W. M. Kephart, "A Quantitative Analysis of Intragroup Relationships," *American Journal of Sociology*, LX (1950), 544–49.

[15] Paul H. Fischer, "An Analysis of The Primary Group," *Sociometry*, XVI (August, 1953), 272–76.

size of the group increases." Following this same line, Slater [16] found that as the group size increased and people became better acquainted through the course of meeting together, their inhibitions dropped. They may express more freely some of their notions, without having to support them in detail. He noted that "in larger groups physical freedom is restricted while psychological freedom is increased. The member has less time to talk, more points of view to integrate and adapt to, and a more elaborate structure into which he must fit." He also notes that in a larger group members may withdraw from the discussion without being as conspicuous as in smaller groups. They may also ignore some ideas and be more direct and forceful in expressing their own opinions and feelings since they are diffused by the larger number of people.

Noting the change in group structure, as size increases, Shepherd [17] says that "members establish formal rules and regulations and the group becomes more like a formal organization than a small group." This organization Thomas and Fink [18] found is the direct result of the decrease in cohesion, and the felt need for some division of labor in the group along with the development of cliques and possible factions." In other words, as the group grows, the natural tendency is to feel its diffusion, and to react to this phenomenon by restructuring to a different system of control which is more formal.

Hare [19] also noted that there is a tendency for individuals to specialize in some aspect of the interaction process. Members will assume more specified roles as initiator, mediator, clarifier, pacifier, questioner, or giver of information. Since there is less opportunity to participate at will, members must wait to enter the discussion, and will therefore begin to limit the ways in which they participate.

Golembiewski [20] in reviewing the research on group size postu-

[16] Slater, "Contrasting Correlates by Group Size," *Sociometry,* XXI (June, 1958), 135.
[17] Clovis Shepherd, *Small Groups,* p. 4.
[18] Thomas and Fink, "Effects of Group Size," *Psychological Bulletin,* LX (1963).
[19] Hare, *Handbook.*
[20] Golembiewski, *The Small Group,* p. 146.

lates that if group size is increased, the most active participants become more active, while the least active become less active and may even become silent. Thus one finds a small segment of overactive speakers and listeners and a group of passive or nonparticipant members. This produces, suggests Golembiewski, more restraints and less freedom of group interaction and therefore greater dissatisfactions on the part of some of the members, greater pressures on time limits, and greater breaking down into factions and increased divisiveness.

The logistics of increase in group size require, therefore, that there must be clear structural division to provide for maximum participation on a substructural basis because, as Cartwright and Zander [21] observe, there is a tendency for "a smaller proportion of members to become central to the organization, make decisions for it and communicate to the total membership." In order to ensure full participation of all members of larger groups, their work must be divided into small committees or task forces. Similarly, in discussion group "as there is increase in size, fewer people can have the floor and the chairman must exercise strong control, address the group rather than individuals and more persons become peripheral." The chairman will need to be particularly sensitive to bring in the people who tend to become peripheral.

The role of the social worker or person in leadership position in larger sized groups needs to be understood. Hare [22] concludes that "when there is a desire for intimate and highly developed relationships or a need for fine coordination there will be a tendency toward reduction in size." On the other hand, he notes that it may be possible to retain a larger size by having the leader establish distinguishable relationships with each of the members, helping them to create supportive subgroups within the larger group and by carefully coordinating these relationships and the flow of communication and action. He postulates that leadership may be in part an alternative to actual reduction in size, but the "demands upon the leadership role may be more numerous and exacting, and members'

[21] Dorwin Cartwright, and Alvin Zander, *Group Dynamics* (3d ed., New York, Harper & Row, 1968), p. 499.
[22] Hare, *Handbook*, p. 230.

tolerance for leader-centered direction of group activities become greater." If then a larger size group is necessary, either because it provides greater resources for problem solving, or because as an autonomous group, it arrived large size at the agency, or because a large number of people request the service, the worker will need to recognize that he may need to assume a fairly central and coordinating role, or facilitate indigenous or elected leadership to do so in order to help all of the participants to work together. Furthermore, some system of subdividing the group activity so that the members can contribute and can work more closely with some other members will need to be devised.

While smaller sized groups would seem to be indicated for informal discussions, or groups where the focus is on the individual participant, problem solving task-oriented groups frequently need to be somewhat larger. Regarding size of problem solving or task groups, Thelen [23] developed the principle of "least group size," which refers to the "smallest group in which it is possible to have represented at a functional level all of the social and achievement skills required for the particular activity." He refers particularly to groups where some division of labor may be required, and the resources of several persons' skills may enrich the process. For instance, a committee formed to explore the problem of drug abuse in the suburban community would include not only the experts on drugs but also representatives of those who are closest to the problem; teachers, religious leaders, doctors, social workers, young adults and teenagers, parents, juvenile authorities, law enforcement officials, among others. While there might be a small coordinating committee eventually appointed by the group, at least initially the exploratory committee would of necessity have a large membership.

Enlarging upon functional size, the research of Thomas and Fink [24] using experimental groups found that four-man groups solved more problems than two-man groups, and that the quality

---

[23] Herbert Thelen, *Dynamics of Groups at Work* (Chicago, University of Chicago Press, Phoenix Books, 1954), pp. 187–88.

[24] Thomas and Fink, "Effects of Group Size," *Psychological Bulletin*, LX (1963).

of solutions to complex problems was greater in groups of twelve and thirteen than in groups of six to eight. Hare [25] concluded that "although a larger group has a greater variety of resources for problem solving, the average contribution of each member diminishes and it becomes difficult to reach consensus on a group solution."

Thomas and Fink,[26] on the matter of consensus, found that larger groups took longer to reach consensus and compromise because more discussion was needed to reconcile a wide variety of initial opinions, but in most instances, their performance in problem solving was superior. On the basis of efficiency, smaller groups were better than larger ones because they took less man-hours, since fewer participants were involved, but their solutions were not superior.

Many studies show the positive gains for a group of larger size. Groups may have a greater possibility of accuracy in problem solving because of the greater number of checks and balances. There is the possibility of greater variety of opinion and more ideas if the focus of the group is on some cognitive task.

Writing from experience in therapy groups, Geller [27] offers the following propositions: "Psychoanalytical groups approaching depth, breadth and totality of psychoanalytic therapy may take as few as three or four or as many as six to ten depending on the intensity of the therapy and the need to explore thoroughly the data presented by each patient, the close attention to many aspects of interpersonal relations in the group." He continues, "where the analysis is related to the alleviation of major presenting problems a more general approach is taken and the group may range from eight to fifteen. The difference is quantitative not qualitative." He postulates further that where the group exists to develop mass emotional phenomena to support and strengthen the individual's

---

[25] Hare, *Handbook*, p. 225.
[26] Thomas, and Fink, "Effects of Group Size," *Psychological Bulletin*, LX (1963).
[27] Joseph J. Geller, "Concerning the Size of Therapy Groups," in Max Rosenbaum and Milton Berger, eds., *Group Psychotherapy and Group Function* (New York, Basic Books, Inc., 1963), pp. 411–12.

responsive abilities using repressive inspirational techniques, the group may be thirty to fifty. Finally, he suggests that for orientation and guidance on the theoretical and practical aspects of psychological functioning, fifty or more persons may be helped. Obviously this becomes principally a lecture-teaching session. He adds, however, that the larger the size, the less opportunity for individual discussion of questions raised by the material presented.

Ziller,[28] considering group size from the standpoint of open and closed groups, found that "group size is more critical in open groups than closed groups." In very small groups the loss of one or two members may dissolve the group, therefore, the "members of the small group may over-react to the threat of group disintegration." When they fear others will be leaving, they may leave the group prematurely in order to avoid the confrontation of termination. Also, Ziller notes the probability that a new member in the open-ended group will find at least that one member with whom he is compatible increases with a larger size. He concludes that while closed groups may be very small, open groups, whether for task achievement or therapy, should be of a larger size. He does not indicate specific size.

Considering all of the factors that have been examined pro and con large and small groups, the question still remains regarding optimum size. Studies of two- and three-person alliances or coalitions, following Simmel's original theory development on dyads and triads, shows that each person in a dyad has great power since his leaving can dissolve the group. The three-person group always contains the potential for coalition or ganging up of two against one. However, Thrasher[29] observed many alliances of three boys who cooperated in perfect congeniality. Strodtbeck[30] also observed in three-person families, where there were clearly differentiated roles, there was no evidence of two person coalitions.

Within research on group size, the number five appears fre-

---

[28] Robert C. Ziller, "Toward a Theory of Open and Closed Groups," *Psychological Bulletin*, LXIII (1965), 164–82.

[29] Thrasher, *The Gang.*

[30] F. L. Strodtbeck, "The Family as a Three-Person Group," *American Sociological Review*, XIX (1954), 23–29.

quently as the optimum size. Shepherd [31] notes that sizes four through seven seem to be favored for most types of groups, with sizes five and seven having a slight preference, by virtue of the fact that they cannot reach a stalemate on a yes-no vote, or two subgroups of equal power. In a group of five there should be at least two people with enough in common to have some sort of alliance. Berelson and Steiner [32] note that a group of five is "large enough for stimulation and small enough for participation and personal recognition." Hare [33] notes that several studies showed greater member satisfaction in five-person groups. Below five, members complained that the group was too small, demanding too much participation from each, and over five members complained that the group was too large and their contributions were restricted.

In social work groups, which tend to be voluntary, unless the group is mandatory or compulsory, there is always the possibility for absenteeism. This factor should be considered in planning group size. Two more than minimum may be a good estimate for treatment groups. Thus if a group of five is desirable, there would be seven regular members, not too large for discussion if all are present, nor too small if two are absent.

Planning groups may be considerably larger since they generally are composed on a representative basis, and since their composition frequently depends upon the interests or functions needed for the group as well as the segments of society concerned with the problem. Absenteeism would be less noticeable unless a particular point of view or interest was lacking in the deliberations.

Space

The structural element of space may affect size, composition, location, and the physical arrangement which influence interactions. Coyle,[34] in paraphrasing Simmel's notations on space, states that

[31] Clovis Shepherd, *Small Groups.*

[32] Berleson, and Steiner, *Human Behavior.*

[33] Hare, *Handbook,* pp. 245–46.

[34] Grace L. Coyle, *Social Process in Organized Groups* (New York, Richard R. Smith, Inc., 1930), p. 83.

"space has great significance for group relations. . . . It often provides limitations on membership . . . sometimes serves to focus group relations through giving a specific 'home,' [and] carries also certain psychological connotations attached to spatial forms . . . current in the milieu, which interact within the group."

Space and Size

We have already noted Thrasher's [35] observation that the size of boys' gangs was frequently determined by the room in the hangout or the number who could gather on the street corner. The director of social service in a mental health clinic established a new program of group therapy in which all of the groups had eight members and two therapists. The size was determined by the new "group room" which contained a round table accommodating exactly ten chairs. The room, designed for the program, was based on someone's idea that eight was an appropriate size for a therapy group. But the room size had become the determining factor for group size. In another setting, the staff of a hospital ward always had to meet in two sessions, since the conference room was only large enough to hold half of the staff at once. Available room space, then, can sometimes become the master of size of a group, rather than the size of the group determining where the group will meet.

Location of Members and Purpose

The purpose of the group may also limit the area from which membership is appropriate. For instance, groups organized to bring about influence on political leaders will only be effective if they are located within the political jurisdiction of the politicians. Surburban residents who organize to help elect a city mayor can contribute financially and can campaign for him, but since they are not voters within the city, their influence will be limited on political issues. The social workers' association, attempting to carry weight in influencing a city council's decisions on welfare matters, may find itself ineffectual if 90% of the membership lives and votes in the suburbs and has no direct voting influence on councilmen.

[35] Thrasher, *The Gang.*

Service recipients who reside in the city and who vote for the councilmen may have a stronger case if organized. A citizens' committee to affect public schools will not be given much credence if the members, no matter how high a status or how prestigious, reside out of the school district or send their children to private or parochial schools. A more effective committee would be parents of children in the public school districts and some of the older students themselves. While these examples may seem more like matters of composition related to goal, they are directly affected by the matter of space, in the territorial and ecological sense of location of members, and the "limitations on membership due to space" as suggested by Simmel.

Another aspect of ecological space is how far people will travel to participate in a group. Some studies of the subject have been done by settlements and also for grade school children related to how far they can walk. The studies showed that they would travel about a quarter of a mile. Of course, the bussing system in rural areas and in recent years in cities has made a difference as far as physical distance is concerned. Schools, settlements, and Y's have gone into the bussing service, and many parents have become chauffeurs when the economic level is high enough. Taxi service has been provided for older adults and mothers with small children. Park, Burgess, and McKenzie [36] in their initial studies of the ecological zones of the community originally noted that people who had moved out through the concentric zones of the city had resistances to returning to an area they had left. Lloyd Warner [37] and his associates also noticed the sense of social distance related to geography in the studies of social class in the New England community and the Middle West. Particular areas populated by people of a given social class were thought to be off-bounds for activities of people of other classes. Thus a group established in an area

[36] Robert E. Park, Ernest W. Burgess, and Roderick McKenzie, *The City* (Chicago, University of Chicago Press, 1925).

[37] W. Lloyd Warner, and Paul Lunt, *Social Life of a Modern Community* (New Haven, Yale University Press, 1941), and W. Lloyd Warner, Marchia Meeker, and Kenneth Eells, *Social Class in America* (Chicago, Science Research Associates, Inc., 1949).

thought to be outside of acceptable geographical or social limits may not be acceptable for all of the potential members. An outpatient group at a mental health center of a V.A. hospital, located in an area of lower-class population, is difficult for middle-class veterans and their relatives to get to even though there is direct bus service. On the other hand, an outpatient group at a V.A. hospital located in the middle-class suburbs is more psychologically accessible to these people even though it requires two bus changes and takes twice as much time. Veterans from the area near to the hospital have no difficulty getting to the first group.

An exception may be stated for people of ethnic and nationality backgrounds who will return, at least for a period of years, to the old neighborhood for church- or settlement house-related groups or ethnic events. Studies of mobility show, however, that after a period of separation there is less likelihood of people returning even for special events or groups for which they are highly motivated. They tend to disengage from the old and find new associations and groups in their new community,[38] with the exception of the upper, upper class who sometimes comfortably went to lower-class areas for their recreational activities. Thus, physical distance may also carry the influence of psychological distance, or social barriers which people will not cross no matter how rewarding the group experience might appear to be. Hall [39] has stated that social distance is the "hidden band that contains the group" and makes it psychologically safe to be some places and not others.

Groups located in the central city in many urban areas, at Y's, community centers, at some of the urban universities, or at family and youth counseling central offices, may have difficulty attracting members because of the fear—real or imaginary—about the location. Decentralization of services and shopping centers in most metropolitan communities and smaller cities has created a spatial attitude about how far and to what locations people will travel. While some of this attitude is related to traffic arteries and public

[38] Peter Blau, "Social Mobility and Interpersonal Relations," American Sociological Review, XXI (1956).
[39] Edward T. Hall, The Hidden Dimension (Garden City, N.Y., Doubleday & Company, Inc. Anchor, 1969), p. 14.

transportation, it is also influenced by constructs in people's minds and varies from one community to another.

Within the institution, the location of the group meeting also becomes a factor if people need to walk long distances, take elevators, or be taken in wheelchairs. This may result in inclusion or exclusion of members.

Space as Home Base

Another aspect of space is the sense of "home" referred to by Coyle [40] as a geographic location for meeting place that specifies a sense of attachment and may influence group cohesion. Robert Sommer [41] says that "people who spend long periods of time in any environment" get used to certain sounds, smells, and locations of facilities, chair arrangement, etc. Certain chairs or places at tables become the territorial property of certain members, and any newcomer who takes the seat will be told he is in another's chair. Groups which meet over a series of sessions frequently develop a patterned seating arrangement. The group and the institutional setting appear to reinforce this pattern of behavior which Sommer calls "institutional sanctity."

A constant single location reinforces the consciousness of group. The place enhances a solidification of the group as the members come together repeatedly in a location that becomes familiar and provides a sense of continuity. Space and location of the room provide an external structure and anchor for the group. Hall says,[42] "man's feeling about being properly oriented in space runs deep. Such knowledge is ultimately linked to survival and sanity. To be disoriented in space is psychotic." In the same sense, the feeling of familiarity about location of the group keeps continuity and orientation.

If for some reason a group must change its meeting place, there can be a noticeable emotional reaction among the members that is not necessarily conscious. Restlessness, difficulty in getting to

[40] Coyle, *Social Process.*
[41] Robert Sommer, *Personal Space* (Englewood Cliffs, N.J., Prentice-Hall, Inc., 1969), pp. 34–35, 80–83.
[42] Hall, *Hidden Dimension*, p. 105.

174 Size, Space, and Time

work, re-establishment of roles, and bickering may occur. One club group of latency-aged girls which had met weekly in a settlement house in a particular room arrived one day to find the room newly cleaned and still retaining the odor of disinfectant. They ran to the worker, several of them actually in tears, and said that their room had been taken over and ruined by someone. They refused to meet there and finally went home without meeting that day.

Some workers have found that teenage gangs can be reached and engaged by providing a room in which they can meet regularly, and which they can clean and paint and have as their own when they are in session. Such territorial possession of space may provide outer structure and security that provide protection and a sense of belonging.

One consideration faced by a worker in deciding whether a group is capable of a trip, a camping weekend, a picnic, or some activity which takes them out of their usual meeting place, is an assessment of the degree to which the group has internalized its structure and can function without the supports of its usual meeting place. If the room has become a supportive prop, the members may be overwhelmed without the boundaries of the familiar space and the group may disintegrate outside. The worker's activity with the group is, of course, to facilitate the development of an interpersonal structure.

Physical Arrangements

In recent years studies have been made of the spatial arrangements within rooms which may affect the group development and functioning. These factors have been considered in light of studies of the way people respond to each other through their senses of sight, hearing, smell, and touch or reaction to body heat. Edward T. Hall [43] has pioneered in the study of social and personal space and man's perception of it as an elaboration of culture which he has labeled proxemics. He notes, for instance, that there are cultural differences regarding how men perceive different experiences because their senses have been accustomed to respond or not respond to certain aspects of the environment. The physical closeness

[43] Hall, *ibid.*, pp. 44–45.

or distance thought to be appropriate differs among Germans, Swiss, French, English, Japanese, Arabs, and Americans as studied by Hall. He notes that "space perception is not only a matter of what can be perceived, but what can be screened out. People brought up in different cultures learn as children, without even knowing that they have done so, to screen out one type of information while paying close attention to another. Once set, these perceptual patterns apparently remain quite stable throughout life." He cites, for example, the Japanese use of paper screens to separate sight as contrasted to the German and Dutch use of thick walls to separate sound. He also notes the sense of crowding that people develop, depending on whether they have been acculturated to or are personally endowed with a sense of propriety about contact or noncontact with others. He suggests that noncontact people set up "an invisible bubble around themselves," keeping others outside. They feel crowded when this distance is invaded. Others huddle together and require physical contact with each other; they judge those who stay at a distance as cool and aloof and withholding. Distance between people is judged both consciously and unconsciously by sight, sound, smell, body temperature, as well as personality. For some, those things in view are the only reality and anything screened out of view is not part of their personal space; for others, sound invades their personal space, regardless of what they see. Some feel invaded by body odors while others feel lacking in cues if odors of others are not there. He says also,[44] "Significant evidence that people brought up in different cultures live in different perceptual worlds is to be found in their manner of orienting themselves in space . . . virtually everything a man does is associated with experience in space. . . . Man's sense of space is a synthesis of many sensory in-puts: visual, auditory, kinesthetic, olfactory, and thermal. Not only does each of these constitute a complex system . . . but each is molded and patterned by culture. . . . The patterning of perceptual worlds is a function not only of culture but also of relationship, activity, and emotion. Therefore, people from different cultures, when interpreting each

[44] Hall, *ibid.*, p. 70.

other's behavior, often misinterpret the relationship, the activity or the emotion." Although these examples given are of cultural differences by nationality, there may be subcultural differences on the basis of socioeconomic life styles, life experiences, rural, urban, and family styles also.

Room or space arrangements also affects group development. Distances between people are influenced by capacity to see and hear. Given normal vision, a person can usually take in visually large spaces. With normal hearing, the distance of twenty feet is encompassable, and two-way conversation is possible. Beyond that there is rapid deterioration of either one-way hearing or two-way conversation without raising voices. On the other hand, some people like to retain greater distances for deliberation with meaning and closer distances for small talk. Thoreau writing in Walden expressed it well when he stated: [45]

One inconvenience I sometimes experienced in so small a house was the difficulty of getting to a sufficient distance from my guest when we began to utter big thoughts in big words. You want room for your thought . . . to run in steady course before it reaches the ear of the hearer, else it may plough out again through the side of his head. Also our sentences wanted room to unfold and form their columns in the interval. Individuals . . . must have suitable broad and natural boundaries, even a neutral ground between them. . . . In my house we were so near we could not begin to hear. . . . If we are merely loquacious and loud talkers, then we can afford to stand very near together, cheek by jowl, and feel each other's breath; but if we speak reservedly and thoughtfully we want to be farther apart. . . .

Here Thoreau equates the influence of space and distance between people with the matters to be undertaken in the communication.

Hall [46] also notes the influence of temperature on feeling crowded. He suggests that "a chain reaction is set in motion when there is not enough space to dissipate the heat of a crowd." He says that in order to maintain some degree of comfort and lack of involvement a hot crowd requires more space than a cool one. He gives as example how much closer people feel without air condi-

[45] Henry D. Thoreau, Walden (New York, The Macmillan Co., 1929).
[46] Hall, Hidden Dimension, p. 57.

tioning in the heat of a summer day, although the distances between them are the same. Sommer [47] commented that "people like
to be close enough to obtain the warmth and comradeship but far
enough to avoid pricking one another." He says further that "people are able to tolerate closer presence of a stranger at their sides,
than directly in front of them." Mintz, [48] studying the effect of the
surroundings on the individual reaction, conducted an experiment
in which a large number of people were interviewed in three different rooms; one very attractive, the second average, and the third
a very ugly cold room in disarray with cans for ash trays, an exposed light bulb, and a torn window shade, that looked like a stor-
age room. Students were questioned about the experiment
afterward and while only 29% noticed anything about the room,
46% said there was something wrong with the experiment but did
not know what it was; 25% thought the experiment was fine. People may feel uncomfortable in unattractive space without realizing
that they are responding to the discomfort of the room.

Hall [49] gives an example of improving the performance of a mal-
functioning committee by changing the auditory and visual aspects
of the conference room. He writes, "There had been so many complaints about the inadequacy of the chairman that a replacement
was about to be requested. The architect had reason to believe
that there was more in the environment than in the chairman to
explain the difficulties. Without telling his subjects what he was
doing, the architect managed to retain the chairman while he cor-
rected the environmental faults." He worked to reduce the sound
in the room of the busy traffic noise from the street outside that
was intensified by bare walls and floors by making modifications
within the physical arrangements of the room. When the reduction
of auditory interference made it possible to conduct a meeting
without strain, complaints about the chairman ceased.

The arrangement of chairs and tables with open spaces in a
room can have an effect upon how people behave toward each

[47] Sommer, *Personal Space.*
[48] Norbitt Mintz, "Effects of Aesthetic Surroundings," *Journal of Psychology,*
XLI (1956), 459–66.
[49] Hall, *Hidden Dimension,* p. 44.

other. Osmond, [50] a psychiatrist who was responsible for a mental hospital, noticed there were some arrangements that seemed to keep people apart from each other—those he labeled "sociofugal." Chairs in rows or along walls which caused people to look straight ahead seemed to prevent conversation. On the other hand, chairs arranged around small tables, or facing each other in small conversational groups, seemed to draw people together. These he labeled "sociopetal." Once he was able to change the habits of both patients and staff who were used to chairs being lined up against the wall, and to create a sociopetal arrangement of equipment, he discovered that the number of conversations doubled and tripled.

Sommer [51] noted that people tended to talk with each other considerably more if they were facing each other, either across a table or diagonally. In an experiment he conducted of people in a cafeteria, people given their choice of seats for informal conversation chose corner positions where they could have physical proximity and visual contact face to face. If they were working together on a cooperative venture, they tended to choose side-by-side seats to look at something together. They commented that it was easier to share things. People who were competitive chose face-to-face or distant seating and people who were merely working in the presence of others chose diagonal or distant seating. One person commented that distance from each other permitted staring into space rather than into someone's face.

The way people arrange themselves in a group, whether there is a table or not, reflects not only the purpose of the group and the task that it sets out to achieve, or how well people know each other and how comfortable they are with each other, but also reflects individual personality factors of the members and their cultural backgrounds. People who like closeness with others will choose locations in the group where they are surrounded or close to others, while those who prefer distance will probably choose corners of the table or those chairs that are farthest away from oth-

[50] Humphrey Osmond, "The Relationship Between Architect and Psychiatrist," in Charles Goshen, ed., *Psychiatric Architecture* (Washington, D.C., American Psychiatric Association, 1959).
[51] Sommer, *Personal Space*, pp. 58–73.

ers. Schutz [52] in his personality inventory studies discovered that one of the characteristics of people is their desire to be close or distant from others, and these characteristics affect their group or interpersonal activity. If they choose to participate less they will probably seat themselves farther away from the central action.

Given the opportunity to sit wherever they chose, people in some of Sommer's [53] studies revealed that the fear of rebuke tended to increase individual distance, but approval-seeking reduced it. People who thought they would be criticized by group members sat farther away from others, especially those from whom they expected criticism. People seeking approval moved closer to those from whom they sought support. When the whole group feared some outside force, they tended to sit closer together. But if they feared a threat within the group itself, they tended to sit farther apart. It was also noted that people tended to seat themselves farther from a person stigmatized by reputed illness or undesirable characteristics and from people in wheelchairs.

In a study of physical arrangements of people in a discussion group, Steinzor [54] noticed that a person who had had a negative encounter with another in the group changed his seat in order to be opposite his opponent. Steinzor also noticed that people in discussion groups more frequently addressed a person opposite them than one beside them. When a person finished speaking, it was usually a person across from him who replied, rather than one next to him. Hearn [55] found that the direction of comments could be modified with strong or weak leaders. With no leaders or weak leaders, participants addressed more of their remarks to those opposite, while a strong leader had the effect of limiting comments to the adjacent persons.

After a group has had enough sessions for members to acquire some impression of each other, it may be noted that people will

[52] William Schutz, *Interpersonal Underworld* (Palo Alto, Calif., Science & Behavior Books, Inc., 1966).

[53] Sommer, *Personal Space*, pp. 68–70.

[54] Bernard Steinzor, "The Spatial Factor in Face-to-Face Discussion Groups," *Journal of Abnormal and Social Psychology*, XLV (1950), 552–55.

[55] Gordon Hearn, "Leadership and the Spatial Factor in Small Groups," *Journal of Abnormal and Social Psychology*, CIV (1957), 269–72.

choose seats next to or opposite certain people, near or far from others toward whom they feel positively or negatively. After the first arrivals are seated, others may choose their seats accordingly. Others may change their seats after latecomers sit. Some people may regularly choose the same seats and feel deposed if an earlier arrival has selected "their chair." Over a period of time members may become possessive about their location in the arrangement of the group.

As to the effect of room arrangement on group participation, Sommer [56] found that with groups of six around rectangular tables, increased distance across table or between chairs resulted in less friendliness and less talkativeness, except where there was increased eye contact that counteracted the effects of increased distance. People tended to sit closer as room size was increased and also when noise level or interference increased.

There have been several studies of spatial arrangement and leadership. In simulated jury deliberations, Strodtbeck and Hook [57] found a tendency for people from higher economic status, proprietors and managers, to select head chairs. There was also a trend for the persons seated at one of the head positions to be elected foreman. Strodtbeck determined that jurors looked at the occupants of chairs at both ends of the table and then elected the one thought to have higher status. He also noted that people in the head chairs participated more than the others. After deliberations, the members of the group regularly voted that the people in the head chairs had made the most significant contribution to the deliberation. Strodtbeck concluded that in our culture some value prevails that suggests that a person in the head chair is the leader. Such a value not only conditions members to turn to the person in the head chair but also for the person who considers himself to be a leader to seat himself in the head chair. This finding suggests that a social worker should choose his location in the room with a group, depending on whether he wishes to be central or peripheral to the group. However, he may pull the focus to himself wherever

[56] Sommer, *Personal Space*, p. 64.
[57] Fred L. Strodtbeck, and L. H. Hook, "The Social Dimensions of a Twelve-Man Jury Table," *Sociometry*, XXIV (1961), 397–415.

he sits because of his function and his role. In counseling with total families, the social worker should consider where he sits since it promotes or demotes the position and role of the father or mother in the deliberation.

Sommer [58] also noted that leaders of discussion groups, given rectangular tables in a cafeteria, tended to choose the head position at a rectangular table. Other people arranged themselves so that they could see the leader. He concluded that it seemed to be more important to see the leader than to be near him.

Architects and designers have begun to take into account some of these factors in planning arrangements for group meeting rooms, constructing sectional tables that can be put together in squares, rectangles, six-or-eight-sided tables, or in circles. While there is no head or foot to a round table, wherever leadership sits probably becomes the head. There may be also a head associated with the location of door, chalk board, or some other functional or symbolic object.

For social workers with groups, the implications of all of this are that spatial arrangements should be considered in planning the location of the group and the room arrangement. Flexibility in seating may provide for individual choice of members. Attractive surroundings may facilitate group development, and the arrangement may provide group structure, but neither alone, without leadership and supportive group feeling, will make for group cohesion.

Time

The element of time can be examined from the standpoint of duration of group or number of sessions, length of sessions, frequency of meeting, and hour of meeting.

Duration

Merton [59] speaks of actual duration and expected duration of a group as provisional group properties. He says, "In some groups

---

[58] Sommer, *Personal Space.*

[59] Robert K. Merton, *Social Theory and Social Structure* (New York, The Free Press, 1957), pp. 311–13.

membership has a fixed term of duration, both in fact and in expectation. In others one or both are indefinitely extended duration." While some groups have a set limit of duration from the beginning, members may hold the expectation that the group has relative permanence. On the other hand, some groups are established with no anticipated terminal date but members have no intention of continuing the group beyond a few sessions.

Merton theorizes that "whether the group is established temporarily to meet a need which once met involves self-liquidation or established with expectation of unlimited duration for the indefinitely prolonged future, will presumably affect the self-selection of members, the kind and degree of involvement, the structure of organization and other properties." For instance, if the group is expected to be temporary for meeting a particular need, people may move in rapidly, focusing on the problem, but not investing much in relationships, because there is no expectation of permanency. A task force to design a new program is a good example, or a six-session, parent-education group. The content is the major point of attraction. If the group is formed with the expectation of permanency, a great deal more is invested in order to create the kind of structure that will be more solid. The creation of a new family is a good example. Ideally, time and attention are given to the courtship, for the "honeymoon," time for initial phase of marriage, for it is presumed usually at the outset that the group will grow and be nurtured and extended through the lifetime. Many socialization groups and some therapy groups are created with the expectation of relative permanence, at least for an extended period of time.

Of such groups, Coyle [60] says traditions are maintained and they develop a sense of continuity with past individuals. Other groups are "established with the expectations of unlimited duration for the indefinitely prolonged future." Coyle notes that "many groups expect immortality," they maintain consciously cultivated traditions, their emotional attachments are deep and enriched. Other groups do expect to persist and attempt to go on for years, gradually acquiring institutional forms and traditions of self-perpetuating attachments. Of some of these groups, Coyle states that they may

[60] Coyle, *Social Process*, pp. 79–82.

cease to perform any useful social function and may even dwindle in members, but "it would outrage the finer feelings of its members to suggest termination."

Coyle notes that in groups formed with the expectation that they will exist only for a short period, members carry a consciousness of limited duration which will permeate relationships and prevent the growth of deep-rooted attachments. Policies established in these groups do not have to be viewed in light of the effect in the distant future and therefore may not become institutionalized.

Some people are willing to become part of groups which they feel will not last long. Cartwright and Lippitt [61] note that "a person may sustain his deviancy in a group through the conviction that his fate is temporary." If one has question about joining a group, serving on a committee, associating or working with people who are not necessarily to his liking, such an assignment may be palatable to the person if he knows that he can escape in a short time, because of the short duration of the group.

The knowledge of limited duration may also encourage a group to work and to complete the objectives as soon as possible, while a group that anticipates a longer period of time will probably arrange to take it. More diversions may be pursued, more alternatives examined.

For problem-solving groups, a method has been created of setting time periods in which certain operations are expected to be completed, and therefore for estimating duration in advance. This procedure is called PERT [62] (Program Evaluation and Review Technique), which is a useful device for task-centered groups, especially in community organization, development and planning, and administration where tasks may be fairly specifically determined in advance. Using the problem-solving procedure of stating the problem, looking at its various aspects, gathering facts about the problem, looking at alternative solutions, choosing direction

[61] Dorwin Cartwright, and Ronald Lippitt, "Group Dynamics and the Individual," in Warren G. Bennis, Kenneth D. Benne, and Robert Chin, eds., *The Planning of Change* (New York, Holt, Rinehart & Winston, Inc., 1961).

[62] A brief discussion of the PERT approach appears in Gerald Phillips, *Communication and the Small Group*, pp. 88–108.

from among the alternatives, and moving to solution, the PERT approach assigns a time estimate to each of the procedures which gives deadlines to each part of the operation in light of a terminal date for completion of the task and critical events or decisions to be made along the way. Phillips [63] evaluates PERT as "a realistic method applied to the discussion process which tends to preserve the constructive elements of traditional problem solving, while adding a new dimension of emphasis on discussion output." But from the standpoint of frequency of meetings, the mere factor of setting estimates in advance, tends to push groups and subgroups toward the completion of their piece of the task, or the stage of the task, and therefore to determine how frequently they will need to meet.

From the standpoint of social work practice, duration of the group is an important factor. As mentioned in Chapter III on group phases, frequently the end is built in the beginning if a group has a set number of sessions, or length of time span in which it is to meet. The duration may also be related to a task to be achieved or changes within individual members. Difficult as it may be sometimes, the social worker may have to bring the group to a close. He may have to confront the group that its duration has come to an end.

Duration has also been seen from the standpoint of length of time it may take a group to develop cohesion, norms, and sense of entity. Dittes and Kelley,[64] for instance, found that some groups could establish a specific norm in a single session. Merei,[65] on the other hand, reported that it took from three to six meetings of children to change from an assemblage into a group "with rules, habits, traditions entirely of its own."

Frequency

Frequency of meeting has been studied on the basis of the effect on participants and on the group of repeated interaction. Josephine

[63] Phillips, *Communication and the Small Group*, p. 108.

[64] James E. Dittes, and H. H. Kelley, "Effects of Different Conditions of Acceptance upon Conformity to Group Norms," *Journal of Abnormal and Social Psychology*, LIII (July, 1956), 100–107.

[65] Ferenc Merei, "Group Leadership and Institutionalization," *Human Relations*, II (1949), 23–39.

Klein [66] found that interaction over a period of time increases the amount of information available and increases sentiments. Bovard [67] similarly found by testing members feelings about each other before and after a period of interaction that the members moved significantly toward a condition of liking after the interaction.

In a study of the development of relationships among members who were initially strangers to one another, over a series of ten meetings, Klein [68] found that members tend to agree more and more in their ranking of each other. She concludes that there was a tendency toward consensus of opinion where members participate in discussion in the group and had no contact outside of the group to compare notes. Their participation together over a period of time and with some frequency provided them with an opportunity to judge each other and rank each other by status in the group. This supports the thesis of the tendency of group members to reach a similar level in their judgments.

Klein also found that people who were strangers initially, over a series of ten meetings, came to rank each other more similarly to each other. The repeated association apparently had the effect of making their judgments become similar.

Experience in working with gang groups over the past twenty years produced the evidence that both boys and girls who associated together in these autonomous groups tended to be together almost constantly. Austin [69] noted the street workers were available almost daily, and had frequent formal sessions with the groups.

Crisis intervention groups [70] in hospitals and clinics, as well as social agencies, have met from three to five sessions a week, at least during the crisis. Community organization committees called together for crisis, especially during racial disorders or following

[66] Josephine P. Klein, *The Study of Groups* (London, Routledge and Kegan Paul, Ltd., 1967), pp. 90–94.

[67] E. W. Bovard, Jr., "The Experimental Production of Interpersonal Affect," *Journal of Abnormal and Social Psychology*, XLVI (1952), 521–28.

[68] Klein, *Study of Groups*, p. 92.

[69] David M. Austin, "Goals for Street Workers," *Social Work*, II (1957), 43–50.

[70] Martin Strickler, and Jean Allgeyer, "The Crisis Group: A New Application of Crisis Theory," *Social Work*, XII (July, 1967).

disasters, have met daily for a period of great pressure, tapering off to weekly thereafter. The urgency of the problem and the nature of the problem, and people's concern about it may be the determining factor in frequency of meeting.

In open-ended groups, where the turnover may be rapid, frequency of meeting becomes a means for retaining some continuity of participation. Ziller [71] says, "Members of open groups are aware of the transitory nature of these relationships. The future is indistinct, the present dominates. . . . If the present membership is to benefit from a given group action, the action must be taken in the immediate future." Thus frequency of meeting would be implied for open-ended groups.

Groups in hospitals, especially in pediatrics services where the stay may be from five days to two months, meet daily or five times a week. The intensity of need of the children separated from their families, plus the anxiety created by the medical treatment, in addition to the open-ended nature of the group, make frequency of sessions imperative.[72]

Those who plan T groups [73] and some of the sensitivity training sponsored by the National Training Laboratories and others have developed the marathon—groups which convene continuously for three to five days, with short intervals for rest periods. The principle behind the plan is that people in constant association will interact more, influence each other more, and engage more in the process of change. The theory rests on Lewin's [74] research on individual and group change discussed in Chapter Two.

There is some assumption that the more frequently that people interact together, the more they will move toward similarity of opinion and the closer they will become personally. There seems to be both support and refutation of these notions in the research. If

[71] Robert C. Ziller, "Toward a Theory of Open and Closed Groups," *Psychological Bulletin*, LXIII (1965), 165.

[72] Grace L. Coyle and Raymond Fisher, "Helping the Hospitalized Child through Social Group Work," *The Child*, XVI (1952).

[73] George Bach, "Marathon Group Dynamics," *Psychological Reports*, XX (June, 1967), 995–1172.

[74] Kurt Lewin, *Field Theory in Social Science* (New York, Harper & Row, 1951).

there are group antagonisms they may not be resolved, but rather may be increased by frequency of interaction. Depending on the groups and the members, and whether they are personal-social groups or task groups, their interaction may increase hostilities or dislikes or resolve tensions and increase liking. They may solidify differences or move toward consensus and similarity of opinion.

Length of Session

The length of a session is largely a matter of preference and capacity of members. Short sessions may produce good and conclusive work if the participants have learned to work together and are in the phase of group development wherein they can concentrate on the job at hand and do not have to spend too much time on group maintenance. Short sessions of forty-five minutes to an hour may be as long as the interest span of the members can be sustained if the participants are young children, or people with certain emotional or nervous conditions. Longer sessions may be necessary when at least part of the session must go with group functioning and maintenance, as well as achieving the purpose of the group, whether that be help to members, or task achievement, problem solving and decision making. Sometimes unstructured sessions which are permitted to go on too long, especially if they are functioning at a high emotional level, may produce too much fatigue and lead to diminishing returns. If a session is scheduled to run for several hours, unless the intent is to operate on the fatigue factor and the contagion factor of breaking down defenses, it is wise to plan for long interval breaks, for releasing of tension—both body fatigue and emotional and mental fatigue—and to provide an opportunity for informal discussion among participants.

The lack of research in this area may be due to the concern of the social scientists with process rather than time in producing results. Arbitrary time limits seem to be set for experimental groups and observation of natural-state groups, but rationale for time limits are not given.

Time Location

When a group meets, the hour of the day or night, whether on a weekend or a weeknight, the season of the year depending on the climate of the region will affect composition or who is willing or able to participate, or available at the time. Many working people are not available during daytime hours. If potential members feel urgency to participate in the group because it is the only way they can achieve certain results, they may make sacrifices to attend at inconvenient times. For instance, if people can obtain therapeutic relief that they need, they may be willing to take time off during working hours, but the chances are that they will feel pressure about missing work, may have to work overtime to make it up, and therefore will bring the current problems of the work situation with them into the session. Since they will be returning to the same, the thought and emotion from the job impinges on their group participation. If it is a task group where the urgency is helping someone else to solve problems or working on some common concerns, the reward of group participation will have to be larger than the penalties of attending at an inconvenient time. If an emergency occurs at work, or at home, or if the travel time to and from the committee or task group is greater than the length of the meeting itself, people may find excuses not to get to the group during working hours. The often heard remark from a person who lives or works in the suburbs, at a university, or some other outlying institution is, "I had to take half a day to go downtown, find a place to park, attend the meeting and return, and we really didn't accomplish anything after I got there. It isn't worth the time." At another time of day the feeling might be the same if the group did not accomplish anything, but the chances are the members might have more to invest and feel less negative about the group if it were held at a more convenient time.

On the other hand, many people react against evening meetings away from home and family, or in areas where it is difficult or dangerous to travel at night. For example, a Girl Scout worker attempting to form a parents' advisory group in the inner city found that practically all of the mothers were employed and could not attend daytime meetings; they needed to be home with their families at the dinner hour, and they felt it was dangerous to be very far from home after dark in the evening. A Sunday afternoon was the only time this group could meet.

A youth counseling agency attempted to have groups of parents of the adolescents in treatment meet at 5:30, or immediately after work in order to include both parents. When they had a high rate of absenteeism they discovered that the mothers, who were not employed, did not like to travel into the city during rush hour, nor did they like to be away during the dinner hour. The husbands did not necessarily work in the inner city so they, too, had to travel at rush hour, and they did not like to attend without their wives. An after-dinner session at 8:00 P.M. proved to be more satisfactory.

A worker setting up a group in a housing project, of mothers of young children who wanted some parent education, asked the women what their preference would be for time of a group session. It had been anticipated that a morning hour would be most desirable. The women suggested 1:30 P.M. They said they had housework and shopping to do in the morning and needed to be home at noon to give the children their lunches. By 1:30 the children had returned to school, and they could be more leisurely about getting to the group. They would then be home by the time the children returned in the afternoon.

In a school, the social worker organized a counseling group of children who were having school-related personal problems. The alternatives offered by the administration for time were immediately after school, before school in the morning, or some release time during class or study period. When the children were asked their preference, they thought it too conspicuous to walk out of class or study period because they got stigmatized as the "kids with problems." After school they had recreation or homework or the group seemed like punishment. Some of the children and their families found it too difficult to get to school before hours. A compromise was reached in having the children bring lunches and meet during the noon hour with their worker in a room designated for meetings and activities.

On a pediatrics ward in a hospital, the group program was offered just after dinner and before and during visiting hours. Since parents did not visit everyday, this provided little conflict. This seemed to be the "lonely hour" at dusk or nightfall, and after the major activities or treatments of the day were completed. This also seemed to be a time when many children missed home the most. The group, offered primarily for socialization, and dealing with anxieties about being away from home, and the unknowns of medical treatment, provided a good opportunity to prepare the children for sleeping and for the treatment day ahead.

These examples of practice decisions on hours are inserted in lieu of any social science research on the factor of meeting time of a group as it affects composition, goal achievement, and the freedom of people to engage to some measure in the group activity. It may be concluded that the hour of a particular group offering should take into consideration the intent, wishes, and conveniences of the potential members, the purpose for which the group is offered, and also, of course, availability of space and staff resources. The importance of time in facilitating group functioning, while it has received very little attention in social science research, should not be underestimated. The feeling of the participants about time or the hour of the session may not only affect their attendance, their decision to participate, but also the pressures or freedom to participate that they feel once they are present in a session.

Summary and Conclusions

In this chapter we have examined some of the research and observations regarding the influence of size of group, spatial factors, and time elements of group development and functioning for many types of person-focused and task-oriented groups. We have seen that while these are not independent variables from each other or from other group factors, they are very important in group composition, development, and accomplishment.

Depending on the purposes of the group, and the capacity of members, groups may need to be small—three to seven members, or large—eight to twenty-five. If the operations are simple and the interaction of the members important, the group should be small. If the activity and task production are important, groups may need to be larger for more possible ideas and division of labor. Size of group will be a consideration also in capacity of members related to age, social development, and interpersonal capacity. Smaller groups need fairly simple organization and large groups require more formal organization and leadership direction. If the group is closed, size may not be a factor for consideration, but an open-ended group must be large enough to sustain itself through losses of members, and to provide enough variety that each member will find someone with whom to associate.

Space available to a group or its location may influence how many and who will be able to participate in the group. Also, the location and purpose of the group may affect who will meet eligibility criteria. Location will determine who may be able to reach the group or will feel attracted to it or repulsed from it. Cultural differences among members may also influence their perceptions of each other and their sense of closeness or distance, and the factors which affect what they see, hear, feel, and take in from a given situation, a field labled "proxemics." The location of the group and its meeting place may become a home base for members, to which they may become so attached that changes become difficult. This is not only true for geographical location, but also for the room itself, its arrangement and particular chairs. Some spatial arrangements drive people apart—"sociofugal"—and others draw them together —"sociopetal." In fact, physical arrangements of meeting space may facilitate or encumber communication, the flow of interaction, and capacity of the group to make decisions. Location of leadership in the room also affects the group process.

The time aspects of duration of group and length of session, frequency of meeting and hour of meeting are affected by the expectations of members, but also influence the composition and process of the group. The research is not yet conclusive as to whether frequent interaction makes a group closer or more distant. Members obviously know each other better after more association and while some research suggests this may draw people closer, others have shown that "familiarity breeds contempt." The method of PERT was reviewed as a procedure for facilitating time use in task groups. While very little research exists on length of session and time location by hour of day, or day of week or session, some observations would suggest that the particular group members, group purpose, and urgency of the group content will influence decisions about time and length of session.

INTERACTION PROCESS
AND INTERPERSONAL
RELATIONSHIPS

When people are convened with the intent of forming a group, they engage in what Eric Berne [1] calls "social rituals and pastimes." People begin to connect with each other in various ways through introductions, stereotyped conversations, finding mutual interests in places, people, things, and events. While underneath these actions they size up each other in the hope of finding someone interesting with whom they might like to form a continuing relationship. Berne says there is a tendency for "people with similar or complementary attitudes, interests and responses to seek each other out and stay together." People communicate through words, through eye contact, sounds, touch or smell. Their responses may

[1] Eric Berne, *The Structure and Dynamics of Organizations and Groups* (Philadelphia, J. B. Lippincott Co., 1963).

be cognitive through thoughts and ideas or emotive through feeling reactions. From the first encounter, preceding any formal session, people begin to interact, to express themselves consciously, and in ways of which they are not aware. They may try to impress others with themselves and at the same time be assessing each other. In that way the interpersonal relationships of any group begin. From this initial engagement on, if a group forms, people have some degree of influence on each other, choose each other, reject each other, or ally themselves with each other on the basis of various attractions. Patterns of affiliation and relationships emerge and some of these patterns become organized into the group structure.

As these relationships develop, the essence of the group emerges and members begin to function together in taking action, deliberating, establishing group goals, and working to satisfy members and to achieve goals. Coyle [2] calls this "a discernible process by which people are connected to each other, and around which the group takes its shape and form."

The interpersonal relationships form an intricate network of emotional, intellectual, and communication patterns which shift constantly with the give and take responses of members to each other, and to the group as a whole or segments of it. Within these patterns, roles, or expected behaviors are created for the members to perform inside and then outside of the group. Through these patterns each person makes his contribution and is influenced by the others. Subgroups emerge and a group structure develops.

At least five types of interpersonal relationships take place within the group organization. These include: (1) affectional or emotional acceptances or rejections; (2) interest alliances; (3) status ratings; (4) leader and follower patterns (formal and informal); and (5) communication patterns. Each of these types will be discussed separately though they are not mutually exclusive, and all of them exist simultaneously in any group. The form of interpersonal relationships in any group depends on the people and the purpose of the group.

[2] Grace L. Coyle, *Group Work with American Youth* (New York, Harper & Row, 1948), p. 91.

Sociometry [3] emerged as a technique to assess personal attractions and rejections among members and the interpersonal relationships within groups. Newstetter,[4] whose work was noted in Chapter Two, was concerned that the results of both individualistic studies, or those which measured individual's traits and drives, and situational studies which analyzed given social situations and conditions, did not give a true reading of the internal processes in small groups. He therefore invented a method for examining and understanding the interaction process as it takes place within the group. Newstetter observed, "An individual with the same natural endowments will manifest totally different patterns of social behavior when the distribution of forces within a group differs." He noted that the "social process in a group at a given time" is a "series of psychological interactions between the individual and other members of the group" and by "study and analysis of the nature of these manifestations" behavior in a group may be understood, predicted, and made manageable to some extent. Newstetter's scheme focused on determining the relationship or the position and status of two or more people in their associations together, their feeling of attachment to each other, and their overt and covert interactions with each other. Preferences of individuals were given through interviews and were correlated with observations of the actual associations of people. Newstetter's major finding showed that an individual's group status was not so much a result of his behavior toward others as it was in their behavior toward him. Thus status came to be defined as a ranking by group members of each other.

Generally credited with originating the idea of sociometrics is Moreno,[5] whose work was carried on simultaneously to Newstetter's, but they apparently worked without knowledge of each other. Moreno also designed techniques and instruments to elicit prefer-

[3] Gardner Lindzey, and Edgar Borgatta, "Sociometric Measurement," in Gardner Lindzey, ed., *Handbook of Social Psychology* (Reading, Addison-Wesley Publishing Co., Inc., 1954), pp. 405–48.

[4] W. I. Newstetter, Marc J. Feldstein, and Theodore Newcomb, *Group Adjustment* (Cleveland, School of Applied Social Sciences, Western Reserve University, 1938), p. 13.

[5] Jacob L. Moreno, *Who Shall Survive?* (rev. ed., Beacon, N.Y., Beacon House, 1953).

ences of individuals for each other and to chart the interactions among group members. His methods take into account quality as well as quantity of interpersonal relationships and interactions. Lindzey and Borgatta [6] state that a "sociometric measure is a means of assessing the attractions and repulsions within a given group. It usually involves each member privately specifying a number of other persons with whom he would like to engage in some particular activity and with whom he would not like to participate." These authors suggest that through sociometric techniques "the web of interpersonal relations, attractions, repulsions, and indifferences that characterize individuals in daily interaction, the informal organization, and social status" may be measured.

Modifications [7] of sociometric techniques have been made by other investigators. Methods include asking members whom they like, making direct observations of time people spent together, observing visiting patterns, asking or giving assistance, or consultation in work, analysis of children's drawings of group activities, and observing behavior in groups when certain individuals are removed.

Typical Sociogram

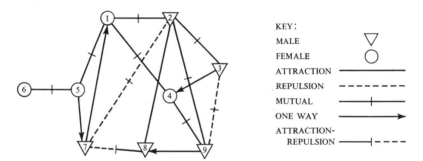

While this digression to a discussion of a method of small group research may divert us from findings on interpersonal relationships temporarily, it is introduced with the notion that social workers

[6] Lindzey, and Borgatta, "Sociometric Measurement," in Lindzey, ed., *Handbook*, pp. 405–407.
[7] A. Paul Hare, *Handbook of Small Group Research* (New York, The Free Press, 1962), pp. 408–409.

desiring to facilitate interpersonal attachments within groups may find the use of sociometric techniques useful. Also, sociometric observations done at close range may provide a worker with a keener awareness of the interaction and alliances within the group.

One other aspect of sociometric procedures is the constructing of sociograms, an instrument also credited to Moreno and his associate, Helen Hall Jennings.[8] The sociogram is a graphic representation of the choices or the association of group members, using symbols for people and their interactions.

Some of the people who have used sociograms have attempted to show status by location at top or bottom of the chart. Others have attempted to show strength of ties by locating the symbols for people closer together or farther apart.[9] Others have used different colors to show attractions, repulsions, or strength of relationships. Some have attempted to construct three-dimensional sociograms. Readings of groups may be taken for specific activities and at different points in the phasing of groups. The comparisons of sociograms of a single group at different times will show stability or shifts in relationships and associations.

When a sociogram has been constructed for a group it is possible to notice isolates, pairs, triads, coalitions, rivalries, and competitive alignments that may not be so clear in the activity with group members. Hare [10] warns that the sociogram is useful in identifying the positions of individuals in informal structure of the group, but it does not reveal actual behavior of members. It shows position without describing role. Therefore, social workers may find a sociogram useful in locating group members in relation to each other and in gaining a clearer view of the subgrouping and isolates.

Another method of observing the internal processes in groups was developed by Robert F. Bales and called *Interaction Process Analysis.*[11] His system has been used so extensively for many types

[8] Helen Hall Jennings, *Leadership and Isolation* (New York, Longmans Green, 1950).

[9] Lindzey, and Borgatta, "Sociometric Measure," in Lindzey, ed., *Handbook,* p. 445.

[10] Hare, *Handbook,* p. 126.

[11] Robert F. Bales, *Interaction Process Analysis* (Reading, Mass., Addison-Wesley Publishing Co., Inc., 1950).

of research on small groups that it bears some discussion here. Also, many social workers who have used Bales' scheme find it helpful in observing high and low participators as well as substantive analysis of content discussed in the group, and the roles taken by various group members. Bales' scheme was developed by his observations of teaching seminars, leadership training groups, committees, labor negotiating teams, juries, classes, and therapeutic sessions.

Bales established a set of twelve categories of types of interactions in which people engaged when they deliberate. These categories then divide into positive and negative acts in each of six areas: (1) defining the situation (orientation); (2) developing a value system for evaluating alternative solutions (evaluation); (3) influence by members on each other (control); (4) making a decision; (5) dealing with tensions; (6) maintaining the group (integration). Half of the categories are in the problem-solving task area; communication or orientation, evaluation, and control. These are instrumental to task performance. The other half are in the social-emotional area; group organization, personal relations, and integration. They are expressive, dealing with members' feelings.

Shepherd [12] notes that "as members interact they express agreement or disagreement with each other and the decisions they are making, they display tension or tension release as they feel interested, bored, satisfied, or disturbed; and they show solidarity or antagonism as they feel a sense of or lack of integration, helpfulness· to each other or friendliness."

The results of use of the Bales scheme for analyzing the interaction process in many kinds of groups over a period of years has produced some rather significant and useful findings. Bales [13] notes that about two-thirds of the acts in a group session are focused on the group task, or doing what the group is in business for, goal setting, and goal achievement. The other one-third of the comments and actions are geared to socio-emotional aspects, such as reassur-

[12] Clovis R. Shepherd, *Small Groups* (San Francisco, Chandler Publishing Co., 1964), p. 28.
[13] Robert F. Bales, "How People Interact in Conferences," *Scientific American,* CXCII (1955), 31–35.

ing someone, giving support, releasing tension, or disagreeing, attacking, or other negative reactions. Apparently in most groups, the positive acts are twice as frequent as the negative ones.

A group in which the task activity takes up more than two-thirds of the meeting period with very little socio-emotional content, such as giving support, maintaining the group, or releasing tensions, it may be concluded that members are exceptionally task-oriented. Hare [14] notes that groups may be highly task-oriented for several reasons. They may know each other very well and have other places to work out their socio-emotional relationships so they can concentrate on the task in the group. They may have developed their group level so well that they can proceed with the task without needing to give support or release tension. Or, they may be using the work of the group as a defense against dealing with their anxieties about their interpersonal conflicts which they do not wish to bring out in the group.

In therapeutic groups the content focus is apt to contain a disproportionate amount of socio-emotional acts and less on task-focused acts. This was found to be true by Munzer and Greenwald,[15] who used Bales' scheme for studying the interactions in therapy groups. Bales' scheme also was used to study group development through phases as discussed previously in Chapter Three.

Affectional or Emotional Ties

In any contact, people are drawn to or repelled by each other because of similar or complementary qualities. Newcomb [16] notes that the basis for attraction may be similar individual characteristics, common interests and values, similar personality traits. Hare [17] adds to the list similarity in age, intelligence, skills, and ideolo-

---

[14] Hare, *Handbook.*

[15] Jean Munzer, and Harold Greenwald, "Interaction Process Analysis of a Therapy Group," *International Journal of Group Psychotherapy,* VII (1957), 175–90.

[16] Theodore Newcomb, "The Prediction of Interpersonal Attraction," *American Psychologist,* II (1956), 575–86.

[17] Hare, *Handbook,* p. 156.

gies. He says, "once acquainted, persons who are attracted to each other seek each other out" and continue the relationship if they have common interests, values, and ideologies. Heber and Heber [18] found that people who had worked together successfully liked each other better and chose each other, but if their group was unsuccessful, the members were not so attracted to each other. Richardson [19] found that friends and marriage partners resembled each other in intelligence. A study by Lundy shows that individuals tend to seek out others whom they perceive to have what they think are their own positive personality traits.

Thus, as any group of people is convened, subgroups will form around some common or complementary qualities. If any member is strikingly different from others, it can be anticipated that he will either leave the group or remain an isolate unless his qualities complement some other member's. Group composition, therefore, may considerably affect the interaction and attraction aspect of interpersonal relationships and the ultimate group development.

Some group members are attracted to certain others because of personality needs. The dependent person seeks someone to lean on. The aggressive and dominating person needs a subject to control. The interpersonal relationships are used by some group members for the reactivation of the family, some members seeking to move through life stages in a new group, or responding to leadership (either indigenous or assigned) in the manner of a parent, or using the group to work on unresolved oedipal conflicts, or acting out sibling rivalry with peers in the group. They may seek neurotic fulfillment of needs for affection not met elsewhere.[20] While such behavior may be encouraged and used as content in therapy groups, it also appears unsolicited in many groups, including committees,

[18] R. F. Heber, and Mary E. Heber, "The Effect of Group Failure and Success on Social Status," *Journal of Educational Psychology*, XLVII (1957), 129–34.

[19] Helen M. Richardson, "Studies of Mental Resemblance Between Husbands and Wives and Between Friends," *Psychological Bulletin*, XXXVI (1939), 104–20.

[20] Irving Janis, "Group Identification under Conditions of External Danger," in Dorwin Cartwright and Alvin Zander, *Group Dynamics* (3d ed., New York, Harper & Row, 1968), pp. 81–83.

citizen-action groups, educational groups, or even professional staffs. These kinds of interpersonal ties can be very harmful to the ongoing work of the group because they set up internal conflicts not related to group goals and upset both those involved and those who are merely observers. At other times, such pseudo-family relations appear without diverting the group from its work. The work of some groups has been stopped while the members examine the nature of the conflict and consider directly what process is going on. Groups have been known to isolate and exclude members or potential members who distorted or misused relationships with others.

The concept of transference as used in psychoanalytic literature and in some of social work literature is applicable in the group.[21] An individual may endow other group members as well as leaders with qualities he associated with others in his past or present, and behave unrealistically or inappropriately toward them. Generally in social work groups, acting out or working through of such emotional reactions is not the major focus of the group, although feelings and the associated behavior that appears in a group have to be dealt with in some way because they have appeared in the group and all members are aware of their existence. In fact, they become part of the content of the group deliberation.

The patterns of interaction that develop initially in the formation stage of the group often are modified with further associations and acquaintance. Those who found each other interesting initially may find differences in values or beliefs that result in disenchantment and even disengagement later in a continuing group. Thus, the interpersonal alignments often shift. Moreover, people sometimes change in the course of group experience, and thus become more or less attractive to others. Thibaut and Kelley[22] state that "preliminary interaction is viewed as exploring possible outcomes, sampling various aspects as a basis for inferring present adequacy

[21] Helen Durkin, *The Group in Depth* (New York, International Universities Press, 1964), and Helen Northen, *Social Work with Groups* (New York, Columbia University Press, 1969), pp. 57, 159, 193–94.

[22] John W. Thibaut, and Harold Kelley, *The Social Psychology of Groups* (New York, John Wiley & Sons, Inc., 1961).

and forecasting trends in outcomes. Initially, this strangeness in interaction from non-acquaintance or different background produces formality and constraint. Initially people enter tentatively into potentially unstable relationships, engage in acts and responses. As the interaction proceeds, greater diversity of types of cues become available. Members may then modify their first impressions and reform their alliances."

Thibaut and Kelley discuss interpersonal attraction and relationships in terms of rewards and costs of reaching out and responding to one another. They list as rewards the "pleasures, satisfactions, gratifications, whether one's drive is reduced or need fulfilled by the relationship." Under costs they list "factors that operate to inhibit or deter performance of a sequence of behavior: the mental or physical effort required, the embarrassment or anxiety caused by the relationship." Their study showed that within groups, people were chosen as friends or work mates if they were able and willing to help others and if they acted with a minimum of tension and restraint in the group. Persons were rejected if they did not help others or if they increased group anxiety or tension.

Other studies showed that for task groups, individuals tended to choose others who appeared to be successful in previous experiences. People seem to want to be associated with a winner—and tended to reject the person who was not successful.

Affectional alliances are, of course, strong and apparent in family groups. These feelings have years to develop. Sometimes the family subgroups on the basis of age (that is among or between generations), sex (either on the oedipal patterns or the boys and girls against each other), or capabilities become very strong. The social worker intervening in a dysfunctional family may find intensive rivalries, hatreds, and separations, as well as affectional bonds. These need to be understood as well as the individual personality problems. Kluckhohn and Spiegel [23] discovered, for instance, that the interactions and dependencies in some families become so strong that the illness of a family member became the function of

[23] Florence Kluckhohn, and John M. Spiegel, *Integration and Conflict in Family Behavior* (Report No. 27, Topeka, Kansas, Group for the Advancement of Psychiatry, August, 1964).

the total family's survival. Healing of one family member resulted in the illness of another. If one member was an isolate and a scapegoat, his removal, or change in the interpersonal configurations that did not permit him to be a scapegoat, resulted in the family locating another scapegoat.

Interest Alliances

While affectional or emotional affiliations are by definition based on personal preference and feeling of association and attachments, interest alliances are more cognitive or intellectual, yet they also carry emotional tones. Interest alliances tend to be based on common experience or knowledge. They may be categorical similarities such as sex, age, marital state, race. People may join together on the basis of some perceived similarity, such as "we men have to stick together," "the blacks had better agree on issues," the "social workers must stand against the doctors or vice versa." Interest alliances may exist on the basis of reference groups, economic background, or political, religious, or ethical ideological beliefs. People may also identify with each other on the basis of common interests in work, sports, hobbies, and skills.

Interest alliances frequently shift and change in the course of a session related to the issue under consideration or the activity of a group. On the other hand, they may make for strong factional divisions in a group that play into all of the other processes of deliberation and decision making. For instance, a task group working on a problem may arrive at an issue where there is strong division of opinion. Alliances and divisions around strong differences may begin to emerge on bases such as philosophical differences, youth versus age, black versus white, or minority-majority status, which have nothing to do with the problem under discussion.

Stark subgroup divisions on the basis of common concerns or shared concerns usually appear in community planning or citizen-action groups where composition is based on representation of various segments of the community. In the course of the deliberations, alliances will appear on issues and group members may line up the forces for and against an issue, not on its merits alone, but through special interests of common reference groups, such as voluntary vs. public services, volunteers vs. professionals, businessmen vs. laborers, black vs. white.

In a therapy group, a person may register a sense of persecution and blame it on his ethnicity or sex. Although the persecution may be due to his behavior, he may find himself supported by other group members who feel minority role status or sex role identity, or discrimination.

Thus, a group member may project his failures on the fact that he came from a poor family rather than his own behavior which gets in his way of success. Other group members who actually came from poor families or who have felt discrimination may tend to ally themselves with this person in blaming external forces rather than helping him look at his own problem. These examples illustrate the alliances that may form on the basis of interests or qualities in common rather than personal affection.

Types of Relationship

Generally the subgroup formation within a group includes pairs, triads, foursomes, and isolates. Some groups as large as five may operate as a total unit, but generally there are subdivisions among the members that become patterned and begin to condition who addresses whom, who sits together, who comes and leaves together, and even who may meet or talk together outside of the group.

Simmel [24] originally developed extensive theory about dyads and triads and his theories have since been tested by a number of modern social researchers.

Diadic relationships are of several sorts. They include mutual pairs where the give and take between the people is of almost equal strength and the givens are similar or complementary. Secondly are the courtship pairs, that is, one is seeking and the other

[24] George Simmel, "The Number of Members as Determining the Sociological Form of the Group," *American Journal of Sociology*, VIII (1902–1903), 1–46.

is being sought after, usually with certain deliberate behaviors on the part of both. Courtship pairs are not necessarily two sex pairs, but people may court each other for various reasons or interests, if one has something which the other one wants. The desired quality may be status in the group, or outside of it, desirable personality traits, material things, skills, or interests. The one being courted may also enjoy the courtship or the "taming process" as St. Exupery [25] referred to it in *The Little Prince*. In the beginning, some of the courtship or "taming" behavior may accompany any relationship. In a group, if it persists and becomes part of the group experience, the pair may be set apart by others and may even establish some rivalries with other group members.

The third type of pair is dependency-dominance, where one leans and the other controls. In group deliberation the dependent one, while he may be meeting some of his personal needs, may not be totally free to express his own opinions. He may wait until he gets the appropriate cues from his partner to participate, or he may let his partner do all of the participating, while he sits by and nods approvingly.

Diagrams of Pairs

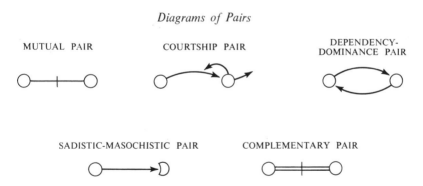

MUTUAL PAIR   COURTSHIP PAIR   DEPENDENCY-DOMINANCE PAIR

SADISTIC-MASOCHISTIC PAIR   COMPLEMENTARY PAIR

A fourth type of pair is the sadistic-masochistic combination of one who needles the other until attacked and then takes it and seems relieved by it. These are the attacked and attacker. In some pairs the behavior is at a verbal level with emotional responses.

[25] Antoine de St. Exupery, *The Little Prince* (New York, Reynal and Hitchcock, 1943).

With others, as in children's groups, it may occur at a physical act-ing-out level; poking, tripping, jumping at, or other physical abuse. Sometimes this pair may be referred to as pairs of enemies, people who are always fighting, but who are nevertheless constantly and consistently together, and thought of together by others, and are satisfying each other's needs, however destructive. This kind of pair may also be harmful to the group if members align themselves with one or the other.

Finally are the complementary pairs similar to the mutual ones. The qualities and traits of one supplement the qualities and traits of the other. The valence between the two may not be as equal as mutual, but there is a blending of differences that makes for the at-traction and persistence.

Triads

Triads have a different quality from the dyads in that should one leave, there would still be a group of two, while in pairs if one leaves, the other is alone. Also, as Simmel [26] theorized, in a triad there is always the potential for the relationship of two to be stronger and one to be left out. Like the pairs, there are several va-rieties of threesomes:

First is the mutual harmonious threesome where there is equal mutuality and similar or complementary quality of contribution. Sometimes each offers a quite different contribution which sup-ports or plays into the other. Thrasher [27] reported finding some of these balanced triads in gangs, and Strodtbeck [28] found them in some three-person families.

Secondly is the triad characterized as the mediator and two be-tween whom there is conflict. In this type of threesome, the roles become diffused and the one is constantly trying to serve to bring together or bridge the difficulty of the other two.

[26] Simmel, "The Number of Members as Determining the Sociological Form of the Group," *American Journal of Sociology*, VIII (1902–1903).

[27] Frederic Thrasher, *The Gang* (Chicago, University of Chicago Press, 1927).

[28] Fred L. Strodtbeck, "The Family As A Three-Person Group," *American Sociology Review*, XIX (1954), 23–29.

Third is the two rivals for one. Two have a single interest, which is the other one, and therefore are constantly attempting to outdo one another for the attention of the third, and each is trying to attract the third one. Mills [29] cites the two suitors for the same girl who have similar interests in the same object, but their goals are competitive not common.

Diagrams of Triads

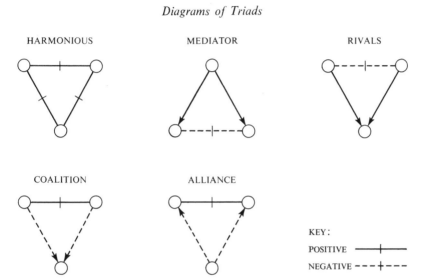

Fourth is the two-person coalition against one, who are ganging up on one. In this case, the one probably is about to leave the triad unless he has a need to be the brunt of the attack. Children sometimes ally against a parent, two students against the instructor.

Fifth is the two-person alliance as a protection against the attack of a third who is thought of as "the enemy."

Foursomes

Foursomes generally divide into two pairs, but they sometimes shift to three and one and they sometimes remain a close four-per-

[29] Theodore Mills, *The Sociology of Small Groups* (Englewood Cliffs, N.J., Prentice-Hall, Inc., 1967).

son mutuality, and sometimes there is partner swapping, or shifts in identification, or alliances within the pairs of the foursome.

Isolates

The social isolate is the person who is present but generally ignored by the others. He does not seem to reach out to others, or he reaches out but is rejected. His lack of affiliation with others in the group may be due to lack of capacity on his part to get along with others, or he may differ in values, beliefs, and life-style from the others enough to be a deviant. He is not generally the scapegoat, for if he were, he would be getting attention, however negative. The true isolate is ignored, his contributions go unnoticed, his opinions are not asked for.

Especially in groups of five or more, individuals may be part of more than one pair, triad, or foursome for various activities, interests, or decisions. It is out of these many subgroups and their interlocking relationships that the networks of interpersonal relationships of the total group are established, roles are defined, and group functions undertaken.

These types of patterns, then, generally reflect the internal affiliations of members on an affective or interest basis.

Status Rating

Another type of internal organization is the status rating process. Shepherd [30] states that members of a small group are usually differentiated by rank, a concept referring to man's position in the group relative to other members. Within any group that exists over a period of time, people begin to develop a status hierarchy, ranking each other as higher or lower, giving higher esteem to some rather than others. As in any human process, a person's status or ranking within the group may shift within the activity. A person who has acquired a fairly high rating within the group on the basis

[30] Shepherd, *Small Groups.*

of his functioning may gain or lose his position because of a particular act in the group, or information about him introduced to the group, or sometimes his behavior outside of the group.

Status in the group, the process of ranking and rating of members by each other goes on at all times in the process of group functioning. Hopkins [31] defines rank as the "generally agreed upon worth or standing of a member relative to other members." He suggests that the status of a member "derives directly from the group interaction system and is obtained by considering the differences among the members with respect to each other." Golembiewski [32] defines status similarly as the relative position on a group roster, ordered with respect to the comparative degree to which they possess or embody some socially approved or generally desired attribute or characteristic. While Berelson and Steiner [33] refer to status as a rough ranking of the members, implicit or explicit, they further link the rating to the extent that the person reflects or realizes the group norms and also his provision of services which the group needs. Bales [34] associates a member's status in the group as the degree to which he has access to resources needed by the group, the degree to which the member has control over others, the degree to which the member shows identification with the group, and the degree to which the person has prestige or status.

These definitions tend to leave status to an acquired position within the group based either on desirable qualities or contributive behavior. Status may also be derived from sources outside of the group. Thus a person may bring prestige to the group on the basis of his high ranking or highly valued behavior elsewhere in the social system. The group may benefit by his pre-eminence elsewhere. Likewise, he may bring low status to the group because he is low-ranked elsewhere, and his presence may cast a negative reflection on the group.

[31] Terence Hopkins, *Exercise of Influence in the Small Group* (Totowa, N.J., The Bedminster Press, 1964).

[32] Robert T. Golembiewski, *The Small Group* (Chicago, University of Chicago Press, 1962), p. 118.

[33] Bernard Berelson, and Gary A. Steiner, *Human Behavior* (New York, Harcourt Brace Jovanovich, Inc., 1964).

[34] Bales, *Interaction Process Analysis*.

It should be noted then that the basis of rating of members may be relevant to the group's purposes and functioning but also not relevant. Dependent on the particular activity of the group, or its period of development, his status may differ. Relevant factors may include the degree to which the person reflects and carries out the values and the goals of the total group or is effective in helping the group to move toward its objectives. Status which is not relevant to group purposes may be derived from a person's association with other high status persons within the group or the capacity to influence high status people. The best friend of the chairman, or a person thought to be a special friend of the worker, may be rated high, not in his own right, but because of his association. Other nonrelevant factors given status may include such things as age, sex, race, ethnicity, social position, or occupation. Seniority confers prestige in certain groups, while in others youth brings higher status. In a racially segregated society, race carries differential status. Men may be more prestigious than women in certain groups or vice versa. Members in esteemed occupations, such as medicine, law, or business, are more prestigious than members in teaching, nursing, or skilled trades in some groups. In groups that exist for leadership training, therapy, or community action, the member's occupation has no relevance, but his position in the ranking in the group will be based, at least initially and sometimes throughout the life of the group, on his occupational status derived elsewhere.

To the extent that the group's objectives are vague, undirected toward any special interest, and purely social, the ranking will be based on personal characteristics of amiability, charm, and personality, according to Berelson and Steiner.[35] If the group has a clear contract and clear direction, the ranking or status hierarchy which evolves on the basis of group purpose will be relevant and pertinent to appropriate group functioning.

Status ranking within the group effects the functioning, contribution, and participation of all of the members. In fact, those who are able to assume or achieve leadership, to give the group direction, and to help the group move toward its goals, depends upon the

[35] Berelson and Steiner, *Human Behavior.*

ranking process. Homans [36] found that the higher a man's rank in the group, the more closely he conforms to the norms, but he also has the most leeway in conforming. That is, his nonconformity is either overlooked or his deviancy becomes the norm for the group. He also noticed that the higher ranked members had more interaction with people outside of the group. Berelson and Steiner [37] found that the highest ranking and most secure members in the group were most central to the group activity and most influential, while at the same time they were most free to express their disagreement with the group inside and out. The lowest ranked were likely to disagree only privately and to conform in public. Those who were somewhere in the middle were likely to agree in both public and private so as not to risk loss of status. Golembiewski [38] observed that the high status members tended to communicate more with each other than with low status members.

Blau [39] studied the manner in which a new member gains status in an already existing group. He observed that the newcomer seeks acceptance by attempting to impress others with his good qualities and his attractiveness to them. The more impressive the newcomer appears, the more reluctant the members are to accept him. The attractiveness of the person may constitute a potential threat to established relationships and the existent status hierarchy. Members become defensive and suspicious and the more the new member attempts to impress the members, the more unapproachable they may be. Blau concludes that becoming accepted rests on the capacity of the newcomer to impress others with his good qualities while he is demonstrating his approachability with well-chosen modesty.

Status is a factor to which the social worker needs to be sensitive. He carries a special status by his expertise in his profession, but he may enter any group with an additional predetermined sta-

---

[36] George C. Homans, *Social Behavior: Its Elementary Forms* (New York, Harcourt Brace Jovanovich, Inc., 1961).

[37] Berelson, and Steiner, *Human Behavior.*

[38] Golembiewski, *The Small Group.*

[39] Peter M. Blau, "Theory of Social Integration," *American Journal of Sociology*, LXV (1960), 545–56.

tus due to his age, sex, or ethnicity. For instance, in certain segments of society, regardless of his expertise and facilitating role or
capacity, a social worker may not have very high status. He may
need to demonstrate his helpfulness before he moves out of a low-
status position in the group. He may find with teenagers or young
adults he cannot know anything if he is over thirty, until he can
achieve an acceptable status. A woman may have to demonstrate
her competency in order to be acceptable in a community organization or development committee. However, regardless of ascribed
status, a person can achieve a different status through behavior.

When a social worker enters an already existing group, a family,
a gang, a neighborhood clique, or when he replaces another
worker in an ongoing group, he may well consider the findings regarding the acceptance of the newcomer in the group.

Leadership and Organization

Bales [40] discovered that in any group there emerges task or instrumental leadership and socio-emotional or affective leadership. The
task leadership facilitates the work. It helps to organize and divide
the labor, specify the goals, and move the group toward achieving
its goals. The affective leadership, on the other hand, focuses on
feelings, mediating differences, soothing ruffled tempers, supporting members, and helping them feel good. Group members rate the
socio-emotional leaders higher than the instrumental leaders. Socio-emotional leaders were more popular. Usually the two roles are
not carried within the same person. A popular person who is a
good socio-emotional leader of the group is sometimes elected or
moved to a formal role in which he has an instrumental function,
and he ceases to be able to deal with the emotional components
and must focus on getting the job done. Whether the socio-emotional role and the task role can be incorporated in one person
may depend also on the size of the group and the need for differentiation or the closeness of the members, as well as the capacities
of the person in the leadership position.

[40] Bales, *Interaction Process Analysis.*

In therapeutic groups where the worker tends to be central, in educational groups where the instructor has a central role, in planning groups with an appointed chairman and staff worker role, indigenous leadership probably will emerge from the participants in the informal structure. People will naturally take on helping and facilitating roles and others will turn to them. It is rare for this phenomenon not to happen in a group of any duration. In fact, any group which does not evolve some internal leadership is either totally captive by assigned or designated leadership, or it is moving toward chaos and disorganization—or it may never have organized. Internal leadership may shift from activity to activity or with the passage of time in a continuing group, but it is almost always there when there is continuity of attendance.

Hollander [41] states that "persons function as leaders in a particular time and place and there are both varying and delineating conditions. . . . There are several pathways to leadership, sometimes from higher authority, and other times from consent and sometimes both." Hollander states further, "leaders are made by circumstances even though some come better equipped than others."

Designated chairmen, captains, coordinators, or specified officers are known as formal leadership. Any group with an assigned social worker has formal leadership to the extent that the worker has a specific and assigned role recognized by the group, the members, and the setting. Formal leaders—including the worker—are people in designated positions who are expected to accept special responsibility in the group by virtue of their positions. They achieve their positions either by election, appointment, self-appointment, inheritance, or following a line of succession, volunteering, group consensus, or by chance.

Where there is formal leadership structure in the group, relationships become organized into well-defined positions with clearly spelled out roles and functions. These roles require consciously coordinated effort and interaction in relation to group goals. The functions are overt and avowed.

All groups do not have formal structure. Some groups do not

[41] E. P. Hollander, *Leadership, Groups, and Influence* (New York, Oxford University Press, 1964).

have a designated chairman, captain, or other coordinating person. Such groups do not necessarily lack leadership however, and either have emergent indigenous leaders or rotating leaders for different functions or actions. When a social worker enters he brings a formalized role with defined functions.

The informal leadership emerges out of the group due to the capacity of one or more members to stimulate the group, mobilize action, synthesize thinking, or otherwise control the group. He may acquire the leadership position through special ability to lead or inspire the response of the members to him. Sometimes the informal structure within a group may not be recognized by all members nor by those outside of the group, and yet it functions to facilitate group action.

Sometimes there are competing forces of informal leadership within groups. Such structure may tend to split or disintegrate the group unless it can be brought into the open, recognized, and dealt with. Competing leadership may develop factionalism and friction within the group to the extent that the differences cannot be bridged.

In characterizing leadership, Hollander [42] states that "leadership has competence in providing for some group function, linked to the social forces at the time and place. If he meets the function as related to the group purpose, he is likely to become influential." He states further that the individual, to become a leader, must be in the group sufficiently long to develop in others a degree of trust or esteem for him and to take his helpful role.

The function of leadership,[43] whether formal or informal, is to facilitate the group's achievement of its goal, to keep it on the focus, to provide for a division of labor or responsibility, or, in other words, to see that all members have an opportunity to engage in the group process, appropriate to their capacity and interest. This may mean the assignment of duties, responsibilities, and to distribute power. He must help to establish relationships between individuals and subgroups or at least their roles. Thibaut and Kelley [44]

[42] *Ibid.*
[43] Cecil A. Gibb, "Leadership," in Lindzey, ed., *Handbook*, pp. 877–920.
[44] Thibaut, and Kelley, *The Social Psychology of Groups.*

refer to the desirability of centralizing some functions and distributing or delegating others.

The amount, kind, and functions of leadership in any group will, of course, be related to size. Larger groups need more organization. Smaller groups need less leadership where decision may be made and carried out by the whole. This was discussed in Chapter Six. Similarly, group purpose determines necessary leadership. A committee may need a chairman and a secretary. Groups with more complicated tasks may have highly organized structures. A therapeutic group may need beyond the therapist only a spokesman, if that, or an initiator. Other leadership roles may be picked up by members. For instance, group members may assume tasks of room arrangement, procuring coffee, initiating the discussion, clean up after the session.

Coyle [45] reflects upon how the surrounding culture also may influence the style of leadership structure. Some groups imitate the pattern of open elections of officers, or highly structured leadership organization which is not necessary or appropriate for the type of group or the age and capacity of members, but is the custom of the setting. Other groups that need a minimum of organization may attempt to operate by consensus, and by the group of the whole, when it would be better to differentiate leadership.

According to Coyle [46] an unauthorized or subversive leadership and organization may appear in groups where members feel they cannot gain access to the decision-making process. This may be particularly true when the group has a highly controlling or autocratic leadership either in the formal or the informal system. Unauthorized or competing leadership may occur when an individual or a subgroup feels the best interests of some members are not being met by the actions and administration of the group. When the use of the usual channels does not bring about the kinds of changes which the member or the subgroup hopes to achieve, a counter organization may be established to work on these matters. The result of such an organization process may be to eliminate the present

[45] Coyle, *Group Work with American Youth.*

[46] Grace L. Coyle, *Social Process in Organized Groups* (New York, Richard R. Smith, 1930).

leadership by one of many methods, or may be to set up a counter organization process that ultimately splits off into another group. Although subversive and unauthorized leadership and organization may be destructive of the original group, a group that has leadership which is too strongly controlling may find it necessary to use this means to establish free discussion and decision making. The technique of organizing unauthorized leadership structure to counteract an existing structure becomes widely used in some aspects of community organization focused on system change.

Establishment of Roles

All of these types of internal organization and interpersonal relationships—affective, interest ties, status rating, and leadership —result in patterns of structure which create roles for all of the group participants. People functioning within the group begin to establish roles for themselves, and groups develop expected roles for members.

Roles, as defined by Linton,[47] are expected behaviors within a given social situation. Within any social organization there are various positions or statuses and with each of these positions are expected behaviors, a collection of rights and duties. When the individual is performing these rights and duties and expected behaviors, he is performing his role. As the group develops, the interaction process will differentiate specific roles for the various members. In a social work group with a worker present, there is already a role defined by the agency and understood by the worker who is performing it, but the group member will only understand the worker's role and come to accept it and function in relation to it as he hears the role described and defined, and experiences the worker performing in it.

Roles for the members will begin to develop when the group is in operation. Roles are related to the expressions of individual needs in the affectional ties, status rating, interest alliances, and

[47] Ralph Linton, *The Study of Man* (New York, Appleton-Century-Crofts, 1936), pp. 113–19.

leadership organization. Roles like group clown, or the overactor, or the silent one may emerge. There will also be roles in relation to the group development and functioning, the initiator, the mediator, the promoter, the denoter. Benne and Sheats [48] made a list of group roles which closely resemble the Bales categories. They are as follows: energizer, who prods the group to action; information seeker; information giver; initiator; contributor; elaborator; opinion giver; evaluator; critic; group builder and group maintainer; harmonizer; expeditor; and encourager.

As people function in certain of these roles within the group they will come to be expected to function this way and begin to create particular statuses for themselves in relation to each other. Thus the group members may learn to wait for the initiator to initiate, or the mediator to mediate. When one person has established himself in a particular role and others have accepted it, it is possible that no one else will pick up on this particular role. When a role is vacated by absence or loss of a member, the group may feel it intensely and suffer in its functioning until the role is picked up by someone else.

Thus there may be interpersonal group roles, and there may also be subgroup roles in relation to the smaller configurations of dyads and triads as described in the affective and interest alliance portions of this chapter. Members may serve each other's personality needs for unconscious purposes, as siblings, parents, children in the group functioning. The total group may accept or reject this type of role behavior without being aware of the roles that are being played. Group leadership may become a symbol of authority for some of the group members who respond to the role, but not to the person in the role.

The group sometimes establishes certain individual roles for a member which the member may or may not request by his behavior, such roles as scapegoat, the person upon whom the group may place its discomforts, or the ego ideal, the person endowed with all of the group members' expectations. These roles are dysfunctional for members when they are not free to be themselves.

[48] Kenneth D. Benne, and Paul Sheats, "Functional Roles of Group Members," *Journal of Social Issues*, Vol. IV, No. 2, (1948), 41–49.

One danger in any establishment of roles within the group, whether related to individual functioning, to group functioning, to task achievement, or to fulfilling group members' needs individually or collectively, is the establishment of stereotypes. A person may be so typed within the group that he cannot move out of the set of expected behaviors. Thus he may be caught in a type of behavior he cannot change and his participation and contribution may be limited. For instance, the person who has become the clown may not be able to make a serious and substantial contribution to the group because regardless of what he says, everyone laughs. If one person has established a high status as the initiator, others may not be able to initiate for fear of threatening his position. If one has established himself in a dependency role in a pair or subgroup, he may not be able to function freely until he gets cues from his subgroup partner. Another kind of example is the person who has become typed "the good mother" in the group so that she can never express anger, boredom, or frustration with her mother role.

Mills [49] concluded from an examination of the research on the various types of interaction process "that a newcomer entering a group is likely to be cast into a behavioral role and to play that particular part whether he and others are aware of it or not. This role is likely to affect his view of the group. . . . what he can and cannot do, and how he feels about himself and others."

In social work groups, the functions of the social worker in the emergence of such a structure and the creation of roles may be to reinforce those roles which are consistent with group organization and the pursuit of the group goals, and to discourage those which are hindering individual and group development for the benefit of each. The group actually operates as a result of the structure and functioning of members in roles in relationships.

Communication Patterns

The fifth type of interpersonal relationships and internal structure is the structure of the communication pattern that evolves. All

[49] Mills, *The Sociology of Small Groups*, p. 65.

other interpersonal patterns, the interaction process, the affective process, the interest alignments, and leadership patterns are dependent upon communications, verbal and nonverbal. But there are also patterns of relationships that are based primarily on communication, or who talks to whom, who sends messages to whom, and who receives messages, what they hear, how they hear it, and how they interpret what they hear, or who understands whom.

Communication is the interaction by symbols through which people convey meaning to each other, stimulate each other, and react to each other. A certain minimum of communication is essential for the group's existence, because without it nothing else can happen among people.

The initial research in this area, much of which was done by Bavelas [50] and his associates, was based primarily on spoken and written language. Bavelas also emphasized the giving and receiving messages in various patterns. Somewhat later there was research on nonverbal communication, pictures, sounds, and appeals to the senses. There followed study of the subliminal—the appeal to the unconscious or preconscious through a combination of sight, sound, feel, smell, taste, suggestion, and perception.

Marshall McLuhan [51] and his associates suggest that the various communications media that exist today, television, radio, newspapers, magazines, and advertising instruments, engage people in a total emersion and involvement with each other and with the environment. He suggests that people who grew up in a world of television and radio have become used to engaging with all of the senses of sight and sound, feeling and touch, and emotion, and of screening in and screening out certain stimuli and responses. This factor conditions the expected behavior of group interactions.

Current experiments in group or interpersonal involvements such as some sensitivity training, encounter groups, and T groups make a deliberate and conscious effort to use the concept of total involvement and communication of people with each other.

[50] Alex Bavelas, "Communication Patterns in Task-oriented Groups," in Cartwright and Zander, eds., *Group Dynamics*.

[51] Marshall McLuhan, *Understanding Media* (New York, McGraw-Hill Book Co., 1964).

Communication has always been a central part of social work practice, since the helping process is by and large based on verbal means. Within group practice there has been emphasis, not only on talking and discussion, but also on interacting with nonverbal program activities which convey meanings and feelings, and relationships through action.

Diagrams for Patterns of Communication

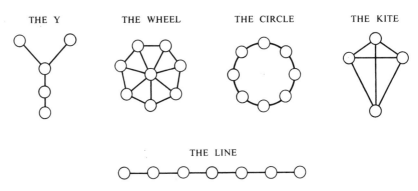

The social psychological research on communication by Bavelas [52] and his associates has suggested that there are patterns of communication such as: the Y, the circle, the wheel, or the kite, which locate key centers of information and directions from which this information proceeds.

From these patterns Leavitt [53] concluded that the location of a person in the physical arrangement of the group affects the rate of communication and the patterns of interaction. For instance, one's position in the communication pattern affected his chance of becoming a leader, as well as one's satisfaction with the group and the role one takes in the group. The position also affected the quantity of one's contribution and the use the group made of one's contribution. People tend to address those who are directly across from them; they have easier eye contact and nonverbal response.

[52] Bavelas, "Communication Patterns," in Cartwright and Zander, eds., *Group Dynamics.*
[53] Harold J. Leavitt, "Some Effects of Certain Communication Patterns on Group Performance," *Journal of Abnormal and Social Psychology,* XLVI (1951), 38–50.

On the other hand, informally, they may address, whisper, pass notes to, or otherwise contact the person on either side of them. Therefore, people may choose to sit next to others with whom they have easier informal contact and communication.[54]

According to the findings of Leavitt [55] it may be concluded that the leader (formal or informal) who remains located in a central position will keep the flow of group thinking and deliberation proceeding through him, with himself as a moderator. If he wishes to move to a less central position, or peripheral to the group, he locates himself off to one side of the central activity of the group, and encourages direct communication between and among others rather than through himself.

The position in the communication system refers to seating arrangement in a group session, but it also refers to position in the process. For instance, the leadership person who keeps a close hold on all activity and interchange between or among members, who requires that all matters be checked with him, who firmly enforces penalties, or is critical of any interchange of which he is not advised, if not engaged, will keep himself central to the group. The leader who delegates, who encourages members to go off and work by themselves, who frees the participants to talk with each other becomes more peripheral to the communication system. In the former process, the leader will use considerable direct contact and confrontation with each member and every subgroup. His communication system will be considerably more formal. In the latter, the leader will rely on informal communication, feedback, casual encounters, and will assume that the networks between and among members will get information back and forth.

Other research indicates that the people who speak the most frequently and have the highest number of contributions also receive the greatest number of responses.[56] About half of a person's contributions are directed to the group generally and half to individual

[54] Edward T. Hall, *The Silent Language* (Garden City, N.Y., Doubleday & Co., Inc., 1959).

[55] Leavitt, "Some Effects of Certain Communication Patterns on Group Performance," *Journal of Abnormal and Social Psychology*, XLVI (1951).

[56] Hare, *Handbook*, p. 277.

members. Once the status of a person is established in the group, it will affect his participation and his communication patterns, but his participation, of course, establishes his status in the group in the first place to a large degree.

Another aspect of the research [57] on communication which comes from electronics also is related to interpersonal relations. This is the effect of static and interference in the process. There can be actual noise, distractions from outside the room, street or sky noises that block or interfere with hearing. But there is also the interference inside the room of the behavior of members and their attitudes or feelings. Something about the personality, style, or appearance of one or more of the members may interfere with their being heard—or may even interfere with others being heard. Behaviors, such as whispering, note passing, passing of glances between subgroups of pairs or triads, may not only interfere with the participation of those engaged but also may interfere with others. It has been noted that one silent person in a group, or one person who appears to be bored or uncommitted to the group purpose, may interfere with the interaction of the entire group.[58]

Stereotypes which members hold about each other, or even about themselves, may render a free flow of messages practically impossible. For instance, if certain group members are thought to be obsolete and out of date, or too youthful and impetuous, what they say, no matter how significant, will not be heard by those holding the stereotypes. The effect is the same as static in radio and TV, the irrelevant noise interferes with passing or receiving a clear message. On the other hand, sometimes because people have to strain extra hard to hear and to understand, may mean that they finally understand better.

The generation of people who grew up to study with radio background, the next generation that studied with the television set on,

[57] G. A. Heise, and G. A. Miller, "Problem Solving by Small Groups Using Various Communication Nets," *Journal of Abnormal and Social Psychology*, XLVI (1951), 327–36; M. E. Shaw, "Some Effects of Irrelevant Information Upon Problem Solving by Small Groups," *Journal of Social Psychology*, XLVII (1958), 33–37.

[58] Edward T. Hall, *The Hidden Dimension* (Garden City, N.Y., Doubleday & Company, Inc., 1969).

and the following one that learned to work only with the very loud beat of rock music have become used to communicating, taking in and giving out with some kinds of static or interference. Silences seem to crowd such people—whether working alone or participating in groups. Their anxiety seems to come not from too much interference, but from too little.

Much has been done with sound research on musical background, the sound effects behind the presentation of an idea, and the piping of certain types of music into industrial plants, grocery stores, study halls, and doctors' offices to create various desired atmospheres and to shut out certain other sounds. The principle is similar to the use of perfumes, mouthwash, or room deodorizers to cover up certain other odors. These provide an interference. Thus it is in a group that certain verbal and nonverbal media may be used to create an atmosphere that facilitates or hinders communication.[59]

Note should be taken that some people communicate clearer messages to others without words, by the way they present themselves, their dress, their physical manner of walking, standing, sitting, looking. In a group, a person who turns his back on the group, looks out the window, remains silent, taps his fingers, yawns, looks inattentive or bored may say a great deal to the group. The person who overdresses, or looks dressed for a cocktail party upon arrival at the group meeting, or dresses slovenly or informally for a formal group meeting is conveying a message to the others. Such behavior is not always conscious on the part of the one who is behaving, but it frequently is. For some people, their dress, hair style, decoration or lack of it in jewelry is a manner of simple presentation of self without too much consciousness of the image they are creating. For others, every single aspect of dress, hair, and appearance is a deliberate and conscious effort to present a particular image. They labor over it and spend considerable time and energy in planning it. This may be true for people who are color coordinated, immaculate appearing, and for those in disarray, unkempt and informal. They wish to convey a message to others in the group, to create an image for themselves, a set of expectations, and

[59] *Ibid.*

a role. The person whose appearance in color and style is striking and aggressive may want to be noticed, while the person in grays and tans and conservative style may hope to sink into the walls.

Communication in a small group becomes a fairly complex process, affected by internal and external conditions of the group and the particular people who compose the group. The symbols used in communications may be verbal, movements and gestures, slight sounds, or symbolic objects or acts. Verbal symbols may be spoken or written language, including tone of voice, choice of words, and other types of verbal expression. Movements and gestures include body language, hand motions characteristic of particular ethnic groups, or characteristic of internal pressures of the speaker, or deliberately used to emphasize certain words. Slight sounds include giggles, laughs, snickers, tongue clicking, negative, critical, or disapproving sounds. Symbolic objects and acts include pictures, drawings and cartoons, graphic, or such things as statues, flags, crosses, uniforms, or insignia on uniforms. Acts include such things as bowing, kneeling, standing, sitting, saluting. Symbols may also be combined; for instance, the speech with slides or blackboard drawings, or the speech with gestures. The combination of words and body language, such as facial expression, eyes, hands, and tone of voice, makes emphatic expression that may not be consistent with the words. The gesture of sending flowers with the card that conveys the message is another combination of behavior and words to reinforce each other. Some people put considerable interpretation on late arrivals as resistance, early arrivals as anxiety, or on-time arrivals, compulsive. Symbolic behavior in the group probably will be reflected mostly in spoken language, behavior, and the development of rituals around objects and acts.

Symbols may be cognitive or related to knowledge or knowing, emotive or carrying positive or negative affect, connotive or referring to something else, or evaluative carrying some weighting. Cognitive symbols appeal to thought, or intellectual factors, such as an agenda, a set of bylaws, or a constitution. Emotive symbols appeal to feelings, the "the tear jerking" or emotionally stimulating images. One sees these in appeals for funds, campaigns for safety, antiwar promotion, or the use of sex symbols in advertising of various personal products. Symbols of fear also fall into this category with intent of arousing the emotions of anger, hatred, or anxiety as inhibitions or controllers of behavior or association. Connotive symbols refer to something other than the object itself, such as use of colors; red is associated with anger, danger, or political symbolism. The intent is to create associations that will stimulate responses to the symbol rather than the actual associative object or event. Evaluative symbols refer to assessing or putting some weight or value upon an object or act. Raising of eyebrows, making critical or condemning sounds, or sounds of approval, applause, are acts that are evaluative. The appeal is to both reason and emotion. The group leadership or membership may use these various types of symbols of communication to interact with each other. All of these aspects of communication are crucial to the interaction process among group members as they learn to work together and may adopt symbolic shorthand for words.

In any communication system and set of communication relationships in the small group there are both facilitators and barriers to the free-flowing interaction. The more heterogeneous and complex the group, the more barriers there may be, and the more homogeneous, the more facilitating in many instances. One barrier that may occur in any group is a language difference due to ethnicity, professionalism, social class, regionalism, education, or literacy. There may be accuracy or confusion in the use and meaning of words. Slang and certain socio-economic and ethnic in-group language may have different connotations in both the meanings and pronunciation of words. Difficult or complicated words as professional language, or as a reflection of education may set up alliances which cause some to feel inside and others to feel outside in subgroups. People with limited social associations may also have limited vocabularies. People who move almost exclusively in professional circles may develop a technical language not understood by the person outside of his profession. There are also changing meanings and interpretations to words through time such as "black is evil" or "black is bad" to "black is beautiful." Sometimes subgroups of two or three within a larger group may tend to separate themselves from others by using a technical or ethnic language, or have their own "in-group" meanings for things that are not shared with others. Their exclusiveness within larger group conversations will set them apart and cause discomfort on the part of the larger group. It may also result in their exclusion or rejection by the others.

Sometimes difference in language that creates barriers is used without any awareness of setting people apart. Other times it is used with an intent to separate, or increase one's status or prestige in the group, or to establish an exclusive subgroup relationship for one's own security within the larger group.

A second type of barrier to open and free communication may be the establishment of restraints in a hierarchy that does not permit informal talking between certain people or people in certain positions. When the structure is formal, or when certain relationships that are emotionally charged with rivalry, competition, or other inhibitions exist informally, it may prohibit communication between some of the members of the group. Lack of channels for feedback, or the free flow of communications back and forth among members or subgroups, may also set up barriers. Messages which only go one way lack the opportunity for correction. They also lack nurture and the increase in quality of contribution that results from exchange of ideas.

Emotional factors may also serve as inhibitors to communications. For instance, if certain people represent symbols to others, such as the authority, the father figure, the white race, the Negro race, the rightist position, or unions, other people may not be able to participate freely out of their emotional reaction to what these people represent.

While these language differences, structural factors, and emotional factors may provide restraints to free interchange in any size group, they may also be facilitators that will open the communication system. Most groups that are together any length of time begin to develop their own words and meanings, their group language which becomes a shorthand for the members. They develop or adapt meaningful symbols for their own use out of the experience of being and working together. They create instruments such as rules and regulations that may get spelled out in writing as codes of behavior or expectations. They may adopt symbolic figures in persons who have achieved what the group would achieve; the founders, or the leaders, or group members who have left or achieved something special outside of the group.

Groups may also develop certain rituals as communication, such as times and ways of beginning meetings, certain activities before and after sessions, certain ways of responding to members and to leadership, the use of food, the place of meeting, the seating arrangement, and who sits where, or things people bring to each other or to the group. Groups sometimes go through a ritual of a series of jokes or anecdotes before beginning. Groups sometimes adopt a ritual for ending a session. Youth groups, service and religious groups particularly may have a special song, prayer, repetition of some oath or code, which is intended to set a particular atmosphere for the group.

Communication, then, both facilitates and symbolizes group cohesion, the interaction process through which people are joined together, act and react together, and arrive at some coalescence that produces the groupness. When the group forms it will develop a recognizable communication pattern that is unique to itself.

In this chapter we have examined five types of interaction process and interpersonal relationships which develop in any group, affective relations, interest alliances, status ratings, leadership structure, and communication networks. We note that the findings related to these aspects of interaction have been studied by sociometrics, interaction process analysis, and communication research. The social worker finds that his interventions with groups will necessitate his sensitivity to all of these forms of interaction whether he is focused on facilitating groups for treatment of their members or for changing some system external to the group. Patterns of relationships and roles become established as groups continue through time. These patterns then affect individual participation as well as group activity and production. All five of these types of interactions take place simultaneously and influence each other.

DELIBERATION
AND DECISION MAKING
IN THE GROUP

All groups engage in deliberative process and decision making as they take shape through the interaction processes considered in the last chapter. In fact, it is through the activity of thinking together, exchanging ideas, and arriving at some conclusions or decisions that the group organizes and establishes its uniqueness. Decisions are the products of the particular collection of people, not as individuals but as a group. The process of deliberation and making decisions rests upon the interactions, the interpersonal relationships, the communications system, and the individual members' motivation to belong and participate. Yet, some collections of people convene, talk with one another, exchange ideas, relate to a worker, and never engage in a focused discussion which leads to a group decision. Participants may be so focused on themselves, or on a task, that they do not give attention to the group purpose, what they hope to accomplish together, and how they are to proceed as a group. Until the collection of individuals has made some decisions together, it is unlikely that the aggregate has become a group. Surely no group can arrive at a contract until there is some discussion and agreement.

In any deliberative process there is the flow of thought, ideas, and the flow of emotion or feelings. As Bales [1] discovered, the behavior of participants includes both cognitive and affective acts. A continuous stream of thought is sometimes most difficult to achieve, because people are not in the habit of listening to each other, as McLuhan [2] and others in the field of communications have noted. Self-oriented people are inclined to speak what is on their minds without consideration of what else has been said. They follow along in their own line of thinking, stimulated by the contributions of others, but still operating in their own line of thought. Most people either have to be taught or must discipline themselves to learn to listen and to make use of the contributions of others in the flow of ideas. It takes skillful discussion leadership to keep the group members focused on the idea at hand and to work through one idea long enough before jumping to another. Most people believe that they are good communicators, so they are convinced that confusions, misunderstanding, or getting the subject off the track is the problem of someone else.

It has been suggested that each interchange between people begins with the world of ETC.[3] Every person brings to his encounters with others leftover thoughts, ideas, and emotions from what he has just previously experienced and from previous unfinished business with these same people if there have been contacts before. Thus no experience begins totally new for the individual and the group. All deliberative process begins with some antecedents.

[1] Robert F. Bales, and P. E. Slater, "Role Differentiation in Small Decision-Making Groups," in Talcott Parsons, et. al., eds., *Family Socialization and Interaction Process* (New York, The Free Press, 1955), pp. 259–306.

[2] Edmond Carpenter, and Marshall McLuhan, *Explorations in Communication* (Boston, Beacon Press, 1960).

[3] "Communications," *Kaiser Aluminum News*, XXIII, No. 3 (1965). Public Affairs Department, Kaiser Aluminum and Chemical Corp., Kaiser Center, Oakland, Calif.

There is always more to start with than can be taken into account in any deliberative process and there is more to say than can be said. Therefore, people not only see and hear through a screen, but if they are not explicit in their use of words, there is room for misunderstanding, misreading of signs, misinterpretation of implicit meanings, through nonverbal signs as well as words. Ideas are always partialized in the language shorthand of conversation, for no one takes time to fill in all of the detail of any thought, and even if he did, no one would listen to the entire statement. People tend to tune each other out as their thoughts jump ahead on a track stimulated by the first part of the speaker's statement.

People respond to each other, not only through the things that they hear and see but they also respond to their association of those things with the other experiences they have had in life. What they think they heard may be distorted by associations and impressions. Experimentation with tape recorders has shown that people are startled to hear a discussion the second time. Comment was once made, "When you hear two or three eye witness accounts of a single event, don't you wonder about history." Each person sees or hears a somewhat different thing and makes a somewhat different interpretation. He also remembers different parts of what he has seen or heard even within the same group session. Tagiuri, Bruner, and Blake's [4] studies showed that in small groups, interpersonal perceptions were influenced by how people felt about each other and responded to each other. Bruner [5] also concludes that once a person has had his interests and expectations conditioned by his society, he will tend to judge other things that he sees and experiences in light of this conditioning. Thus in small group deliberation, discussion, and decision making there is always room for misunderstanding and conflict as well as for pooling of ideas, thoughts, and feelings into a common plan. Through a careful and

[4] Renato Tagiuri, Jerome Bruner, and Robert Blake, "On the Relation between Feelings and Perception of Feelings among Members of Small Groups," in E. Maccoby, T. Newcomb, and E. Hartley, *Readings in Social Psychology* (New York, Holt, Rinehart & Winston, Inc., 1958), pp. 110–116.

[5] Jerome Bruner, and Renato Tagiuri, "The Perception of People," in Gardner Lindzey, *Handbook of Social Psychology* (Reading, Mass., Addison-Wesley Publishing Co., Inc., 1954), pp. 634–54.

well-managed deliberative process, people may learn to listen, to contribute, and to use each other's thoughts, and to follow a logical procedure for problem solving or help giving.

Another problem that occurs in group deliberation comes from individuals who speak what is on their minds without thought of the effect on the receiver or the recipient of the message. The self-oriented person may have a clear idea in his own mind which he does not put into the context of the hearer or the receiver. The receiver may not have the background and may not know what is in the other person's mind. The emotional tones or the choice of words, or even the tone of voice, or the manner of speaking may convey a meaning that is quite different from the message that was intended. Leadership role in a group deliberative process may, therefore, need to serve a bridging function, to demote certain words, paraphrase ideas, work for linkages between the giver and the receiver, mediate misunderstandings, so that the focus may be put upon the work at hand.[6]

Conversations and ideas must be divided into little pieces in sequences, or as McLuhan[7] has suggested in "linear language," but at the same time there are other supports, such as supplementary actions, facial expressions, body posture, gestures, voice tone, demonstrations, use of diagrams and pictures, which augment and may dramatize what the speaker wishes to convey. The bits and pieces together form the total panorama. Just as the eye can see a great deal more than a binocular lens can encompass, or a camera lens can capture on film, the mind perceives more ideas than the words can express.[8] Thus the spoken contribution to the group deliberation must of necessity be selective. People can learn through group discussion to be selective of those thoughts or comments that make the greatest contribution to the flow of ideas since no one person in a group could possibly say all that is in his mind and still provide

[6] M. G. Preston, and R. K. Heintz, "Effects of Participatory Versus Supervisory Leadership on Group Judgment," *Journal of Abnormal and Social Psychology*, XLIV (1949), 345–55.

[7] Carpenter and McLuhan, *Explorations in Communication.*

[8] Edward T. Hall, *The Hidden Dimension* (Garden City, N.Y., Doubleday & Co., Inc., Anchor, 1966), pp. 42–43.

opportunity for others to say anything, or survive the frustration of having only to listen.

Often in discussions, one individual or several go into more detail than is necessary, interesting, or appropriate, or than the other participants are able to absorb about a particular issue or problem. Although it is incumbent upon the group to discipline itself and control such activity, it may rest with the leadership actually to focus and control such participation.

It should be noted that much participation in the deliberative process is a discharge of energy or an expression of emotions of the participant through the means of words.[9] Thus, "what" he says may be less important than "how" he contributes it and the emotion with which he delivers his message. People may become repetitious as their feelings are aroused in the session and they may use words to release feelings of anger, frustration, affection, or connection with the other participants. Leadership needs to be sensitive to this aspect of the deliberative process also, and to help group members to see what is happening.

While the "self-oriented" person may speak his mind without much regard for others, until he learns to be sensitive to getting his message across, the "other-oriented" person may condition his responses so much to what he thinks other group members, or at least prestigious group members, wish to hear, that he never quite expresses his own views.[10] The studies of Asch or Sherif, referred to elsewhere in this book, show clearly the tendency of many people to say what they think others want to hear, or to agree with the crowd. Enough is known from jury deliberations and other studies of negotiation, compromise and consensus processes to recognize that for any group agreement, people must be influenced by each other and modify their positions. Strodtbeck has shown this process may take place on the basis of reason, logic, and collaborative

[9] Robert Sears, Eleanor Maccoby, and Harry Levin, "The Socialization of Aggression," in Maccoby, Newcomb, and Hartley, *Readings in Social Psychology* (New York, Holt, Rinehart, and Winston, 1958), p. 352.

[10] Leon Festinger, "Informal Social Communication," *Psychological Review*, LVII (1950), 271–82.

thinking, or it may be the result of coercion and pressures.[11] A "Peanuts" cartoon showed Charlie Brown, Lucy, and Linus lying on a hillside looking at the clouds. Lucy says, "What do you see, Linus?" and he responds, "Oh, I see a map of British Honduras, and a Picasso sculpture, and an outline of the Apostle Paul." Lucy says, "What do you see, Charlie Brown?" and he responds, "Well, I was going to say I see a duckie and a horsie, but I've changed my mind." Based on the clues that they have, people often state what they think others expect to hear or refuse to speak because they feel their contribution is insignificant, as compared to the comments of others.

The Festinger studies of cognitive dissonance [12] suggest that people may even contribute thoughts and ideas which they do not believe, if the group situation is such that it seems appropriate to do so. They may even come to believe what they say, if they have to say it often enough, and if the rewards for taking the position are not very great. Festinger's studies indicate that given tangible rewards, people can repeat certain facts or positions that they may not necessarily hold to. But if the rewards are small for taking positions about which they do not believe, they may convince themselves that the position is correct. Deliberation and decision making are linked to the concept of group cohesion. The degree to which a person wants to be part of a group, to belong, to be gratified by those aspects of the group which are attractive to him, will condition how much he will risk what he says in the group. He must weight the merits of speaking what he believes, with what he thinks others in the group believe, if the two are different.[13]

Contributions of individuals in the group will most probably be associated with the opinions or contributions of "significant others" in the group or in one's life, and with the general trend of the discussion in the group. The skilled leader in the group, or social

[11] F. L. Strodtbeck, Rita Jones, and C. Hawkins, "Social Status in Jury Deliberation," *American Sociological Review*, XXII (1957), 713–19.
[12] Leon Festinger, *Theory of Cognitive Dissonance* (Evanston, Ill., Row Peterson, 1957).
[13] Dorwin Cartwright, and Alvin Zander, *Group Dynamics* (3d ed., rev., New York, Harper & Row, 1968), "Pressures for Uniformity in Groups," pp. 139–51.

worker, may need to create the kind of permissive atmosphere, at least initially, that permits a free flow of ideas and acceptance of diversity in both cognitive and affective responses. Once this tone of open and free discussion and participation has been established, it will probably become a part of the group culture and continue throughout the life of the group unless someone disturbs it.

Coyle [14] notes that although a group may be composed of people who have something important in common, or some similarity that provides a good rationale for the group, difference is an ultimate trait. No two persons are completely identical in personality, values, styles of thinking, or beliefs, and therefore, some conflict is destined to be a constant factor in deliberation. People are more alike in their needs, wishes, and expectations than they are in the capacity to move toward agreement. The types of interpersonal substructures, such as pairs and triads based either on emotional attachments or interest alignments, will influence the group process in deliberation and decision making. Rivalries, status seeking, supports, likes, identification, personal ambitions will influence who will contribute, who will capitulate, who will attempt to control, who will put on a special performance in the deliberative process and in helping or hindering the group in making a decision.[15]

From the beginning of a session to the end, or from one session to another, many things occur which have both emotional charge and intellectual content. People may be stimulated to think differently or they may be emotionally influenced to change their minds in the course of group deliberations. Therefore, people do not always remember what they have said, or what has been covered in the course of a group discussion. Periodic summaries are, accordingly, important during the course of a session, at the end of a session, or at the beginning of a new one. Formal groups have minutes. Some groups have found that listening to sections of a tape recording of a previous session to be useful in recall of previous

[14] Grace L. Coyle, *Social Process in Organized Groups* (New York, Richard R. Smith, 1930).

[15] H. A. Simon, and Harold Guetzkow, "A Model of Short and Long Run Mechanisms Involved in Pressures toward Uniformity in Groups," *Psychological Review*, LXII (1955), 56–58.

content. Indigenous or professional leadership may planfully summarize the ideas so that the group may move ahead and not go over the same territory. This procedure is as important for a therapeutically oriented group as it is for a problem-solving or task group, such as a committee. People in a group may feel a certain sense of satisfaction if they are not permitted to roam about in a free association, nondirective fashion, and see their accomplishments. If they can have periodic anchor points, which occur in a review of the content which has been covered or the actions that have been taken, they gain a greater sense of order and achievement. The group itself may be involved in creating the summary rather than having leadership summarize.

The form of collective thinking used in any group will depend upon the purpose of the group, the capacity of members, the size of the group, and the authority of the group to make decisions and take actions. There are several forms of collective thinking for exchange of information, problem solving, provision of help and support, for affecting attitudes of members, and for bringing about change of some system outside of the group. The simplest form is the lecture method, which engages each person in taking in his own content and provides the quickest and clearest way to give accurate information. It has the limitation that unless it is followed by questions and answers, or discussion, it does not give any opportunity for feedback to the lecturer to know whether his message is getting across, nor for the listeners to test out whether they are receiving the message. Hare [16] concludes from examining much research on communication, "When an individual lectures to a group, the effects may be similar to forced one-way communication." Research by McKeachie [17] and others does show that where there is straight information to be given, a well-organized lecture provides better learning than a simple group discussion where confusions may arise from erroneous interpretations of the information pooled through group deliberation. However, where the informa-

---

[16] A. Paul Hare, *Handbook of Small Group Research* (New York, The Free Press, 1962), p. 290.

[17] W. J. McKeachie, "Student-Centered Versus Instructor-Centered Instruction," *Journal of Educational Psychology*, XLV (1954), 143–50.

tion is to be put to use through a changed style of behavior, it has greater effect if group members had an opportunity to talk over the information that they received. Thus, the form of lecture plus group participation may be more effective for group learning. Even in very small groups, the lecture-discussion method may be used for orientation and education when certain specific facts or procedures are to be given.[18]

Another means of imparting information is the use of a symposium of two to five people who express different points of view, discussing, or even debating and engaging audience participation. The panel discussion is another type of information giving, where several persons having a range of special knowledge add to the dimensions of understanding their particular views. Again, there may or may not be group discussion depending on the purpose of information giving. Committees may use this means for fact gathering in their process of problem solving. Therapy groups sometimes request that there be some presentation of information on certain types of problems by one or more experts. Educational groups, whether formal or informal, may have speakers or panels of outside experts or group members who prepare themselves on certain subjects. Even socialization groups or developmental groups may use this approach when they wish to add to their resources through an expert in knowledge or skill, in cognitive ideas or information like sex education, or health, or in skills like ceramics, poetry writing, or basketball. The role of presenter in any of these styles of groups may be assumed by some of the group members, the worker, or visiting experts from outside of the group.

Task-focused, problem-solving groups are usually faced with a process of confronting and clarifying the problem, fact gathering, analyzing, interpreting, proposing a solution, planning, and engaging in appropriate actions. While they may use a speaker, forum, or expert for some stage in fact gathering, they are more inclined to engage the total group in deliberation and decision making in informal or perhaps formal discussion. If they are person-centered problem-focused groups, they may use the same procedure. They

---

[18] Kurt Lewin, *Field Theory in Social Science* (New York, Harper & Row, 1951).

may use the highly structured parliamentary procedures with formal motions and action, or they may follow a flow of informal deliberation. Their consideration will include both the presentation of facts and the expression of feelings, drawing upon experience and many types of actions. They will dispose of their business through voting, mutual consent, reference to other authority. Generally, a problem-solving group has some method of recording its actions through minutes or records.

Where the intent of the group is provision of help to the members, the deliberative process will generally take the form of informal discussion. The problem is presented, and sometimes a specific problem is considered in depth. Sometimes the problem is generalized or universalized by the worker if others in the group have similar feelings or experience to add to it. Many people, when put into a group situation for discussing personal problems, will engage in giving advice to each other, rather than thinking through the problem and considering alternatives from which the person with the problem can draw his own conclusions and plan for action with the support of the group. Direction and control of focus of the discussion must be assumed by the worker until the members learn to engage in a deliberative and problem-solving approach. On the other hand, a skilled social worker must exercise caution not to engage the person with the problem in a dialogue with the worker, with group members looking on. In this latter instance, the other members of the group become passive and the use of group as the instrument of help is lost rather than maximized. The group deliberative and problem-solving process takes longer and the worker's skill becomes that of helping the group to think through possible alternatives as well as offering corrective suggestions when nonhelpful or erroneous suggestions are made. Although this focus on engagement of members is more taxing on both worker and members, this deliberative process does maximize the group effect. It should be the intent in use of group method for dealing with personal change to engage all of the members, otherwise, individual counseling of worker and client would be simpler and quicker, but would not have reinforcing and supportive effect of the group.

When the purpose of the group is educational or affecting attitudes, that is, cognitive and emotional learning or relearning, the group discussion must take into account the authority of knowledge or the expertise of the teacher or those group members who have expertise. The teacher's role is instructor through the informal discussion method and is different from that of a chairman. While he has the responsibility for mediating or moderating the discussion and helping it focus as an instructor, he also has the responsibility for intellectual or knowledge inputs, for correcting erroneous information, for holding to a free flow of discussion, and the use of the resources of knowledge of group members and the widest engagement of group members in use of this knowledge. Research [19] gives evidence that there is greater change in attitudes and incorporation of knowledge when the group members have a chance to work over the content in a group discussion, and they feel better satisfied if they are dealing with more than information. As indicated previously, for orientation or information giving, the lecture does as well. But for information in a different style of behaving, or in attitude change, or use in problem solving or behaviors, discussion combined with lecture, or discussion itself, may produce better results. Therefore, it falls upon the social worker in form of teacher-discussion leader to be able to be expert in the subject matter, but skilled in engaging group members in their own and each other's learning.

Where groups are used for catharsis or talking things out that are full of tension or conflict, the free-floating nondirective discussion may provide the best means.[20] Such a group should not continue too long or too unstructured so that it merely creates more conflict and more tension rather than relieving those. In commu-

[19] See the following studies for example: R. F. Bales, "Social Therapy for a Social Disorder—Compulsive Drinking," *Journal of Social Issues,* I (1954), 14–22; L. Coch, and J. R. P. French, Jr., "Overcoming Resistance to Change," *Human Relations,* I (1948), 512–32; W. J. McKeachie, "Students, Groups, and Teaching Methods," *American Psychologist,* XIII (1958), 580–84; L. I. Mitnick, and E. McGinnies, "Influencing Ethnocentrism in Small Discussion Groups through a Film Communication," *Journal of Abnormal and Social Psychology,* LVI (1958), 82–90.

[20] Irving L. Janis, "Group Identification under Conditions of External Danger," in Cartwright and Zander, *Group Dynamics,* pp. 80–90.

nity situations, as well as personal and interpersonal conflicts, a group may be used to bring people together to talk out their concerns at least as a preliminary step in action about the problem. Getting an expression of the feelings is sometimes an important beginning. But unless the talk moves toward some suggested solution, people may leave feeling more angry and frustrated than before the session. When youth gangs have been warring, family members arguing, people in a community feeling interracial tensions, or individuals feeling anxiety about an impending treatment or about their personal problems, a chance to talk together with others in a free and open atmosphere without too much structure and no decisions to make, at least in the beginning, may provide relief and release. The leadership role in such groups is to facilitate the expression of all sides of an issue, and provide an opportunity for everyone to speak. Sometimes the major emotional issues can be expressed in one session and sometimes it takes more. But ultimately, after talking out their concerns and relieving some of the emotion, people are usually ready to confront the issues and think out plans for what they want to do about the situation whether personal or social. Allport has discussed experiences in helping people to move in looking at problems after they have talked out their anger.[21] The social worker in a situation of this nature may intervene in the deliberative process to help the group to look at various alternatives for themselves, each other, or the social situation.

Decision making in a group may be arrived at by majority rule or taking a vote, attaining consensus or working through to some common agreement, or compromise of the opposing positions. Usually the majority rule vote is reserved for formal types of structures, though sometimes informal groups take votes on things. Attaining a consensus generally takes longer than a majority vote where someone wins and someone loses. Small groups frequently arrive at agreement without formally voting or taking action on an issue. This process is called "consensus." Phillips [22] says, "Some-

[21] Gordon W. Allport, "Catharsis and the Reduction of Prejudice," *Journal of Social Issues*, I (August, 1945), 3–10.

[22] Gerald M. Phillips, *Communication and the Small Group* (Indianapolis, The Bobbs-Merrill Co., Inc., 1966), p. 8.

times consensus is built on agreements about minor points over a period of time. Sometimes it is a major insight that suddenly reveals a solution that all members can accept." He also thinks that "consensus is the result of careful interpersonal communication in which members subordinate some of their personal feelings and desires to demonstrated facts or necessity." He also suggests that consensus does not happen until after much interaction. When a group has worked through together their various differences or an idea or issue, they have achieved a greater sense of groupness than when some have given in to the will of the group. Similarly, a compromise means that someone has yielded to the wishes of others.

As a group is deliberating toward reaching a decision, inputs may come from the members which add to or detract from the decision. Not only are there cognitive and emotional contributions but members also will use various methods of persuasion and influence. People's judgments may be skewed by strong reference groups or subgroups, by high status or low status members, by those with whom one is allied, or by those with whom one differs.[23]

Labeling by negative connotations of people or their ideas may be used in order to discredit them. Other ideas may be given positive sanctions by reference to support of the view of someone of high status in knowledge and experience. Labeling will tend to influence the attitude or opinion of members toward an idea. Leadership may need to help a group to sort out the fact and the merit of particular ideas and separate these from inferences and distortions. He may also need to keep the group pursuing alternatives in cases where they have not done so or want to come to closure too soon.

Group decisions, then, come about as the result of group members' exploring in some orderly manner the various possibilities of alternative issues in the matter under discussion, whether the subject be the selection of group goals, setting criteria for group membership, setting a plan for group action, or deciding how a particular member should proceed in facing a conflict in his life, or preparing for a new treatment form. Having explored the possibili-

[23] Kurt W. Back, "Influence through Social Communication," *Journal of Abnormal and Social Psychology,* XLVI (1951), 9–23.

ties then, through some discussion process, the group may reach a decision. Frequently, decisions made in a group have more influence on the individual than decisions arrived at alone. Lewin,[24] for instance, found that people who had committed themselves in public and to each other held more to their decisions than people who had decided on their own. Thus, group discussion may be very reinforcing and supportive to the group members.

The attitudes and behavior of leadership can have considerable influence on the communication network and the group discussion and decision process, according to Hare.[25] He comments on the implications of the Lewin, Lippitt, and White leadership studies that permissive leaders who managed the discussion process without injection of their own opinions, who operated to protect minority opinions from social influence, increased the probability that the individual with the right solution would be able to convince the majority. The studies of Preston and Heintz,[26] previously noted, indicated that members of groups were more satisfied when leadership kept channels open and participated himself in the group deliberation. Leaders who expressed no opinion created an anomalous and frustrating state of affairs in the group. Actually, in some types of sensitivity training and in some types of therapy, this approach is used in order to create enough frustration that the group and its members are forced into action on their own behalf. It would appear that groups can be as facilitated in learning to deliberate and come to decision if their goals are clear and they can contribute constructively.

Summary

We have examined the deliberation and decision-making process of the group as a major process in group development and continuous functioning. Factors which influenced deliberation, open com-

[24] Lewin, *Field Theory*.
[25] Hare, *Handbook*, p. 288.
[26] Preston, and Heintz, "Effects of Participatory Versus Supervisory Leadership on Group Judgement," *Journal of Abnormal and Social Psychology*, XLIV (1949).

munication, and the capacity of the group to come to a decision include perception of the members of each other, and of the subject matters under consideration, level of group development, degree of self and other orientation of members, level of emotion in the group, the nature of the interpersonal network, process within the group, and functioning of leadership. Deliberation may take many forms, including lecture, discussion, and a combination of these. Decision making in a group may take place through consensus or through a voting procedure depending on size, intimacy of members, and time available. Whether the purpose of the group is problem solving for individual members, or a social situation, it appears to be essential for direction from leadership to facilitate the process and to channel the flow of ideas and feelings.

COHESION

Group cohesion is the development of the feeling of group identity or group spirit, referred to by Cooley [1] as "we-feeling," and by Coyle [2] as "bond." Festinger, Schachter, and Back [3] have referred to cohesion as "the degree to which members desire to remain in the group." Evidence of cohesion appears when the members begin to refer to themselves, each other, and the group as "we" and when they take hold of an idea or problem and work together on it.

Cooley,[4] who first noted this phenomenon, wrote of the feeling of belonging together, of sympathy of the members for each other, and mutual understanding. Freud [5] described the phenomenon of

[1] Charles Horton Cooley, *Social Organization* (New York, Charles Scribner's Sons, 1909).

[2] Grace L. Coyle, *Social Process in Organized Groups* (New York, Richard R. Smith, 1930).

[3] Leon Festinger, S. Schachter, and Kurt Back, *Social Pressures in Informal Groups* (New York, Harpers, 1950).

[4] C. H. Cooley, *Social Organization*.

[5] Sigmund Freud, *Group Psychology and the Analysis of the Ego*, authorized translation by James Strachey (London, International Psychoanalytical Press, 1922).

members' identification with each other and feeling of empathy for each other. Argyle [6] referred to cohesion as a measure of the extent to which members like each other.

The essence of the group as reflected in its cohesiveness is expressed in the way members feel about the rightness or goodness of being together, their pride in belonging, the gratification that the group gives to them and they to each other, and the degree to which they can move and act together with coordination, synthesis, and comfort.

Some of the major studies of cohesion conducted by Festinger, Schachter, and Back [7] focused on determining the nature of cohesiveness, the conditions that bring it about, and the evidences that indicate its presence. Festinger [8] defines group cohesion as "the resultant of all of the forces acting on members to remain in the group." These include the attractiveness of the group by virtue of its purpose or goals, its position in the hierarchy of other groups in its context, the attractiveness of its members or composition, or the degree to which members gain satisfaction or gratification with the group activities and outcomes. Group cohesion embraces the synthesis of satisfactions or fulfillment of member's needs, interest, and expectations that are compounded in the development of "groupness."

Cartwright [9] says that the individual member's attraction to the group will depend upon four major factors: (1) the incentive nature of the group, its goals, program, size, type of organization, and position in the community; (2) the motivation of the person, his needs for affiliation, recognition, security, and other things he can get from the group; (3) the attractiveness of other persons in the group; and (4) if the group serves as a means for satisfying needs outside of the group, that is, helps the person to achieve with the

[6] Michael Argyle, *The Scientific Study of Social Behavior* (London, Methuen Co., 1957).

[7] Festinger, Schachter, and Back, *Social Pressures.*

[8] Leon Festinger, "Informal Social Communication," *Psychological Review,* LVII (1950), 271–82.

[9] Dorwin Cartwright, "The Nature of Group Cohesiveness," in Dorwin Cartwright and Alvin Zander, eds., *Group Dynamics,* 3d ed. (New York, Harper & Row, 1968), pp. 91–109.

others what he could not achieve alone. The composite of all of the individual members' attractions effects the group cohesion.

Attractions on the part of each of the members is, of course, crucial to the coalescence within the group, but cohesion is more than the addition of each person's individual attraction. Cohesion is a group phenomenon, the product of the interaction, the outcome of the other group processes that culminate into a synthesis or an integration of individual factors and the achievement of group factors. Terence Hopkins [10] refers to this phenomenon as "collective identity." Golembiewski [11] formulates cohesion not only as the "stick togetherness" or "member attraction" but also as the coordination of efforts of members and the level of motivation of the group members to do a task with zeal and efficiency. Shepherd [12] has characterized cohesion as the quality of a group that includes commitment, meaning, ability to weather crises, and ability to maintain itself over time.

Evidences that a group has become cohesive, according to Cartwright and Zander,[13] are that attendance remains high, people speak of the group as "we," everyone seems to be friendly, there is expression of loyalty to fellow members, members work together for a common goal, everyone is ready to take responsibility for group tasks, members show willingness to endure unpleasantness or frustration for the sake of the group, and members defend each other and the group against external criticism and attack. Other evidences of cohesion include willingness on the part of a member to put group demands above individual demands or desires. Another evidence of cohesion may be action by the group in expelling nonconformers or deviants, or pressure on these members to conform to the group values and processes.

The members usually create group symbols, endowed with feel-

[10] Terence Hopkins, *The Exercise of Influence in Small Groups* (Totowa, New Jersey, The Bedminster Press, 1964), p. 24.

[11] Robert Golembiewski, *The Small Group* (Chicago, University of Chicago Press, 1962), p. 149 ff.

[12] Clovis Shepherd, *Small Groups* (San Francisco, Chandler Publishing Co., 1964).

[13] Dorwin Cartwright, and Alvin Zander, *Group Dynamics* (2d ed., New York, Harper & Row, 1960), pp. 69–70.

ing about the group, including rituals of induction, initiation, or orientation to the group of new members, or material symbols, such as badges, name tags, special group nicknames. A study by Aronson and Mills [14] hypothesized that people who endured pain, sacrifice, or trouble to achieve something tend to value it more highly than people who achieve the same thing by little or no effort. By virtue of their study, they concluded that people who go through a severe initiation to get into a group will tend to feel a stronger attraction to the group and put a higher value on belonging than those who were not initiated. Thus cohesion in the group may be increased as belonging becomes more attractive or more difficult to achieve. Many groups, once they are formed, establish some sort of induction ritual or testing process through which any new member is expected to pass—induction fees, requirements to learn history of the group, or given bodies of content, such as a statement of group purpose or a code of ethics. While these rituals tend to symbolize the group cohesion, they also help to facilitate the process by standardizing and repeating certain behavior which creates a regularity or continuity and cause the group climate to become familiar.

Symbolic actions which reflect a developing sense of cohesion include such practices as developing a style of seating for which members take responsibility. For instance, the members may rearrange chairs or other equipment in a certain position for the session which become an automatic procedure at the beginning of each meeting. While this behavior is an emergent cultural manifestation, it reflects a sense of order about the group and responsibility which members express in their attachment to the group. Rituals appear around seating location or the "ownership" of certain chairs, places in the room, or places in relation to each other, or the leader, as reflected in the research of Sommer [15] cited in Chapter Six. Groups may establish a practice of regularly beginning on

[14] Elliot Aronson, and Judson Mills, "Effect of Severity of Initiation on Liking for a Group," *Journal of Abnormal and Social Psychology*, LIX (1959), 177–81.

[15] Robert Sommer, *Personal Space* (Englewood Cliffs, N.J., Prentice-Hall, Inc., 1969).

time, punishing those who deviate by imposing fines, or subtly ig-
noring latecomers. At the second meeting of a parent education
discussion group of fifteen people who were not acquainted, one of
the members brought large cards and markers for members to
make name placards. She said that she felt that the group would
feel closer if they knew each other's names and used them. Thereafter, the ritual was established by group members who could not
begin the meeting without distributing the cards which were then
carefully collected after the meeting and given to a member for
safe keeping. One meeting was delayed in beginning, despite the
worker's efforts to start, because the person with the cards was late
in arriving. The procedure had become so much part of group culture that it was an instrument for their operation, as well as a reflection of their togetherness.

If a group exists for long, it may adopt elaborate rituals and
symbols as a reflection of the feeling of belonging, including rituals
for the beginning and ending of meetings. A group that has developed much cohesion may have some sort of dramatic ritual when it
approaches termination. For instance, a committee may plan a dinner for the closing meeting. Workshop and institute groups, parent
education groups, and even therapy groups sometimes collectively
plan a gift or a testimonial speech for the leader or resource person, or may exchange small tokens among themselves. Task forces
may have a ritualized final meeting to evaluate their work, or to
hand over their report to the governing body which established
them. Clubs frequently have parties, classes, summaries, therapy
groups, evaluations. The degree of cohesion may show as the
group faces dissolution and reducing their attraction to each other,
to the group, and to their group achievement. A person leaving a
cohesive group while it continues will probably be shown ritual in
a separation party, or may himself express ritualistic gestures toward the other members.

Groups may be attractive to members without intimate personal
ties binding the members together. There may be forces other than
personal ones, such as program or goals, the prestigious nature of
the group, or the satisfactions of achievement. In fact, the participants may feel deeply committed to the purpose and program of a

group while they do not care particularly about each other. They become coalesced at a high level out of their zeal for achieving their objectives.

Homans [16] speaks of the "pull" factors and "push" factors of group attraction. The "pull" factors are those inside of the group that make it attractive, such as mentioned above, the people, the sense of achievement, the objectives, or even an attractive process such as the feeling that the group can make suggestions and get things done so that people feel good as a result of their time together. "Push" factors, on the other hand, are forces outside of the group that drive people together. Homans cited for example the sense of isolation that gang members felt as alien to their culture and their community. They were held together, not so much by a common bond inside of the group, but as a coalition against a threatening outside world. Some groups are bound together by a common enemy, hostile society or community that cause people to want to cling to each other. Sometimes groups are allied protectively against an autocratic or controlling administrative structure within which the group exists. An assigned leader from outside of the group may provide the external force around which the group will coalesce. A poorly organized collection of people may group rapidly and form a strong cohesion when confronted with new leadership who may be seen as alien.

Conclusion has been drawn by many authors that the Lewin and Lippitt [17] studies of autocratic, democratic laissez-faire leadership showed that democratically led groups tended to have a higher degree of cohesiveness. It may also be concluded that some autocratically led groups tend to coalesce around a rebellion against the control of the leader.

Changes in Group Cohesion

Over time there are changes or fluctuations in the degree of cohesion of the group. As the group forms, it is expected that the cohe-

[16] George C. Homans, *The Human Group* (New York, Harcourt Brace Jovanovich, Inc., 1950).

[17] Kurt Lewin, and Ronald Lippitt, "An Experimental Approach to the Study of Autocracy and Democracy," *Sociometry*, I (1938), 292–300.

sion will increase, but as the group encounters conflicts and read-justments, the cohesion may decrease. To the degree that conflicts are resolved so that the group can get on about its work, the members will draw close together and work together. But to the degree that conflicts are not resolved, the members may remain alienated and separated, and cohesion is lowered.

Members' need for the group also fluctuates. As they grow so-cially, or find their needs satisfied through a particular group, they may move to seek satisfaction elsewhere, pairing off with another member and leaving the group or selecting a new experience else-where. The old group loses its attractiveness and the cohesion di-minishes as the group diminishes. For instance, in the socialization process, at a particular stage in adolescence, the one-sex gang-type peer group no longer gratifies the social needs. Coeducational groups of teenagers or young adults frequently are followed by pairing. Long-term autonomous groups that began in early latency tend to dissolve in late adolescence or young adulthood as mem-bers begin families, move into new occupational associations, and assume civic and social responsibilities through groups. "The old gang" may disappear and be replaced by new types of social and recreational groups centered around the family.

In open-ended groups established for therapeutic purposes, a member may resolve the problems that brought him to the group and therefore may leave it. When a member has achieved social and emotional growth for which the group was established, he is ready to leave the group. As members do leave, the group goes through a process of reorganization and regrouping, and the pro-cess of cohesion also fluctuates. The cohesion of an open-ended group will tend to be low so that new members can enter and old ones leave without destroying the group.

Open-ended groups, where members come and go, will probably be in a constant state of flux in their coalescence. As mentioned previously, the interaction process and patterns must begin over with each addition or loss of a member. Thus, the strength of at-traction and the comfort which emerges from acquaintance and working together will fluctuate. Cohesion tends to be low in open-ended groups. Observation of open-ended groups that continue over a period of time with individual members who remain in the group no longer than six weeks, for instance, in hospitals, correctional institutions, or crisis groups in clinics, some cohesion and group development occurs over time, carried by those who continue even though membership shifts. A feeling of group unity occurs that is passed from members to each other and sustains the group with its additions and losses, even with the shifts in composition.[18]

If the status of the group changes in the hierarchy of groups, or the surrounding society, groups may change in their degree of cohesion. A group that has developed a successful program, has been rewarded or acknowledged as having special merits, may reach a high level of cohesiveness. On the other hand, a group that has failed or that has come in for criticism or negative sanctions from its surrounding culture may be less attractive and therefore less cohesive. Members may resign or drop away or express the desire not to be associated with the group. A task force recommending unpopular procedures may come in for criticism from peers outside of the group. Some members may be uncomfortable about the criticism and leave the group. A group that has been criticized, however, may become a rallying point for martyrdom! The members may cling together, support each other, and elevate the group because of its negative position. It may become stronger in alliance against a common enemy.

Effects of Cohesion

The research of Festinger [19] has shown in a variety of situations that as group cohesion increases, the power of the group over its membership also increases. Thibaut and Kelley [20] found that a group could not induce control over its members greater than the

[18] Robert Ziller, "Toward a Theory of Open and Closed Groups," *Psychological Bulletin*, LXIII (September, 1965).

[19] Leon Festinger, "Laboratory Experiments: The Role of Group Belongingness," in J. G. Miller, ed., *Experiments in Social Process* (New York, McGraw-Hill Book Co., 1950), pp. 31–46.

[20] John W. Thibaut, and Harold H. Kelley, "Experimental Studies of Group Problem-Solving Process," in Gardner Lindzey, ed., *Handbook of Social Psychology* (Reading, Addison-Wesley Publishing Co., Inc., 1954).

strength of the members' motives to belong. Hagstrom and Selvin [21] noted that highly cohesive groups tend to have more extensive group norms and standards resulting in greater uniformity of behavior. Therefore, one may conclude that so long as the group is satisfying and provides a satisfactory experience for its members, so long as it resolves its conflicts and moves toward task achievement and membership gratification, it will be a strong force on the members. If members' feelings about the group are ambivalent, they are dissatisfied or apathetic, they will not be so much influenced by group norms or expected behaviors.

Horowitz [22] has concluded on the basis of the above findings that the more attractive the group the more a person may fear being rejected, since cohesive groups apply sanctions more readily than noncohesive ones. The effect on the individual may, therefore, be one of conformity or carefully adhering to group expectations in order to remain in good standing.

Riecken and Homans [23] equate cohesiveness with motivation of members to take part in the group and to work on the group task, because the cooperative action of the group or the environment can get the individual what he desires or because he values the association with the others for its own sake. If he does not value these, his rank in the group, his interaction with others, and his share in the achievement of the group, or if he can get these elsewhere, he will not mind being rejected by the group. To the extent that any member or members feel this way, the group as a whole will be less cohesive. Frank,[24] considering cohesion in therapy groups, said that there is a force operating with people to attempt to form cohesive groups. He said, "Members strive to make the groups they are in the kind of groups they want to belong to," that

[21] Warren O. Hagstrom, and Hanan Selvin, "Two Dimensions of Cohesiveness in Small Groups," *Sociometry*, XXVIII (March, 1965).

[22] Murray Horowitz, "Conceptual Status of Group Dynamics," in Warren G. Bennis, Kenneth D. Benne, and Robert Chin, eds., *The Planning of Change* (New York, Holt, Rinehart & Winston, Inc., 1961), pp. 284–85.

[23] Henry W. Riecken, and George C. Homans, "Psychological Aspects of the Social Structure," in Lindzey, ed., *Handbook*, p. 817.

[24] Jerome K. Frank, "Some Determinants, Manifestations, and Effects of Cohesiveness in Therapy Groups," *International Journal of Group Psychotherapy*, VII (1957), 53–63.

is, they "try to find bases for mutual attraction." He said further, "A cohesive group with proper standards protects and enhances the self-esteem of its members, fortifies their ability to consolidate and maintain beneficial changes in behavior or attitudes, helps resolve conflicts and facilitates constructive release of feeling." From this he concludes that "the cohesive group not only exerts pressure on the members to change but strengthens their ability to maintain the changes it has helped to bring about." Thus the goal of achieving cohesion in the group can be seen as the means to provide helpful influences for the members.

In a study of industrial groups, Seashore [25] discovered that members of highly cohesive groups showed less anxiety than members of low cohesive groups who felt jumpy and nervous about their work, under pressure to achieve more, and lack of support from the management. The cohesive groups provided effective support for the individual in his encounters with anxiety-provoking aspects of his environment, thus allaying his anxiety. There seemed to be an association between the satisfaction of belonging to a well-formed group and anxiety reduction.

Deutsch [26] found that in more cohesive groups the members made a greater effort to reach agreement and were more influenced by the discussion than low cohesive groups, no matter what the basis of attraction to the group. However, there were certain differences in groups on the basis of attraction. Those who were attracted by liking the other members tended to be more chatty or social. People who were attracted because of the prestige of the group were more cautious and less related to other members. People who were attracted to a group as a means of goal achievement were more impersonal and task-oriented. The implication of these findings suggests an examination of service goals for a social work group, as well as intake, composition, and what may be said to potential members about reasons for belonging.

One additional note may be made with regard to open-and-

[25] S. E. Seashore, *Group Cohesion in the Industrial Group* (Ann Arbor, Institute of Social Research, 1954).

[26] Morton Deutsch, "Field Theory in Social Psychology," in Lindzey, ed., *Handbook*, pp. 181–222.

closed groups and the levels of cohesion that may be desirable and possible. Lasswell and Kaplan [27] state that "a tightly built group significantly means both a difficult-to-enter group and one whose members are closely identified with each other. The less permeable the group, the more value is attached to membership and, in turn, the more intense the adherence to group perspectives."

Further, Van den Haag [28] comments, "the existence of intensive ties among members is often associated with exclusiveness among groups, but where groups accept newcomers readily the bonds which are so easily lengthened often become less stringent." Depending on the purpose of the group then, the desired composition and the ongoing level of group development, it may be more or less desirable to stimulate a high level of cohesion.

Deutsch [29] looked into those factors which would induce or increase cohesion. He found that groups actually could be encouraged to coalesce if it was emphasized to the members that they would like each other, or like the group, or be interested in the task, or that belonging to the group would be prestigious. His study showed the suggestability of the potential members where the group potential was to meet some specific need or interest, which they had.

French [30] noted that people who knew each other before they joined in a group produced more cohesive groups. Obviously, they did not have to go through the process of getting acquainted. However, it might be postulated that some people who know each other in advance would not appreciate being together and might not form a cohesive group because they knew each other. In my study, groups that had a high level of development in the first session showed some losses as they reorganized with a worker present. The intervention of a worker into an already cohesive group may threaten the group at least temporarily. New groups coalesced

[27] Harold D. Lasswell, and Abraham Kaplan, *Power and Society: A Framework for Political Inquiry* (New Haven, Yale University Press, 1950), p. 35.

[28] Ernest van den Haag, *Passion and Social Constraint* (New York, Stein and Day, 1963), p. 100.

[29] Deutsch, "Field Theory," in Lindzey, ed., *Handbook.*

[30] J. R. P. French, Jr., "Group Productivity," in H. Guetzkow, ed., *Group Leadership and Men* (Pittsburgh, Carnegie Press, 1951), pp. 44–54.

quicker with the worker present. For groups with a social worker, it might be more beneficial for group formation to begin with groups where there is no previous acquaintance or attraction.[31]

Deutsch [32] found that cohesion was higher in groups that were rewarded for their cooperation than groups that were rewarded for competition. It would follow that competitiveness is not a quality that promotes sharing, trust, empathy, and support as does the stimulation of cooperation.

Thibaut [33] found that members who felt that their group was consistently high in status and successful tended to form more cohesive groups while those who felt failure and low status had low cohesive groups. It follows that nothing succeeds like success, and people want to be attached to a group and work for it if it is high status or has high value.

Group Morale

Hollander [34] defines morale as "a complex of attitudes towards the total experience of the setting." He says that morale is a psychological state reflecting satisfactions and security.

Group morale or group climate is frequently considered with a discussion of cohesion and sometimes the two concepts are confused. Morale has to do with the feeling tones or mood about the group which come from group experience. Some authors refer to esprit de corp. There is an association between cohesion and morale; however, they do not necessarily rise and fall together. Good feeling will draw members together, poor feeling tends to separate them. High coalescence generally engenders good feeling, while feeling of distance or separation engenders a low feeling. However, a group may sense low morale because of some problem of a mem-

[31] Margaret E. Hartford, "The Social Group Worker in the Process of Group Formation" (unpublished Ph.D. dissertation, University of Chicago, 1962).

[32] Morton Deutsch, "An Experimental Study of the Effects of Cooperation and Competition upon Group Process," *Human Relations,* II (1949), 199–231.

[33] Thibaut, and Kelley, "Experimental Studies," in Lindzey, ed., *Handbook.*

[34] E. P. Hollander, *Leadership, Groups, and Influence* (New York, Oxford University Press, 1964).

ber or of the group activity while still being strongly coalesced. For instance, the death or separation of a member may cause low individual and group morale. The defeat of an action toward which the group has been working may bring discouragement, a distinct loss of morale. At the same time members may be drawn more closely together by the loss. A group may also disband at a very high level of morale because of its achievements, thus its cohesion is low while morale is high. On the other hand, a dip in morale may affect members to such an extent that they wish to get out of the group and cohesion may drop along with morale.

Morale seems to fluctuate in time in the phasing of a group. It does not exist or is low at the initial stages of a group but generally rises rapidly with the hopes, expectations, and anticipation of the members and as the members begin to coalesce. It drops when the initial phase of formation moves into some conflict, or testing, or disappointment, if the group does not meet every expectation. With the resolution of conflicts, the reintegration and the movement toward doing the group's work, morale again picks up. When a group is confronted by termination—if it has had any satisfactions as a group—it will probably have another morale dip.

Other losses in morale come with addition of members or losses of members, though new members sometimes boost morale. It depends on how much readjustment must take place. If a group fails or has difficulty achieving its goals, it will also tend to be demoralized. On the other hand, successes, achievements of individual members which reflect on a group, acquisition of new leadership, establishment of new structure, or even a new image, may be morale boosters.

Size may also be a factor in morale according to Hare,[35] who states that "as a group increases in size and as time is limited in activity, each person has less time for individual participation, morale declines since former intimate contact is no longer possible."

The social worker attempting to improve the morale of a group may seek out ways to help the group feel a sense of success in

[35] A. Paul Hare, *Handbook of Small Group Research* (New York, The Free Press, 1962).

meeting the group goals and to help members feel a sense of satisfaction in meeting individual goals or expectations for the group. Group morale cannot be artificially created or enhanced, it must grow out of actual group experience and feeling, but groups can be facilitated in resolving conflicts, in working together on tasks, on feeling a sense of satisfaction, and on achievement of goals. These actions generally lead to morale building. Furthermore, when faced with losses or defeats, the group may be helped to face these problems, talk them out, and deal with them as a group. This procedure leads to a rallying force to begin anew and to increase group spirit.

Summary

Cohesion, then, is a product of group processes in which individual needs, interests, or expectations for the group are met. The level of cohesion varies with time, the activity of the group, and the members. It is a desirable state for the group to achieve from the standpoint of the development of the group as an instrument of service delivery. Once a group has coalesced it has greater meaning for the members and greater influence on them. A social worker who has interest in stimulating the cohesive process so that the group may be maximized to achieve both the service goals and the group goals will, therefore, consider those factors which lead to group attraction, member motivation, and member satisfaction in the group, and group goal achievement. He will attempt to help members to be attractive to each other, to help them set achievable and interesting goals and tasks, and facilitate a process that is satisfying to the members.

Recognizing the ebb and flow of morale within the time passage and action of the group, the social worker may want to plan for interventions or group activities that will be morale boosters at the times of cyclical low morale or at the times of events that might tend to lower morale. The worker might deliberately wait out the building of high morale to introduce to the group some problem which it might have to confront, but could cope with better when the cohesion and morale were at high levels.

Cohesion is a phenomenon that can be seen to exist through evidences of other group processes that occur when there is a feeling of bond, friendliness, working together, giving high priority to group, and feeling of good morale. It is crucial to the existence of the group. Further, it is a phenomenon unique to groups. Cohesion does not exist in an individual because there are no separate units to be coalesced, and it is difficult to observe in the wider society or community because of the complexity of the organization of these entities. Cohesion, therefore, is the ultimate in achievement of group formation, integration, and entity, and the group capacity to act as a whole. Yet for open-ended groups to which new members may be added frequently, cohesion has to be low enough to permit the addition of newcomers. The phenomenon of losing and adding new members in an open-ended group will in itself prevent cohesion from becoming too high.

GROUP INFLUENCE AND CONTROL AND THE EVOLUTION OF GROUP CULTURE

As a group becomes a cohesive entity with uniqueness among all other groups, creates norms of expected behavior, and develops organization of the relationships between and among the members, it takes on meaning for the participants which has influence and control over them both within and outside of the group. Inside of the group, individuals and subgroups influence each other and sometimes influence the entire group as a result of the significance that they come to have for each other. This influence process has been referred to as group control. Control is defined as the exercise of power or the capacity to influence men and move material to bring about some change.

Hare [1] states that "through social control, behavior is confined to acceptable limits which maximizes the possibility of survival for the individual in the group." In other words, the pressure which is felt by the group member to modify his beliefs and behaviors and the degree to which he responds to this pressure will ensure his remaining within the group and accepting the support which the group has to offer him. Hare classifies these controls as "formal," that is, rules or regulations developed within the group and thereby imposed on the members, and "informal," or social pressures of the small intimate group which may be subtle and not as clearly recognized.

Collections of individuals convened with tasks to perform in each other's presence have shown evidence of interpersonal influence, even though they have not developed a group. The Asch and Sherif experiments referred to earlier showed that people may be influenced by collective pressure of expressed opinions of others even when the collective is not a group in the sense that the concept has been used here. Asch [2] says, for instance, that "confronted with opinions contrary to their own, many subjects apparently shifted their judgments in the direction of the views of the majorities." He concludes, "Apparently the sheer weight of numbers or authority sufficed to change opinions . . . without reference to its merits." Many people are influenced by the pressure of opinions of others who have no ongoing connection with them. An individual may be influenced to change his ideas or expressed opinions contrary to his rational judgment because of sheer strength of unanimous group pressure of opinion against him. It was noted in a pervious chapter that in a mean measure of a great many tests of aggregates, using the Asch experiment, only 36.8% of the subjects changed their expressed opinions under group pressure, while 25% were completely independent and willing to stand alone, unchanged, and the others vacillated between changing and remaining constant in their expressed opinions. It is also worthy of note

[1] A. Paul Hare, *Handbook of Small Group Research* (New York, The Free Press, 1962), p. 25.
[2] Solomon E. Asch, "Opinions and Social Pressure," *Scientific American,* CXCIII (November, 1955), 31–35.

that in tests where even one person agreed with or supported the person, he did not change his opinion from his original judgment. It may be concluded that an individual in a minority position, given the support of one other member, may withstand collective pressure to change.

There is generally a relationship between the level of group cohesion and the degree of influence which the group has on its members, but at least for their public utterances, many people will be influenced by the mere weight of social pressure of unanimous agreement of others against them regardless of their attachment to the others. In evaluating the findings of studies, such as those of Asch and Sherif, it should be kept in mind that the matters under consideration in those experiments were not really matters of consequence to the individual. To change one's opinion in a judgment of the length of a line or the movement of a light does not compare with group pressure to change one's habits, indulgences, beliefs, life style, values, or roles. If people will change under the pressures of insignificant others (or people with whom they are not invested), the influence of significant others has an even greater meaning. But it may also be true that people may hold on more tenaciously to their values, beliefs, or positions which they have acquired over a long period of time, while they yield more easily to group pressure or judgment of matters in the gestalt of the group. Evidence is not conclusive in this area. It may be recalled from Chapter Two that Cooley theorized that the groups provided the medium and the context for individual socialization and change. Therefore, while there is evidence that people may change merely by their response to others, they may change in more permanent matters, such as behaviors or norms because of their attachment to the instrument of change—the group.

Deutsch and Gerard,[3] in a follow-up study of a modified Asch experiment, found that people were more influenced in normative behavior in organized groups which had become meaningful to them than by the opinions of others in an aggregate. To the extent

[3] Morton Deutsch, and Harold Gerard, "A Study of Normative and Informational Social Influence upon Individual Judgment," *Journal of Abnormal and Social Psychology*, LI (1955), 629–36.

that people matter to each other and have a sense of belonging together, to that extent it will matter to a person how far he deviates from expected behavior and to what degree he conforms to majority opinion.

In the organized group, the sources of control may be structural, interpersonal, coercive, or cultural. Structural control is control implemented by organization, leadership, or group government. Interpersonal control is personal influence exerted by members over each other. Coercive control is the use of force, fear, or threats that cause others to do one's bidding. Cultural control is created through the establishment of group values and norms that have a regulatory effect on group members as to what "we do here" or "things our members do not stand for."

Structural Control

Group organization brings about structural control. In formal groups the officers or leadership provide a clear hierarchy of control with defined roles of authority and lines of responsibility. Through designated functions or collective action within the group, the leadership provides structural control through regulating individual impulses, coordinating the power and interests of the members, creating a collective authority and exerting pressure to keep members in line with the general will of the group. Cartwright and Zander [4] have referred to these functions of leadership as the operation of social power. They conclude that leaders contributing to some group function "require[s] influencing behavior of others in some way: activities must be coordinated, instructions must be given and accepted, persuasion must be accomplished, motivation to strive for group goals must be generated and harmonious interpersonal relationships must be engendered."

The informal structure within the group may shift with each activity from member to member, depending on the activity to be un-

---

[4] Dorwin Cartwright, and Alvin Zander, "Leadership and Performance of Group Functions," in Dorwin Cartwright and Alvin Zander, eds., *Group Dynamics* (3d ed., New York, Harper & Row, 1968), p. 309.

dertaken and the capacity of particular members. The leadership functions, however, still need to be carried out and the power or authority to do so must be granted by the members. The socio-emotional leader as designated by Bales,[5] in helping members to feel more comfortable, and in mediating differences among members, can only assume this role if the members grant him the power by responding to his efforts. The "instrumental leaders" can only help members achieve their tasks so long as they respond. Thus he acquires power and control.

Within the group there are inherent and derived sources of power of leadership and members. Inherent power is due to some capacity or quality of the person, or believed to be there by the members who respond. Gibb [6] refers to many studies that show a correlation of leadership, particularly indigenous leadership with such personal qualities as intelligence, physical stature and bearing, and conditions of charisma. It has been said that power follows the charismatic leaders like a comet's tail. They have the facility to get others to do their bidding in any area of group functioning. In a review of the research on personal qualities that are associated with natural or inherent leadership, Gibb says, "There is abundant evidence that member's personalities do make a difference to group performance and do affect that aspect of group behavior to which leadership applies." [7]

A person may establish a leadership and power-endowed role for himself by a series of innovative actions or initiative acts, so that the group comes to believe that he has special wisdom or leadership attributes. Or he may instill fear in the members and thus inherently possess the source of power and influence on the group. He is in the position to control the other members of the group because of his skills or their esteem of him and response to him.

Derived power is the explicit delegation of authority to a person or people by their placement in a particular role or position, such

[5] R. F. Bales, *Interaction Process Analysis* (Reading, Mass., Addison-Wesley Publishing Co., Inc., 1950).

[6] Cecil A. Gibb, "Leadership," in Gardner Lindzey, ed., *Handbook of Social Psychology*, Vol. II (Reading, Mass., Addison-Wesley Publishing Co., Inc., 1954), pp. 877–920.

[7] *Ibid.*, p. 889.

as election or appointment to an office or leadership responsibility. The influence and control is derived from the various aspects of the role. People may also have power in a particular group derived from power elsewhere. The social worker, for instance, has weighted authority or power in a group for which he provides professional leadership, derived from his staff position in the agency or his standing in the profession. In a committee, people from high status positions, professions, or business may have power not relevant to the functions of the group, but derived from their organizational or institutional positions, their economic status or social position. Their contribution as group leaders may derive not from their behavior in the group, but from their leadership roles elsewhere. Their contributions to group deliberation may carry considerable power and influence, not on the merits of their ideas, but on the basis of the prestige they bring from their positions.

In either inherent or derived power, the individual or subgroup, or people-in-position, only have power so long as they exert it and group members respond to their influence. When a president leaves office he may still have a following, but he no longer has the authority of the role or position. He may influence many of the members unofficially. When a gang leader loses face he no longer has influence. A chairman, who does not fulfill the leadership role in line with group expectations, may lose the authority and respect of group members even though he still remains in the position he holds.

It may be assumed, therefore, that whether a group has formal leadership organization or informal leadership, there will be centers of power carrying influence over group members. Not only will the social worker with the group have power derived from his position, but he also will have greater or lesser power depending upon the roles he assumes and the position he accepts within the group. If he maintains a central position through which all activity and communication must flow, he will have a very high power position. He may also have considerable influence if he is well liked. He may be well liked due to his personality, or because he supports the group members and facilitates their achievement of their individual and group goals. The structured position or location of the worker in the group, however, grants him derived power at the outset.

Interpersonal Control

Personal influence is as powerful as the interpersonal relationships in any group. As people become involved in subgroups of twos, threes, and fours, they may acquiesce to the dominant or influential partners, or to the more aggressive initiators to the extent that the relationships between or among them have particular meaning. Group members may turn to each other for cues or approval, or be responsive to the proverbial kick under the table from friend or colleague. Thus as interpersonal patterns emerge within the group, whether they are due to feelings of attraction or repulsion, interest alignments, or antagonisms, these will exert strong natural controls on individuals and subgroups and ultimately influence the operations of the group.

Polansky [8] and others examining the phenomenon of personal influence and power in groups used the concept of behavioral contagion developed by Redl.[9] They indicate that contagion is the pick up of behavior from one individual to another when the originator has no intention of having the others follow him. They found that high status group members were more apt to cause others to contage their behavior. People seem to want to emulate others whom they think have more prestige or power in the group than they have. Therefore they take on behavior, values, and life styles. The person thus influencing the behavior of others may possess very great power, sometimes without even recognizing it. The stronger the group cohesion, the more the total group may be affected by the contagion factor of one or more members.

Out of group cohesion, the pressures develop within the group

[8] Norman Polansky, Ronald Lippitt, and Fritz Redl, "An Investigation of Behavioral Contagion in Groups," *Human Relations,* III (1950), 319–48.

[9] Fritz Redl, "The Phenomenon of Contagion and Shock Effect in Group Therapy," in W. Healy and A. Bronner, eds., *Searchlights on Delinquency* (New York, International Universities Press, 1949).

toward uniformity which tends to establish each member to try to change the opinions of others and tends to redefine the boundaries of the group to exclude those who hold deviant opinions, according to Cartwright and Lippitt.[10] The pressures toward uniformity then are related to the degree to which a person wishes to stay in the group. The more attractive or cohesive the group, the more the members may want to stay in the group and yet may also try to influence others and resist being influenced by them.

Festinger [11] conducted several studies of the effect of group cohesion on influence, which showed that the stronger the group cohesion the more pressure there is for members to conform to group norms. They noted that the pressures toward uniformity were related to the degree to which the person wishes to stay in the group. The more attractive or cohesive the group the more the members wish to remain in the group and therefore the more willing they are to conform. They also found that if persistent efforts to change the deviant in line with group expectations fail, then the group begins to reject the deviant, particularly when the deviance is on an issue relevant to the group goal. Cohesion, then, binds in the members and tends to control them or keep them in line with group expectations.

However, Walker and Heyns [12] maintain that cohesion is not enough to cause individual behavioral change toward group norms. They maintain that people conform to group pressure and to change their behavior out of personal need. If their needs are gratified by conforming they will do so, but if not, they will deviate from group expectation. If members deviate, of course, they run the risk of rejection by group, according to studies by Schachter.[13] Therefore, it may be assumed that cohesion, norms, and con-

[10] Dorwin Cartwright, and Ronald Lippitt, "Group Dynamics and the Individual," in Warren G. Bennis, Kenneth D. Benne, and Robert Chin, eds., *The Planning of Change* (New York, Holt, Rinehart & Winston, Inc., 1961).

[11] Leon Festinger, S. Schachter, and Kurt Back, *Social Pressures in Informal Groups* (New York, Harpers, 1950).

[12] Edward L. Walker, and Roger Heyns, *An Anatomy of Conformity* (Englewood Cliffs, N.J., Prentice-Hall, Inc., 1962).

[13] S. Schachter, "Deviation, Rejection, and Communication," *Journal of Abnormal and Social Psychology*, XLVI (1951).

formity go hand in hand. From the standpoint of social work practice, the conclusion may be drawn that if a group develops a high level of cohesion, then the individual member will be caught up in pressure from the group to behave in accordance with group expectations if its norms of functioning are conducive to health, growth, action, and problem solving. He may also feel support if he goes along with the group.

Group Cultural Control

Golembiewski [14] thinks that perhaps the strongest type of control is cultural, the establishment of group norms and values and their operation within the group to influence individual members and the group as a whole. Members bring to the group their own individualities, their own ideas, values, life styles, as well as their personalities and roles from other aspects of their lives. As they begin to interact with each other, to take on meaning, and to influence each other, the unique characteristics of the group emerge within it. These characteristics may be called group culture. Kluckhohn [15] defines culture as the interacting values and norms that evolve out of group life, and act to determine the norms of behavior for group members and for the group as a whole. A value, according to Parsons, [16] is an explicit or implicit conception of the desirable, which influences the selection from the available modes, means, and ends of action. A norm is a standard of what ought to be, as established within the group. Norms affect not only the behavior of the group as a whole but also the behavior of individuals in the group and frequently away from the group. According to Homans, [17] "group norms are ideas in the minds of members about

[14] Robert T. Golembiewski, *The Small Group* (Chicago, University of Chicago Press, 1962), p. 21 ff.
[15] Clyde Kluckhohn, "Culture and Behavior," in Lindzey, ed., *Handbook*, Vol. I.
[16] Talcott Parsons, and Edward Shils, *Toward a General Theory of Action* (Cambridge, Mass., Harvard University Press, 1951).
[17] George C. Homans, *The Human Group* (New York, Harcourt Brace Jovanovich, Inc., 1950), pp. 122–23.

what should and should not be done by a specific member under specified circumstances."

According to Parsons,[18] values may be cognitive, ethical, or aesthetic. That is, values may include ideas, beliefs, ideologies, or theories about the "truth," "right" or "wrong," "good" or "bad," and tastes about "beautiful" or "ugly," or "appropriate." Group culture may include all these aspects or types of values from which are developed expectations, and standards are set not only for group behavior and for group members but also standards for people outside of the group. They serve to control the beliefs, the behavior, and the knowledge of members of what is to be included and what is screened out.

The values and expectations brought to the group by individual members are modified as people in the group influence each other in their activity together and as they assess their expectations for the group. New cultures unique to the group then emerge as the group takes on its own character. This culture not only develops within the group but also is influenced by the surroundings of the group, the prevailing customs and norms of the community, and also the nature of the world and general customs of the time. Normative behavior develops out of the cultural expectations of a particular group at a specific time.

Some group culture is expressed through customs, styles, or "the way we do things here," and also may be codified into acts or rules or regulations which become norms. Group culture may be expressed through behaviors like beginning meetings on time or late, serving refreshments before the session or after the session, or not at all, seating arrangements, dressing up for a session or dressing informally, following a particular procedure in addressing people. Culture may also be expressed through the establishment of rituals before, during, or after the session. Codes of rules or regulations, posted or read at meetings or circulated and understood by members, are also part of group culture. Styles of leadership, informal or formally elected or otherwise designated leaders, characterize particular groups. The names given to the group by members and

---

[18] Parsons and Shils, *Toward a General Theory of Action.*

sometimes by people outside of the group, the wearing of uniforms, badges, or items of clothing which may be formally adopted or informally accepted, are other symbolic expressions through which group uniqueness is expressed.

The student worker of a boys club in a settlement house carried an attaché case containing supplies for the group to group meetings. His colleagues referred to this as his security blanket and encouraged him not to take it to group meetings. Finally at one session he left his case in the office. At that meeting all of the little boys who were members showed up with various types of brief cases, either school bags or used brief cases their mothers had bought at the Thrift Shop. They said they were known as the "Brief Case Boys," and everyone had to get a bag, to be like the leader, but also to distinguish them from other boys clubs. The bags had become a symbol and the culture that emerged took on the name, even though the cases had no functional relationship to the club purpose or activity.

Whether the culture is acknowledged and expressed in what ought to be and how to behave by informal custom or specified in rules and regulations, members acquire cues for their behavior and know what is expected of them and what to expect of others by the existence of the culture. Group culture is a strong instrument for control over individual impulsiveness and over personal behavior, style of dress, manner of speaking, development of group jargon or special words, phrases, and the ways in which members are expected to behave toward each other. Culture which grows out of the group may also become the context which regulates individual and group behavior.

According to Hare,[19] members conform to norms or rules of behavior which they have established as the proper ways of acting and which have been accepted as legitimate by the group. The specific kinds of behavior that are expected from group members will be derived from the goals which the group has set for itself. The shared expectations of behaviors, including role performance, develop as the group evolves and goes through the process of culture building.

[19] Hare, *Handbook.*

Berelson and Steiner [20] conclude from their review of research that members are ranked within the group on the basis of the degree to which they conform to the group's norms. Those in the middle status will strive harder to conform and tend to deviate less. The high status members will feel freer about nonconformity and become innovators, while the low status members will be apathetic or may even be deviant since they have nothing to lose. On the other hand, the group controls may have another effect. For says Berelson and Steiner,[21] the closer that the individual conforms to the accepted norms, the better liked he will be, and the better liked he is, the more he conforms. Similarly, if he does not conform he may be disliked. If the members were part of the group when the culture was being evolved, then their deviation from the norms would be a result of moving away from procedures or standards they helped to create. If, however, they are members who were added after the group culture was established, they entered the group on the assumption that they accepted the prevailing norms. Their deviation, therefore, is from something they do not like about the procedures of the group which they have joined.

Sometimes the symbols of culture—a name, rituals, procedures, a language, a particular set of words, or a style of relating and of expressing relationships with intimacy or aloofness—are taken as the culture itself. A person who works with a group may tend to think he can change the group by changing the symbols. For instance, if a group has adopted a derogatory name for itself that reflects a poor group image, it will not help members feel any better about themselves or the group to change the name. If group activities and achievements improve, the members will usually voluntarily adopt a new name that reflects their improved sense of themselves. If a group is having difficulty in organizational structure, the members themselves must evolve their own indigenous structure, and/or accept it before they can coalesce into a well-functioning group; no superimposed symbols of culture will form a group. On the other hand, the development of the group will be

[20] Bernard Berelson, and Gary A. Steiner, *Human Behavior* (New York, Harcourt Brace Jovanovich, Inc., 1964).
[21] *Ibid.*

accompanied by the emergence of the culture and its symbols, and the resulting aspects of group control.

In research that has been undertaken to determine why group norms tend to have so much influence on members. Argyle [22] concludes that the personality factors in individual members which cause them to need acceptance from the group influence their response to group pressures. Other studies link conformity to status seeking on the part of group members.[23] Festinger [24] and others link normative behavior to the fear of the pain to the individual and to the group of being different, holding a different view, or behaving unlike other members or group expectations.

A social worker, participating with a group in its development, offers high status sanctions and judgments by virtue of his position and role. He carries values as a representative of the profession, and expertise in his skill as a practitioner. He also carries various cultural symbols from the agency. The service goal which he expresses by his presence with the group reflects the culture of his agency. Therefore, it may be assumed that worker interventions in group development, the deliberative process, the establishment of goals, will reflect values and culture based on expectations, whether explicit or implicit in his behavior.

Sometimes people are not as aware of their own culture—values, styles of behavior, beliefs of what they consider to be true, right, good, and beautiful. They have been so acculturated into their particular reference groups and their lives have been so infused with their own styles, that they are unaware of their culture. They can see differences in others, even to slightest speech inflections, manners of relating to others, beliefs, and life styles. Social workers may see differences in group members and members may notice differences in each other and in the worker. In the initial phase of group development, these differences may be more evident, and may be a source of conflict and struggle, but as the group emerges and becomes an entity, the group influence and control process

[22] Michael Argyle, "Social Pressure in Public and Private Situations," *Journal of Abnormal and Social Psychology,* LIV (1957).

[23] Golembiewski, *The Small Group.*

[24] Festinger, Schachter, and Back, *Social Pressures in Informal Groups.*

will cause people to become more alike. As people begin to take on meaning for each other, the differences may be submerged into a common culture created within the group. This group culture will then influence group members to the extent that they will take on for themselves some of the values, manners, and style from the group. The emergence of group culture with its norms that control and support behavior will influence members to the extent that they will probably modify some of their beliefs and behavior, not only in the group but also in other aspects of their lives. They will become more like each other with some modification on the part of all of them.

The emergence of group culture will contain worker and member inputs and will be a collective product, constantly open to revision and modification as the group moves through time and varying experiences that produce growth and change. It can happen that group culture and norms can become ossified at a particular stage and freeze the progress of the group. Rituals, rules, bylaws, or customs that encumber the group may be established, rather than freeing the members to innovate and make the best use of the group. This may happen particularly to groups with closed membership, which meet over a long period of time. Task groups, like committees or formal organizational structures, may particularly find themselves with outdated procedures. A part of the deliberative process of any group may need to be the periodic re-examination of the customs and rituals of the group to ensure that the group goals are being achieved and not thwarted by the culture.

Summary and Conclusion

Group influence, or group control, is the power created within the group through the interaction of the participants, including the social worker. This power comes from the organized structure of the group, both formal or designated leadership, and informal or indigenous leadership. It also comes from the personal influence people have over one another through the relationships they develop and the emotional meaning that these relationships take on. There may also be power and influence members feel because they fear certain individuals or group ridicule, ostracization or exclusion; that is, coercive power. Finally, group influence comes from the emergent group culture, the values, norms, and customs which are created within the group and come to be important in the life of the group and to all who participate.

In the final analysis it is the group influence on the member, the effects of the group experience on the participants within the group and outside of the group which provide the essence of the meaning to the use of groups. It is group control that not only results from all of the other group processes but also provides the end to which group participation is aimed. It can cause an individual to conform, but at the same time it can offer an individual support so that he can feel an anchor to move on to express himself and his own creativity, because he knows he belongs. It is through group control also that a disparate collection of individuals may act together to bring about some solution to a problem or some change in the environment of the group, or may influence some system outside of the group. It is to this end that groups have use in social work.

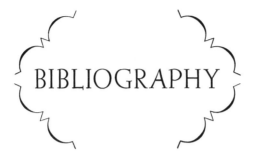

BIBLIOGRAPHY

Adorno, T. W., Else Frenkel-Brunswick, D. J. Levinson, and R. N. Sanford. *The Authoritarian Personality*. New York, Harper & Row, Publishers, 1950.

Albee, Constance I. "Group Work with Hospitalized Children," *Children*, II (1955).

Allport, Floyd. "The Influence of the Group upon Association and Thought," *Journal of Experimental Psychology*, III (1920).

Allport, Gordon W. "Catharsis and the Reduction of Prejudice," *Journal of Social Issues*, I (1945), 3–10.

Allport, Gordon. W. "The Historical Background of Modern Social Psychology," in Gardner Lindzey, ed., *The Handbook of Social Psychology*. Reading, Mass., Addison-Wesley Publishing Co., 1954.

Almond, G., and S. Verba. *The Civic Culture: Political Attitudes and Democracy*. Princeton, New Jersey, Princeton University Press, 1963.

Appelberg, Esther. "The Cottage Meeting As A Therapeutic Tool," in Henry Maier, ed., *Group Work As Part of Residential Treatment*. New York, National Association of Social Workers, 1965.

Aranguren, J. L. *Human Communication*. Translated by Francis Partridge. New York, McGraw-Hill Book Company, 1967.

Argyle, Michael. *The Psychology of Interpersonal Behavior*. Baltimore, Penguin Books, Inc., 1967.

Argyle, Michael. *The Scientific Study of Social Behavior*. London, Methuen Company, 1957.

Argyle, Michael. "Social Pressure in Public and Private Situations," *Journal of Abnormal and Social Psychology*, LIV (1957).

Aronson, Elliot, and Judson Mills. "Effect of Severity of Initiation on Liking for a Group," *Journal of Abnormal and Social Psychology*, LIX (1959), 177–81.

Asch, Solomon. "Opinions and Social Pressure," *Scientific American,* CXCIII (1955), 31–35.

Austin, David M. "Goals for Street Workers," *Social Work,* II (1957), 43–50.

Bach, George. "Marathon Group Dynamics," *Psychological Reports,* XX (1967), 995–1172.

Back, Kurt W. "Influence through Social Communication," *Journal of Abnormal and Social Psychology,* XLVI (1951), 9–23.

Bales, Robert F. *Interaction Process Analysis.* Reading, Mass., Addison-Wesley Publishing Co., Inc., 1950.

Bales Robert F. "How People Interact in Conferences," *Scientific American,* CXCII (1955), 31–35.

Bales, Robert F. "Small Group Theory and Research," in R. K. Merton, Leonard Broom, and Leonard Cottrell, Jr., eds., *Sociology Today.* New York, Basic Books, Inc., 1959, p. 295.

Bales Robert F. "Social Therapy for a Social Disorder—Compulsive Drinking," *Journal of Social Issues,* I (1954), 14–22.

Bales Robert F., and P. E. Slater. "Role Differentiation in Small Decision-Making Groups," in Talcott Parsons, Robert F. Bales, James Old, Morris Zelditch, Jr., and Philip E. Slater, eds., *Family Socialization and Interaction Process.* New York, The Free Press, 1955, pp. 259–306.

Bales Robert F., and Fred Strodtbeck. "Phases in Group Problem Solving," *Journal of Abnormal and Social Psychology,* XLVI (1951), 485–95.

Bavelas, Alex "Morale and the Training of Leaders," in G. Watson, ed., *Civilian Morale.* New York, Reynal & Hitchcock, 1942.

Bavelas, Alex. "Communication Patterns in Task-oriented Groups," in Dorwin Cartwright and Alvin Zander, eds., *Group Dynamics.* 2d ed., New York, Harper & Row, 1960.

Benne, Kenneth D., and Paul Sheats. "Functional Roles of Group Members," *Journal of Social Issues,* IV, No. 2 (1948), 41–49.

Bennis, Warren G., Kenneth D. Benne, and Robert Chin, eds. *The Planning of Change.* New York, Holt, Rinehart & Winston, Inc., 1961.

Bennis, Warren G., and Herbert A. Shepherd. "A Theory of Group Development," *Human Relations,* IX (1956), 415–37.

Berelson, Bernard, and Gary A. Steiner. *Human Behavior.* New York, Harcourt Brace Jovanovich, Inc., 1964.

Berne, Eric. *Principles of Group Treatment.* New York, Oxford University Press, 1966.

Berne, Eric. *The Structure and Dynamics of Organizations and Groups.* Philadelphia, J. B. Lippincott, 1963.

Bernstein, Saul, ed. *Explorations in Group Work.* Boston, Boston University School of Social Work, 1965.

Berry, H., III, Margaret Bacon, and I. L. Child. "A Cross-Cultural Survey of Sex Differences in Socialization," *Journal of Abnormal and Social Psychology,* LV (1957), 323–32.

Berry, Margaret. "Grouping Devices for Interpersonal Goals in Agency Initiated Groups," in *Social Work in the Current Scene.* Selected papers from the National Conference of Social Work. New York, Columbia University Press, 1950.

Bettelheim, Bruno, and Emery Sylvester. "Therapeutic Influence of the Group on the Individual," *American Journal of Orthopsychiatry,* XVII (1947), 684–92.

Bion, W. R. *Experiences in Groups.* New York, Basic Books, Inc., 1961.

Blau, Peter M. *Bureaucracy in Modern Society.* New York, Random House, Inc., 1956.

Blau, Peter M. "Social Mobility and Interpersonal Relations," *American Sociological Review,* XXI (1956).

Blau, Peter M. "Theory of Social Integration," *American Journal of Sociology,* LXV (1960), 545–56.

Blau, Peter M., and W. Richard Scott. *Formal Organizations.* San Francisco, Chandler Publishing Co., 1962.

Blumer, Herbert. "Society as Symbolic Interaction," in Arnold Rose, ed., *Human Behavior and Social Process.* Boston, Houghton Mifflin Company, 1962.

Bossard, J. H. "Law of Family Interaction," *American Journal of Sociology,* L (1945), 292–94.

Bovard, E. W., Jr. "The Experimental Production of Interpersonal Affect," *Journal of Abnormal and Social Psychology,* XLVI (1952), 521–28.

Bradford, Leland. "Hidden Agenda," *Adult Leadership* I, No. 4, (1952).

Bradford, Leland. "Membership in the Learning Process," in Leland Bradford, Jack R. Gibb, and Kenneth Benne, *T Group Theory and Laboratory Method.* New York, John Wiley & Sons, Inc., 1964.

Bradford, Leland, Jack R. Gibb, and Kenneth Benne. *T-Group Theory and Laboratory Method.* New York, John Wiley & Sons, Inc., 1964.

Brim, Orville, Jr. "Adult Socialization," in John Clausen, ed., *Socialization and Society.* Boston, Little, Brown and Company, 1968.

Brim, Orville G., and Stanton Wheeler. *Socialization after Childhood.* New York, John Wiley & Sons, Inc., 1966.

Brown, Louise A., and Margaret E. Hartford. "Effecting Value Change in Race Relations through Group Service Agencies," *Social Work Practice, 1965.* New York, Columbia University Press, 1965.

Bruner, Jerome, and Tagiuri, Renato. "The Perception of People," in Gardner Lindzey, ed., *Handbook of Social Psychology.* Reading Mass., Addison-Wesley Publishing Co., Inc., 1954.

Buxbaum, Edith. "Transference and Gang Formation in Adolescence," in *Psychoanalytic Study of the Child,* Vol. I. New York, International Universities Press, 1945.

Carey, Gloria. "Sex Differences in Problem-Solving Performance as a Function of Attitude Difference," *Journal of Abnormal and Social Psychology,* LVI (1958), 256–60.

Carpenter, Edmond, and Marshall McLuhan. *Explorations in Communication.* Boston, Beacon Press, 1960.

Cartwright, Dorwin. "Achieving Change in People," in Warren G. Bennis, Kenneth Benne, and Robert Chin, eds., *The Planning of Change.* New York, Holt, Rinehart & Winston, Inc., 1961.

Cartwright, Dorwin. "The Nature of Group Cohesiveness," in Dorwin Cartwright and Alvin Zander, eds., *Group Dynamics.* 3d ed., New York, Harper & Row Publishers, 1968.

Cartwright, Dorwin, and Ronald Lippitt. "Group Dynamics and the Individual," in Warren G. Bennis, Kenneth D. Benne, and Robert Chin, eds., *The Planning of Change.* New York, Holt, Rinehart & Winston, Inc., 1961.

Cartwright, Dorwin, and Alvin Zander. *Group Dynamics.* 2d ed. New York, Harper & Row, Publishers, 1960.

Cartwright, Dorwin, and Alvin Zander. *Group Dynamics.* 3d ed., New York, Harper & Row, Publishers, 1968.

Cartwright, Dorwin, and Alvin Zander. "Leadership and Performance of Group Functions," in Dorwin Cartwright and Alvin Zander, eds., *Group Dynamics.* 3d ed. New York, Harper & Row, Publishers, 1968.

Cattell, R. B. "Concepts and Methods in the Measurement of Group Syntality," *Psychological Review,* LV (1948), 48–63.

Cattell, R. B. "Types of Group Characteristics," in Paul Lazarsfeld and Morris Rosenberg, eds., *The Language of Social Research.* New York, The Free Press, 1955.

Chavers, Faye, and Helen O'Rourke. "The Use of Groups with Unmarried Mothers to Facilitate Casework." Mimeographed. Child Welfare League Regional Meeting, Cleveland, 1967.

Child Welfare League. *Group Methods and Services in Child Welfare.* New York, Child Welfare League of America, 1963.

Christensen, H. T. *Handbook on Marriage and the Family.* Chicago, Rand McNally & Co., 1964.

Clark, Kenneth B. *Prejudice and Your Child.* Boston, Beacon Press, 1955.

Cleminger, Florence. "Congruence Between Members and Workers on Selected Behaviors of the Role of the Social Group Worker." Unpublished D.S.W. dissertation, University of Southern California, 1965.

Coch, L., and J. R. P. French, Jr. "Overcoming Resistance to Change," *Human Relations,* I (1948), 512–32.

Collins, Barry, and Harold Guetzkow. *A Social Psychology of Group Processes for Decision Making.* New York, John Wiley & Sons, Inc., 1964.

"Communications," *Kaiser Aluminum News,* XXIII, No. 3 (1965). Public Affairs Department, Kaiser Aluminum and Chemical Corp., Kaiser Center, Oakland, California.

Cooley, Charles H. *Social Organization.* New York, Charles Scribner's Sons, 1909.

Coyle, Grace L. *Group Work with American Youth.* New York, Harper & Row, Publishers, 1948.

Coyle, Grace L. *Social Process in Organized Groups.* New York, Richard R. Smith, Inc., 1930.

Coyle, Grace L. *Social Science in the Professional Education of Social Workers.* New York, Council on Social Work Education, 1958.

Coyle, Grace L. "Concepts Relevant to Helping the Family As a Group," *Social Casework,* XLIII (1962), 347–54.

Coyle, Grace L. Memorandum on "The Bethel Laboratory for Group Development, 1948," to the Faculty of the School of Applied Social Sciences, Western Reserve University. Unpublished.

Coyle, Grace L., and Raymond Fisher. "Helping the Hospitalized Child through Social Group Work," *The Child,* XVI (1952).

Coyle, Grace L., and Margaret E. Hartford. *Social Processes in the Community and the Group.* New York, Council on Social Work Education, 1958.

Crow, Maxine. "Preventive Intervention Through Parent Group Education," *Social Casework,* XLVIII (1967).

Cyrus, Ada Shaw. "Group Treatment of 10 Disadvantaged Mothers," *Social Casework,* XLVIII (1967).

Dashiell, J. F. "Experimental Studies of the Influence of Social Situations on the Behavior of Individual Human Adults," in C. Murcheson, ed., *Handbook of Social Psychology.* Worcester, Mass., Clark University Press, 1935.

Davis, Allison, Burleigh Gardner, and Mary Gardner. *Deep South.* Chicago, University of Chicago Press, 1941.

Davis, James H. *Group Performance.* Reading, Mass., Addison-Wesley Publishing Co., Inc. 1969.

Deutsch, Morton. "An Experimental Study of the Effects of Cooperation and Competition upon Group Process," *Human Relations,* II (1949), 199–231.

Deutsch, Morton. "Field Theory in Social Psychology," in Gardner Lindzey, ed., *Handbook of Social Psychology.* Reading, Mass., Addison-Wesley Publishing Co., Inc., 1953.

Deutsch, Morton, and Mary Collins. *Interracial Housing: A Psychological Evaluation of a Social Experiment.* Minneapolis, University of Minnesota Press, 1951.

Deutsch, Morton, and Harold Gerard. "A Study of Normative and Informational Social Influence upon Individual Judgment," *Journal of Abnormal and Social Psychology,* LI (1955), 629–36.

Dittes, James E., and H. H. Kelley. "Effects of Different Conditions of Acceptance upon Conformity to Group Norms," *Journal of Abnormal and Social Psychology,* LIII (1956), 100–107.

Dollard, John. *Caste and Class in a Southern Town.* New York, Harper & Row, Publishers, 1949.

Drake, St. Clair, and Horace R. Cayton. *Black Metropolis.* New York, Harcourt Brace Jovanovich, Inc., 1945.

Durkheim, Emil. *Suicide.* Translated by John A. Spaulding and George Simpson. New York, The Free Press, 1951.

Durkin, Helen. *The Group in Depth.* New York, International Universities Press, 1964.

Duvall, Evelyn M. *Family Development.* Philadelphia, J. B. Lippincott, 1967.

Eisenstadt, S. N. *From Generation to Generation.* New York, The Free Press, 1964.

Elliott, Harrison. *Process of Group Thinking.* New York, Association Press, 1928.

Erikson, Erik. *Childhood and Society.* New York, W. W. Norton & Company, Inc., 1963.

Erikson, Erik. *Insight and Responsibility.* New York, W. W. Norton & Company, Inc., 1964.

Eubank, E. E. *Concepts of Sociology.* Boston, D. C. Heath & Company, 1932.

Family Service Association of America. *Group Treatment in Family Service Agencies.* New York, Family Service Association of America, 1964.

Faw, V. A. "A Psychotherapeutic Method of Teaching Psychology," *American Psychologist*, IV (1949), 104–109.

Feldman, Frances, and Frances Scherz. *Family Social Welfare: Helping Troubled Families*. New York, Atherton Press, Inc., 1967.

Fenton, Norman, and Kermit T. Wilse, eds. *Group Methods in the Public Welfare Program*. Palo Alto, Calif., Pacific Books, 1963.

Festinger, Leon. *Theory of Cognitive Dissonance*. Evanston, Ill., Row Peterson, 1957.

Festinger, Leon. "Informal Social Communication," *Psychological Review*, LVII (1950), 271–82.

Festinger, Leon. "Laboratory Experiments: The Role of Group Belongingness," in J. G. Miller, ed., *Experiments in Social Process*. New York, McGraw-Hill Book Company, 1950.

Festinger, Leon, S. Schachter, and Kurt Back. *Social Pressures in Informal Groups*. New York, Harper & Row, Publishers 1950.

Fischer, Paul H. "An Analysis of the Primary Group," *Sociometry*, XVI (1953), 272–76.

Follett, Mary. *Creative Experience*. New York, Longmans Green, 1924.

Follett, Mary. *The New State*. New York, Longmans Green, 1918.

Foulkes, S. H., and E. J. Anthony. *Group Psychotherapy*. Baltimore, Penguin Books, Inc., 1957.

Fouriezos, N. T., M. L. Hatt, and Harold Guetzkow. "Measurement of Self-Oriented Needs in Discussion Groups," *Journal of Abnormal and Social Psychology*, XLV (1950), 682–90.

Frank, Jerome K. "Some Determinants, Manifestations, and Effects of Cohesiveness in Therapy Groups," *International Journal of Group Psychotherapy*, VII (1957), 53–63.

Frank, L. K. "Change through Group Experience." *Social Welfare Forum*, *1957*. New York, Columbia University Press, 1957.

French, J. R. P., Jr. "Group Productivity," in H. Guetzkow, ed., *Group Leadership and Men*. Pittsburgh, Carnegie Press, 1951.

Freud, Sigmund. *Group Psychology and the Analysis of the Ego*. Authorized translation by James Strachey. London, International Psychoanalytical Press, 1922.

Frey, Louise, and Ralph Kolodny. "Illusions and Realities in Current Social Work with Groups," *Social Work*, IX (1964).

Garland, James, Hubert Jones, and Ralph Kolodny. "A Model for Stages in the Development of Social Work Groups," in Saul Bernstein, ed., *Explorations of Group Work*. Boston, Boston University, 1965.

Geller, Joseph J. "Concerning the Size of Therapy Groups," in Max Rosenbaum and Milton Berger, eds., *Group Psychotherapy and Group Function*. New York, Basic Books, Inc., 1963.

Gibb, Cecil A. "Leadership," in Gardner Lindzey, ed., *Handbook of Social Psychology*, Vol. II. Reading, Mass., Addison-Wesley Publishing Co., Inc., 1954, pp. 877–920.

Glasser, William. *Reality Therapy*. New York, Harper & Row, Publishers, 1965.

Goffman, Erving. *Encounters*. Indianapolis, The Bobbs-Merrill Co., Inc., 1961.

Golembiewski, Robert. *The Small Group.* Chicago, University of Chicago Press, 1962.
Golembiewski, Robert. "Small Groups and Large Organizations," in James G. March, ed., *Handbook of Organizations.* Chicago, Rand McNally & Co., 1965.
Goodman, Mary Ellen. *Race Awareness in Young Children.* Reading, Mass., Addison-Wesley Publishing Co., Inc., 1952.
Grinker, R. R., and J. P. Spiegel. *Men Under Stress.* New York, McGraw-Hill Book Company, 1945.
Gurin, G., J. Veroff, and Sheila Feld. *Americans View Their Mental Health: A Nationwide Interview Survey.* New York, Basic Books, Inc., 1960.
Hagstrom, Warren O., and Hanan Selvin. "Two Dimensions of Cohesiveness in Small Groups," *Sociometry,* XXVIII (1965).
Hall, Edward T. *The Hidden Dimension.* Garden City, New York, Doubleday & Company, Inc., 1969.
Hall, Edward T. *The Silent Language.* Garden City, New York, Doubleday & Company, Inc., 1959.
Harding, John, Harold Proshansky, Bernard Kutner, and Isidor Chein. "Prejudice and Ethnic Relations," in Gardner Lindzey and Elliot Aronson, eds., *The Handbook of Social Psychology.* 2d ed. Reading, Mass., Addison-Wesley Publishing Co. Inc., 1969.
Hare, A. Paul. *Handbook of Small Group Research.* New York, The Free Press, 1962.
Hare, A. Paul, E. F. Borgatta, and R. F. Bales. *Small Groups: Studies in Social Interaction.* Rev. ed. New York, Alfred A. Knopf, Inc., 1965.
Hartford, Margaret E., ed. *Working Papers Toward a Frame of Reference for Social Group Work.* New York, National Association of Social Workers, 1962.
Hartford, Margaret E. "The Preparation of Social Workers to Practice with People in Groups," *Journal of Education for Social Work,* III (1967), 49–61.
Hartford, Margaret E. "The Social Group Worker in the Process of Group Formation." Unpublished Ph.D. dissertation. Chicago, University of Chicago, 1962.
Hawkins, Gaynell. *Educational Experiments in Social Settlements.* American Association of Adult Education. New York, P. Grady Press, 1937.
Haythorn, W., A. Couch, D. Haefner, P. Langhorn, and L. F. Carter. "The Behavior of Authoritarian and Equalitarian Personalities in Groups," *Human Relations,* IX (1956), 57–74.
Hearn, Gordon. "Leadership and the Spatial Factor in Small Groups," *Journal of Abnormal and Social Psychology,* CIV (1957), 269–72.
Hearn, Gordon. "The Process of Group Development," *Autonomous Groups Bulletin,* XIII (1957).
Heber, R. F., and Mary E. Heber. "The Effect of Group Failure and Success on Social Status," *Journal of Educational Psychology,* XLVII (1957), 129–34.
Heider, F. *The Psychology of Interpersonal Relations.* New York, John Wiley & Sons, Inc., 1958.
Height, Dorothy. *Step by Step in Interracial Groups.* Rev. New York, National Board of the Y.W.C.A., 1954.

Heinicke, C., and R. F. Bales. "Developmental Trends in the Structure of Small Groups," *Sociometry*, XVI (1953).

Heise, G. A., and G. A. Miller. "Problem Solving by Small Groups Using Various Communication Nets," *Journal of Abnormal and Social Psychology*, XLVI (1951), 327–36.

Helanko, R. "Sports and Socialization," in Neil J. Smelser and William T. Smelser, *Personality and Social Systems*. New York, John Wiley & Sons, Inc., 1963.

Hemphill, J. K., and Charles Westie. "The Measurement of Group Dimension," *Journal of Psychology*, XXIX (1950), 325–420.

Hill, Reuben. "Methodological Issues in Family Development Research," *Family Process*, III (1964).

Hill, Reuben, and Donald Hansen. "The Identification of Conceptual Framework Utilized in Family Research," *Marriage and Family Living*, XXII (1960), 299–314.

Hoffman, Martin L., and Lois Hoffman, eds. *Review of Child Development Research*, Vol. I. New York, Russell Sage Foundation, 1964.

Hollander, E. P. *Leadership, Groups, and Influence*. New York, Oxford University Press, 1964.

Hollander, E. P., and Raymond G. Hunt, eds. *Current Perspectives on Social Psychology*. New York, Oxford University Press, 1967.

Hollingshead, Augustus. *Elmtown's Youth*. New York, John Wiley & Sons, Inc., 1949.

Homans, George C. *The Human Group*. New York, Harcourt Brace Jovanovich, Inc., 1950.

Homans, George C. *Social Behavior: Its Elementary Forms*. New York, Harcourt Brace Jovanovich, Inc., 1961.

Hopkins, Terence. *The Exercise of Influence in the Small Group*. Totowa, New Jersey, the Bedminster Press, 1964.

Horowitz, Murray. "Conceptual Status of Group Dynamics," in Warren Bennis, Kenneth Benne, and Robert Chin, eds., *The Planning of Change*. New York, Holt, Rinehart & Winston, Inc., 1961.

Howard, Jane. *Please Touch*. New York, McGraw-Hill Book Company, 1970.

Hunt, C. L. "Negro-White Perceptions of Interracial Housing," *Journal of Social Issues*, XV (1959), 24–29.

Inkeles, Alex. "Society, Social Structure, and Child Socialization," in John Clausen, ed., *Socialization and Society*. Boston, Little, Brown and Company, 1968.

Isaacs, Susan. *Social Development in Young Children*. New York, Harcourt Brace Jovanovich, Inc., 1933.

Israel, Joachim. *Self-Evaluation and Rejection in Groups*. Stockholm, Sweden, Alnquist & Wiksell, 1956.

James, John. "A Preliminary Study of the Size Determinant in Small Group Interaction," *American Sociological Review*, XVI (1951), 474–77.

Janis, Irving. "Group Identification under Conditions of External Danger," in Dorwin Cartwright and Alvin Zander, *Group Dynamics*. 3d ed., New York, Harper & Row, Publishers 1968.

Jennings, Helen Hall. *Leadership and Isolation.* New York, Longmans Green, 1950.

Josselyn, Irene. *Psychosocial Development of Children.* New York, Family Service Association of America, 1948.

Kaiser, Clara, ed. *The Group Records of Four Clubs at University Neighborhood Center.* Cleveland, Ohio, School of Applied Social Sciences, Western Reserve University, 1930.

Kaiser, Clara A. "The Social Group Work Process," in Marjorie Murphy, ed., *The Social Group Work Method in Social Work Education,* Vol. XI. A Project Report on Curriculum Study. New York, Council on Social Work Education, 1959.

Kelley, Harold, and John W. Thibaut. "Experimental Studies of Group Problem Solving and Process," in Gardner Lindzey, ed., *Handbook of Social Psychology.* Reading, Mass., Addison-Wesley Publishing Co., Inc., 1954.

Kemp, C. Gratton. *Perspectives on Group Process.* Boston, Houghton Mifflin Company, 1964.

Kephart, W. M. "A Quantitative Analysis of Intragroup Relationships," *American Journal of Sociology,* LX (1950), 544–49.

Kirzenbaum, Minna, Edward Panzer, and Sol Gordon. "Group Psychotherapy as the Treatment of Choice for the Majority of Patients in a Community Mental Health Clinic." Mimeographed. Orthopsychiatric Conference, 1963.

Klein, Alan. "Exploring Family Group Counseling," *Social Work,* VIII (1963), 23–29.

Klein, Josephine P. *The Study of Groups.* London, Routledge and Kegan Paul, Ltd., 1967.

Klein, Joyce Gale. *Adult Education and Treatment Groups in Social Agencies.* Doctoral Dissertation. Washington, D.C., Catholic University Press, 1960.

Kluckhohn, Clyde. "Culture and Behavior," in Gardner Lindzey, ed., *Handbook of Social Psychology,* Vol. I. Reading, Mass., Addison-Wesley Publishing Co., Inc., 1954.

Kluckhohn, Florence, and John M. Spiegel. *Intergration and Conflict in Family Behavior.* Report No. 27, Topeka, Group for the Advancement of Psychiatry, August, 1964.

Kolodny, Ralph. "The Impact of Peer Group Activity on the Alienated Child," *Smith College Studies in Social Work,* XXXVII (1967), 142–58.

Konopka, Gisela. *Social Group Work: A Helping Process.* Englewood Cliffs, New Jersey, Prentice-Hall, Inc., 1963.

Lang, Norma C. "A Broad Range Model of Practice in the Social Work Group." Paper delivered at the National Conference of Social Welfare, Chicago, 1970. [To be published in *Social Service Review* (in press)].

Lasswell, Harold D., and Abraham Kaplan. *Power and Society: A Framework for Political Inquiry.* New Haven, Yale University Press, 1950.

Lazarsfeld, P. F., B. Berelson, and Hazel Gaudet. *The People's Choice.* New York, Duel Sloan and Pearce, 1944.

Leader, Arthur. "The Role of Intervention in Family Group Treatment," *Social Casework,* XLV (1964), 327–32.

Leavitt, Harold J. "Some Effects of Certain Communication Patterns on Group

Performance," *Journal of Abnormal and Social Psychology*, XLVI (1951), 38–50.

Lebon, Gustav. *The Crowd*. Translated by Fisher. London, Alan Unwin, 1895.

Leichter, Elsa. "Interrelationship of Content and Process in Therapy Groups," *Social Casework*, XLVII (1966), 302 ff.

Leighton, Alexander H. *The Governing of Men*. Princeton, New Jersey, Princeton University Press, 1945.

Levine, J., and J. Butler. "Lecture vs. Discussion in Changing Behavior," *Journal of Applies Psychology*, XXXVI (1952), 29–33.

Lewin, Kurt. *Field Theory in Social Science*. New York, Harper & Row, Publishers, 1951.

Lewin, Kurt. "Forces Behind Food Habits and Methods of Change," *National Research Council Bulletin*, CVIII (1943).

Lewin, Kurt, and Ronald Lippitt. "An Experimental Approach to the Study of Autocracy and Democracy," *Sociometry*, I (1938), 292–300.

Lewin, Kurt, R. Lippitt, and R. White. "Patterns of Aggressive Behavior in Experimentally Created 'Social Climates,' " *Journal of Social Psychology*, X (1939), 271–99.

Lindeman, Eduard. *Social Discovery*. New York, Republic Press, 1924.

Lindzey, Gardner, and Edgar Borgatta. "Sociometric Measurement," in Gardner Lindzey, ed., *Handbook of Social Psychology*. Reading, Mass., Addison-Wesley Publishing Co., Inc., 1954.

Linton, Ralph. *The Study of Man*. New York, Appleton-Century-Crofts, 1936.

Lippitt, R., and R. White. "Leader Behavior and Members' Reactions in Three Social Climates," in Dorwin Cartwright and Alvin Zander, *Group Dynamics*. 1st ed. New York, Harper & Row, 1953.

Lippitt, Ronald, Jeanne Watson, and Bruce Westley. *The Dynamics of Planned Change*. New York, Harcourt, Brace & Co., 1958.

Litwak, Eugene. "Geographical Mobility and Extended Family Cohesion," *American Sociological Review*, XXV (1960), 385–94.

Luchins, Abraham. *Group Therapy: A Guide*. New York, Random House, Inc., 1967.

McDavid, John W., and Herbert Harrari. *Social Psychology*. New York, Harper & Row, 1968.

McDougall, William. *The Group Mind*. New York, G. P. Putnam's Sons, 1920.

MacIver, Robert. *Community*. New York, The Macmillan Company, 1924.

McKeachie, W. J. "Student-Centered Versus Instructor-Centered Instruction," *Journal of Educational Psychology*, XLV (1954), 143–50.

McKeachie, W. J. "Students, Groups, and Teaching Methods," *American Psychologist*, XIII (1958), 580–84.

McLuhan, Marshall. *Understanding Media*. New York, McGraw-Hill Book Company, 1964.

Maier, Henry. In *A Conceptual Framework for Teaching Group Work Method in the Classroom*. Edited by M. E. Hartford. New York, Council on Social Work Education, 1964.

Main, Marjorie W. "An Examination of Selected Aspects of the Beginning Phase in Social Work with Groups." Unpublished Ph.D. dissertation. Chicago, University of Chicago, 1965.

Maloney, Sara E. "The Development of Group Work Education in Schools of Social Work in the U.S., 1919–1948." Unpublished D.S.W. dissertation. Cleveland, Ohio, Western Reserve University, 1963.

Maloney, Sara, and Margaret Mudgett. "Group Work and Casework: Their Similarities and Differences," *Social Work*, IV (1959), 31.

Manis, Melvin. "Social Interaction and the Self Concept," *Journal of Abnormal and Social Psychology*, LI (1955), 362–70.

Mann, J. H. "The Differential Nature of Prejudice Reduction," *Journal of Social Psychology*, LII (1960), 339–43.

Mann, Richard. *Interpersonal Styles and Group Development.* New York, John Wiley & Sons, Inc., 1967.

March, James G., ed. *Handbook of Organizations.* Chicago, Rand McNally & Co., 1965.

Martin, Elmore A., and William F. Hill. "Toward a Theory of Group Development," *International Journal of Group Psychotherapy*, VII (1957), 22–30.

Mead, G. H. *Mind, Self, and Society.* Chicago, University of Chicago Press, 1934.

Merei, Ferenc. "Group Leadership and Institutionalization," *Human Relations*, II (1949), 23–39.

Merton, Robert K. *Social Theory and Social Structure.* New York, The Free Press, 1957.

Mills, Theodore M. *The Sociology of Small Groups.* Englewood Cliffs, New Jersey, Prentice-Hall, Inc., 1967.

Mills, Theodore M., and Steve Rosenberg, eds. *Readings on the Sociology of Small Groups.* Englewood Cliffs, New Jersey, Prentice-Hall, Inc., 1970.

Mintz, Norbitt. "Effects of Aesthetic Surroundings," *Journal of Psychology*, XLI (1956), 459–66.

Mitnick, L. I., and E. McGinnies. "Influencing Ethnocentrism in Small Discussion Groups through a Film Communication," *Journal of Abnormal and Social Psychology*, LVI (1958), 82–90.

Mobley, Albertina. "Group Application Interview in a Family Agency," *Social Casework*, XLVII (1966).

Moreno, Jacob L. *Who Shall Survive?* Rev. ed. Beacon, New York, Beacon House, 1953.

Moreno, J. L. *Who Shall Survive?* Washington, D.C., Nervous and Mental Disease Publishing Co., 1934.

Mossberg, J. W., and A. K. Berliner. "The Developmental Stages in Group Psychotherapy with Hospitalized Narcotic Addicts," *International Journal of Group Psychotherapy*, VI (1956).

Munzer, Jean, and Harold Greenwald. "Interaction Process Analysis of a Therapy Group," *International Journal of Group Psychotherapy*, VII (1957), 175–90.

Murphy, Gardner. "Group Psychotherapy in Our Society," in Max Rosenbaum and Milton Berger, *Group Psychotherapy and Group Function.* New York, Basic Books, Inc., 1963.

Murphy, Lois, and G. Murphy. "The Influence of Social Situations upon the Behavior of Children," in C. Murcheson, ed., *A Handbook of Social Psychology.* Worchester, Mass., Clark University Press, 1935.

Musner, B. "Studies in Social Interaction," *Journal of Social Psychology*, XLI (1955), 259–70.

Mussen, P. H. "Some Personality and Social Factors Related to Changes in Children's Attitudes," *Journal of Abnormal and Social Psychology*, XLV (1950), 423–41.

Neighbor, J. E., Margaret Beach, Donald Brown, David Kevin, and John Visher. "An Approach to the Selection of Patients for Group Psychotherapy," in Max Rosenbaum and M. Berger, eds., *Group Psychotherapy and Group Function.* New York, Basic Books, Inc., 1963.

Neugarten, Bernice. "Social Class and Friendship among School Children," *American Journal of Sociology*, LI (1946), 305–13.

Newcomb, Theodore. *Personality and Social Change.* New York, Dryden, 1943.

Newcomb, Theodore. *The Acquaintance Process.* New York, Holt, Rinehart & Winston, Inc., 1961.

Newcomb, Theodore. "The Prediction of Interpersonal Attraction," *American Psychologist*, II (1956), 575–86.

Newstetter, W. I., Marc C. Feldstein, and Theodore Newcomb. *Group Adjustment.* Cleveland, School of Applied Social Sciences, Western Reserve University, 1938.

Newstetter, Wilbur I. "The Social Intergroup Work Process—How Does It Differ from the Social Group Work Process?" *Proceedings—National Conference of Social Work, 1947.* New York, Columbia University Press, 1948.

Northen, Helen. *Social Work with Groups.* New York, Columbia University Press, 1969.

Osmond, Humphrey. "The Relationship between Architect and Psychiatrist," in Charles Goshen, ed., *Psychiatric Architecture.* Washington, D.C., American Psychiatric Association, 1959.

Pacey, Loren M. *Readings in the Development of Settlement Work.* New York, Association Press, 1950.

Papell, Catherine, and Beulah Rothman. "Social Group Work Models: Possession and Heritage," *Journal of Education for Social Work*, II (1966).

Park, Robert E., Ernest W. Burgess, and Roderick McKenzie. *The City.* Chicago, University of Chicago Press, 1925.

Parsons, Talcott. "Age and Sex in the Social Structure," *American Sociological Review*, VIII (1942), 604–16.

Parsons, Talcott. "The School Class as a Social System," *Harvard Education Review*, XXIX (1959), 297–318.

Parsons, Talcott, and Edward Shils. *Toward A General Theory of Action.* Cambridge, Harvard University Press, 1951.

Parten, Mildred. "Social Play Among Preschool Children,'" *Journal of Abnormal and Social Psychology*, XXVIII (1933), 136–47.

Peirce, Francis J. "A Study of the Methodological Components of Social Work with Groups." Unpublished D.S.W. dissertation. Los Angeles, University of Southern California, 1966.

Phillips, Gerald M. *Communication and the Small Group.* Indianapolis, The Bobbs-Merrill Co., Inc., 1966.

Phillips, Helen U. "Records Kept by Group Working Agencies: Their Form and Values." Unpublished Master's Thesis. Cleveland, Western Reserve University, 1927–28.

Philp, H., and D. Dunphy. "Developmental Trends in Small Groups," *Sociometry*, XXII (1959), 162–74.

Piaget, Jean. *The Moral Judgments of the Child*. New York, Harcourt Brace Jovanovich, Inc., 1932.

Preston, M. G., and R. K. Heintz. "Effects of Participatory Versus Supervisory Leadership on Group Judgment," *Journal of Abnormal and Social Psychology*, XLIV (1949), 345–55.

Psathas, George. "Phase Movement and Equilibrium Tendencies in Interaction Process in Psychotherapy Groups," *Sociometry*, XXXIII (1960), 176–94.

Rapaport, David. *The Collected Papers of David Rapaport*. Edited by Merton M. Gill. New York, Basic Books, Inc., 1967.

Redl, Fritz. "The Art of Group Composition," in Suzanne Schulze, ed., *Creative Group Living in a Children's Institution*. New York, Association Press, 1953.

Redl, Fritz. "Group Emotion and Leadership," *Psychiatry*, V (1942), 573–96.

Redl, Fritz. "The Phenomenon of Contagion and Shock Effect in Group Therapy," in W. Healy and A. Bronner, eds., *Searchlights on Delinquency*. New York, International Universities Press, 1949.

Redl, Fritz, Norman Polansky, and Ronald Lippitt. "An Investigation of Behavioral Contagion in Groups," *Human Relations*, III (1950), 319–48.

Richards, Catherine V. "A Study of Class Differences in Women's Participation." Unpublished D.S.W. dissertation, Cleveland, Ohio, Western Reserve University, 1958.

Richards, Catherine V., and Norman Polansky. "Reaching Working Class Youth Leaders," *Social Work*, IV (1959), 31–39.

Richardson, Helen M. "Studies of Mental Resemblance between Husbands and Wives and between Friends," *Psychological Bulletin*, XXXVI (1939), 104–20.

Riecken, Henry W., and George C. Homans. "Psychological Aspects of the Social Structure," in Gardner Lindzey, ed., *Handbook of Social Psychology*, Vol. II. Reading, Mass., Addison-Wesley Publishing Co., Inc., 1954.

Rodgers, Roy. *Improvements in the Construction and Analysis of Family Life Cycle Categories*. Kalamazoo, Mich., Western Michigan University, 1962.

Roethlisberger, E. J., and W. J. Dickson. *Management and the Worker*. Cambridge, Mass., Harvard University Press, 1939.

Rogers, Carl R. *Carl Rogers on Encounter Groups*. New York, Harper & Row, 1970.

Roseborough, Mary E. "Experimental Studies of Small Groups," *Psychological Bulletin*, L (1953), 275–303.

Rosenbaum, Max, and Milton Berger. *Group Psychotherapy and Group Function*. New York, Basic Books, Inc., 1963.

Rosenthal, D., and C. N. Cofer. "The Effect on Group Performance of an Indifferent and Neglectful Attitude of One Group Member," *Journal of Experimental Psychology*, XXXVIII (1948), 568–77.

Rosow, Irving. *Social Integration of the Aged*. New York, The Free Press, 1967.

de St. Exupery, Antoine. *The Little Prince*, New York, Reynal and Hitchcock, 1943.

Saloshin, Henrietta. "Development of an Instrument for the Analysis of Social Group Work Method in Therapeutic Settings." Unpublished D.S.W. dissertation. Minneapolis, University of Minnesota, 1954.

Sarri, Rosemary, and Maeda Galinsky. "A Conceptual Framework for Teaching Group Development in Social Group Work," in *Faculty Day Conference Proceedings, 1964*. New York, Council on Social Work Education, 1964.

Satir, Virginia. *Conjoint Family Therapy*. Palo Alto, Calif., Science and Behavior Books, 1964.

Schachter, S. "Deviation, Rejection, and Communication," *Journal of Abnormal and Social Psychology*, XLVI (1951).

Schein, Edgar, and Warren Bennis. *Personal and Organizational Change through Group Method*. New York, John Wiley & Sons, Inc., 1965.

Schutz, William C. *F.I.R.O.: A Three-Dimensional Theory of Interpersonal Orientation*. New York, Holt, Rinehart, & Winston, Inc., 1958.

Schutz, William C. *Interpersonal Underworld*. Palo Alto, Calif., Science and Behavior Books, Inc., 1966.

Schvanveldt, Jay D. "The Interactional Framework in the Study of the Family," in F. Ivan Nye and Felix M. Berardo, eds., *Emerging Conceptual Frameworks in Family Analysis*. New York, The Macmillan Co., 1966.

Schwartz, William. "Small Group Science and Group Work Practice," *Social Work*, VIII (1963).

Schwartz, William. In *Working Papers Toward a Frame of Reference for Social Group Work*. Edited by M. E. Hartford. New York, National Association of Social Workers, 1964.

Scodel, A., and Maria L. Freedman. "Additional Observations on the Social Perceptions of Authoritarians and Non-Authoritarians," *Journal of Abnormal and Social Psychology*, LII (1956), 92–95.

Sears, Pauline S., and V. S. Sherman. *In Pursuit of Self-Esteem*. Belmont, Calif., Wadsworth Publishing Co. Inc., 1964.

Sears, Robert, Eleanor Maccoby, and Harry Levin. "The Socialization of Aggression," in E. Maccoby, T. Newcomb, and E. Hartley, *Readings in Social Psychology*. New York, Holt, Rinehart, and Winston, Inc., 1958.

Seashore, S. E. *Group Cohesion in the Industrial Group*. Ann Arbor, Institute of Social Research, 1954.

Seguin, Mary M. "The Small Group as Agent of Socialization: A Model for Social Work Practice with Older Adults." Mimeographed. Unpublished paper delivered at the National Conference of Social Work, Chicago, 1970.

Seguin, Mary M., ed. *Working Paper on the Nature of Social Work Practice in Groups*. National Association of Social Workers Commission on Social Group Work. New York, 1967.

Selznick, P. S. *T.V.A. and the Grass Roots*. Berkeley, University of California Press, 1949.

Shalinsky, William I. "The Effect of Group Composition on Aspects of Group Functioning." Unpublished D.S.W. dissertation, Western Reserve University, 1967.

Shaw, Clifford. *The Jack Roller*. Chicago, University of Chicago Press, 1930.

Shaw, M. E. "Some Effects of Irrelevant Information upon Problem Solving by Small Groups," *Journal of Social Psychology*, XLVII (1958), 33–37.

Sheffield, Alfred. *Creative Discussion*. New York, The Inquiry, 1928.

Shepherd, Clovis. *Small Groups*. San Francisco, Chandler Publishing Co., 1964.

Sherif, Muzafer. *The Psychology of Social Norms*. New York, Harper & Row, Publishers, 1936.

Sherif, Muzafer, and Hadley Cantril. *The Psychology of Ego Involvements*. New York, John Wiley & Sons, Inc., 1947.

Shils, Edward. "The Study of the Primary Group," in Daniel Lerner and H. D. Lasswell, eds., *The Policy Sciences*. Stanford, Calif., Stanford University Press, 1951.

Shoemaker, Louise. "Uses of Groups in A.D.C.," in M. Montelius, ed., *Helping People in Groups*. Washington D.C., U.S. Department of Health, Education, and Welfare, 1964.

Simmel, Georg. *The Sociology of George Simmel*. Translated and edited by K. H. Wolff. New York, Free Press, 1950.

Simmel, Georg. "The Number of Members as Determining the Sociological Form of the Group," *American Journal of Sociology*, VIII (1902–1903), 1–46.

Simmel, Georg. "The Significance of Numbers for Social Life," in A. Paul Hare, E. F. Borgatta, R. F. Bales, eds., *Small Groups: Studies in Social Interaction*. Rev. ed. New York, Alfred A. Knopf Inc., 1965.

Simon, H. A., and Harold Guetzkow. "A Model of Short and Long Run Mechanisms Involved in Pressures toward Uniformity in Groups," *Psychological Review*, LXII (1955), 56–58.

Slater, Philip E. "Contrasting Correlates by Group Size," *Sociometry*, XXI (1958), 129–39.

Slavson, S. R. *The Practice of Group Therapy*. New York, International Universities Press, 1947.

Sloan, Marion. "Factors in Forming Treatment Groups," in *Use of Groups in Psychiatric Settings*. New York, National Association of Social Workers, 1960.

Smith, Peter B., ed. *Group Processes*. Baltimore, Penguin Books, Inc., 1970.

Solomon, Barbara Bryant. "Social Group Work in the Adult Outpatient Clinic," *Social Work*, XIII (1968), 56 ff.

Somers, Mary Louise. "Four Small Group Theories: A Comparative Analysis and Evaluation of Selected Social Science Theory for Use as Teaching Content in Social Group Work." Unpublished D.S.W. dissertation. Cleveland, Western Reserve University, 1957.

Somers, Mary Louise. "Group Process within the Family Unit," in *The Family As Client*. National Association of Social Workers, Pacific Northwest Regional Institute, 1968.

Sommer, Robert. *Personal Space*. Englewood Cliffs, New Jersey, Prentice-Hall, Inc., 1969.

Sommer, Robert. "Leadership and Group Geography," *Sociometry*, XXIV (1961), 99–110.

Spergel, Irving. *Street Gang Work*. Reading, Mass., Addison-Wesley Publishing Co., Inc., 1966.

Sprott, W. J. H. *Human Groups*. Baltimore, Penguin Books, Inc., 1958.

Steinzor, Bernard. "The Spatial Factor in Face-to-Face Discussion Groups," *Journal of Abnormal and Social Psychology*, XLV (1950), 552–55.

Sterling, T. D., and B. G. Rosenthal. "Relationship of Changing Leadership and Followership in a Group to the Changing Phases of Group Activity," *American Psychologist*, V (1950).

Stouffer, Samuel et al. *The American Soldier, Combat and Its Aftermath*. Princeton, New Jersey, Princeton University Press, 1949.

Strickler, Martin, and Jean Allgeyer "The Crisis Group: A New Application of Crisis Theory," *Social Work*, XII (1967).

Strodtbeck, F. L. "The Family As a Three-Person Group," *American Sociological Review*, XIX (1954), 23–29.

Strodtbeck, F. L., Rita Jones and C. Hawkins. "Social Status in Jury Deliberation," *American Sociological Review*, XXII (1957), 713–19.

Strodtbeck, Fred L. "The Case for the Study of Small Groups," *American Sociological Review*, XIX (1954), 651–57.

Strodtbeck, Fred L., and L. H. Hook. "The Social Dimensions of a Twelve-Man Jury Table," *Sociometry*, XXIV (1961), 397–415.

Strodtbeck, Fred L., and R. D. Mann. "Sex Role Differentiation in Jury Deliberations," *Sociometry*, XIX (1956), 3–11.

Suchman, Edward, John P. Dean, and Robin Williams, Jr. *Desegregation: Some Propositions and Research Suggestions*. New York, Anti-Defamation League, 1958.

Sussman, Marvin. "Isolated Nuclear Family: Fact or Fiction," *Social Problems*, VI (1959), 333–40.

Tagiuri, Renato, Jerome Bruner, and Robert Blake. "On the Relation between Feelings and Perception of Feelings among Members of Small Groups," in E. Maccoby, T. Newcomb, and E. Hartley, *Readings in Social Psychology*. New York, Holt, Rinehart, and Winston, Inc., 1958.

Taylor, F. K. "The Three-Dimensional Basis of Emotional Interactions in Small Groups," *Human Relations*, VII (1954), 441–71.

Thelen, Herbert. *Dynamics of Groups at Work*. Chicago, University of Chicago Press, Phoenix Books, 1954.

Thelen, Herbert, and Watson Dickerman. "The Growth of a Group," *Educational Leadership*, VI (1949).

Theodorson, George A. "Elements in the Progressive Development of Small Groups," *Social Forces*, XXXI (1953), 311–20.

Thibaut, John W., and Harold Kelley. *The Social Psychology of Groups*. New York, John Wiley & Sons, Inc., 1961.

Thibaut, John W., and Harold H. Kelley. "Experimental Studies of Group Problem-Solving Process," in Gardner Lindzey, ed., *Handbook of Social Psychology*. Reading, Mass., Addison-Wesley Publishing Co., Inc., 1954.

Thomas, Edwin, and Clinton Fink. "Effects of Group Size," *Psychological Bulletin*, LX (1963), 371–84.

Thompson, J., and W. J. McEwen. "Organizational Goals and Environment: Goal Setting as an Interaction Process," *American Sociological Review*, XXIII (1958), 23–31.

Thoreau, Henry D. *Walden.* New York, The Macmillan Co., 1929.

Thrasher, Frederic M. *The Gang.* Chicago, University of Chicago Press, 1927.

Truman, David B. *The Governmental Process.* New York, Alfred A. Knopf, Inc., 1951.

Tuckman, Bruce W. "Developmental Sequence in Small Groups," *Psychological Bulletin,* LXIII (1965), 384–99.

Turner, John B. *Neighborhood Organization.* New York, National Association of Social Workers, 1968.

United States Department of Health, Education, and Welfare. *Working with Groups.* Washington, D.C., U.S. Government Printing Office, 1963.

van den Haag, Ernest. *Passion and Social Constraint.* New York, Stein and Day, 1963.

Vinter, Robert, ed. *Readings in Group Work Practice.* Ann Arbor, Campus Publishers, 1967.

Vinter, Robert. "Components of Social Group Work Practice," in *Readings in Group Work.* Ann Arbor, Campus Publishers, 1965.

Vinter, Robert. "Social Group Work," in Harry L. Lurie, ed., *Encyclopedia of Social Work.* New York, National Association of Social Workers, 1965.

Vinter, Robert. "Small Group Theory and Research: Implications for Group Work Practice Theory and Research," in Leonard Kogan, ed., *Social Science Theory and Social Work Research.* New York, National Association of Social Workers, 1960.

Walker, Edward L., and Roger Heyns. *An Anatomy of Conformity.* Englewood Cliffs, New Jersey, Prentice-Hall, Inc., 1962.

Warner, W. Lloyd. *American Life.* Chicago, University of Chicago Press, 1953.

Warner, W. Lloyd, and Paul Lunt. *Social Life of a Modern Community.* New Haven, Yale University Press, 1941.

Warner, W. Lloyd, Marchia Meeker, and Kenneth Eells. *Social Class in America.* Chicago, Science Research Associates, Inc., 1949.

Warner, W. Lloyd, and Leo Srole. *American Ethnic Groups.* New Haven, Yale University Press, 1945.

Weiner, Hyman. "Social Change and Social Group Work Practice," *Social Work,* IX (1964), 106–12.

Whitaker, Dorothy Stock, and Morton Lieberman. *Psychotherapy through the Group Process.* New York, Atherton Press, Inc., 1964.

Whyte, William Foote. *Street Corner Society.* Chicago, University of Chicago Press, 1943.

Wilse, Kermit, and Justine Fixel. *Use of Groups in Public Welfare.* California State Department of Social Welfare, September, 1962.

Wilson, Gertrude, and Gladys Ryland. *Social Group Work Practice.* Boston, Houghton Mifflin Company, 1948.

Wilson, Gertrude, and Gladys Ryland. "The Family as a Unit of Service," in *Social Work Practice, 1964.* New York, Columbia University Press, 1964.

Wispe, L. G., and K. E. Lloyd. "Some Situational and Psychological Desire for Structural Interpersonal Relations," *Journal of Abnormal and Social Psychology,* LVII (1955).

Wright, Charles, and Herbert Hyman. "Voluntary Association Memberships of American Adults: Evidence from National Sample Surveys," *American Sociological Review*, XXIII (1958), 284–94.
Yarrow, Marion R., ed. "Interpersonal Dynamics in a Desegregation Process," *Journal of Social Issues*, XIV (1958).
Ziller, Robert C. "Toward a Theory of Open and Closed Groups," *Psychological Bulletin*, LXIII (1965), 164–82.

INDEX